T IS FOR TELEVISION
THE SMALL SCREEN ADVENTURES OF
RUSSELL T DAVIES

T IS FOR TELEVISION

THE SMALL SCREEN ADVENTURES OF
RUSSELL T DAVIES

MARK ALDRIDGE
& ANDY MURRAY

REYNOLDS & HEARN LTD
LONDON

DEDICATED TO

Mark – for my consistently amazing family.

Andy – with love to Catherine and Michael,
my favourite and my best.

First published in 2008 by
Reynolds & Hearn Ltd
61a Priory Road
Kew Gardens
Richmond
Surrey
TW9 3DH

A CIP catalogue record for this book is available from the British Library.

ISBN 978 1 905287 84 0

Designed by James King.

Printed and bound in Great Britain by MPG Ltd, Bodmin, Cornwall.

ACKNOWLEDGEMENTS

Without the unqualified co-operation of Russell T Davies himself, whole swathes of this book would not have been possible, and we're grateful for his time and assistance throughout the long gestation of the project. It's been hugely appreciated.

For kindly sparing the time to talk about their involvement in Russell's career, many thanks to Phil Collinson, Frank Cottrell Boyce, Paul Cornell, Godfrey Evans, Ed Pugh, Gareth Roberts and Nicola Shindler.

For invaluable assistance with research, our thanks to: Gemma Brown, Shauno 'Springhill' Butcher, Roy Gill (of the excellent centuryfalls.co.uk), Alan Hayes, Sarah Perks, Suzette Phillips, Steve Roberts, Goz Ugochukwu and Paul Vanezis.

Special thanks also to Matthew Frost, Gary Russell and Adam Newell. For support and encouragement, heartfelt thanks to Seb Buckle, David Butler, Peter Diment, Richard Donlan, Liz Jones, Paul Lang, Lucy Mazdon, Maureen Murray, Terry Murray, Danny Neville, Tim Sheehan, Garry Watson, Michael Williams, Nicky Williams and Andy Willis.

CONTENTS

T IS FOR TELEVISION

ONE:
SALUBRIOUS PASSAGE

On the face of it, Saturday 27 April 1963 might not have seemed
a particularly auspicious day for British television.

Showing on the solitary BBC channel were six solid hours of sports
coverage under the *Grandstand* banner from 11.00 am. That was followed
by new instalments of imported American shows *Circus Boy* (starring future
Monkee Mickey Dolenz), ranch-based Western adventure *Laramie* and
the UK/US co-production *The Third Man*, 'continuing the adventures of
Harry Lime.' The big variety extravaganza, *The Andy Stewart Show*, offered
guests Ray Allan, Dixie Ingram and The George Mitchell Singers. Then the
big film, *They Won't Believe Me*, and just before Closedown the last in the
current run of groundbreaking satire show *That Was the Week That Was*.

Over on ITV there was an alternative afternoon sports marathon, followed
by swashbuckling yarn *Sir Francis Drake* and yet more imported US family
viewing (*Checkmate*, *Popeye*, *I'm Dickens He's Fenster*, *Wyatt Earp*), then
Episode Five of the Associated British production *The Human Jungle*, and
finally the topical homegrown comedy of *The Braden Beat*.

Meanwhile, over in Wales – specifically, within the south west district
of the County Borough of Swansea – Stephen Russell Davies was born in
Mount Pleasant Hospital. The name Stephen never stuck for the new baby:
in due course he became known to one and all simply as Russell.

The boy's background was middle class. His parents, Barbara and Vivian,
were both Classics teachers who'd set up home in the well-heeled Sketty
area. Between 1947 and 1956, Vivian had played for Swansea Rugby Club,
as had his father before him, as a scrum half. Indeed, he first met Barbara in
the club bar in 1952. The couple already had two daughters, Janet and Susan,
when Russell was born.

The Davies family's newspaper of choice was the *Daily Express*, the front
page of which declared, on the day in question, 'It's Sunshine Today!' The
cause for this buoyancy, it seems, was a series of public pronouncements
by Prime Minister Harold Macmillan. '"The sun's beginning to shine
again. Britain is on the move," Mr Macmillan said last night. "I believe,"

he told Tories in Glasgow, "we shall have from now on a good period of acceleration. So let pessimists beware."' Elsewhere on the *Express'* front page, there was less uplifting news from the other side of the Iron Curtain: 'Russian women who admire frilly Western panties were condemned today by Mr Kruschev.'

That little Russell grew up with a penchant for drama is hardly surprising. Even his earliest moments were eventful. 'My birth was quite extraordinary!' Davies says. 'When I was born they gave my mum too much morphine. I got too much morphine as well, I reckon, and she went mad. She went insane, and was put on a psychiatric ward. She was sectioned. Because I was her third Caesarean birth, they sterilised her at the same time. They thought she'd gone mad because she'd been sterilised, genuinely. It was primitive sixties medicine. Our family would be millionaires now because we'd have sued the fucking arses off them. Of course we didn't because at the time you just went, "Yes doctor, no doctor." But my father comes to the hospital with flowers, I'm lying in a little cot somewhere abandoned, and it was like a horror movie in the ward, with the bed stripped bare, and now she's in the mental ward. Literally, they sat him down and said, "I'm sorry, she's lost her mind! We're really sorry about this."'

Meanwhile, as a result of the morphine overdose, poor Barbara Davies was experiencing what Russell describes as a 'complete 48-hour trip. It was like a science fiction film where she was floating in space, and giant God-like heads were talking to her. They said, "We're sending you back to a parallel Earth." Literally, it's like science fiction. Where she got all this stuff from I don't know. But they said, "We're sending you back to a parallel Earth in which your first-born child, your daughter, is dead. And if you speak to anyone from this parallel Earth you have to stay there forever."'

The bewildered woman then regained consciousness and the hospital staff took note. 'So a nurse comes along and says, "How are you feeling, Mrs Davies?" – and she went berserk and attacked the nurse, pulled down curtains, went bananas. Got sectioned, locked up, and they said, "She's gone mad, she's psychotic." My father was brilliant. He's not a medical man at all, but he just stood there saying, "She is not mad."'

Davies' father Vivian took the initiative and did some hasty amateur research of his own, concluding that a morphine overdose was indeed the cause of his wife's psychotic episode. At the time, one of Vivian's ex-pupils was working as a geriatrics consultant at Mount Pleasant, and Davies Sr persuaded him to intervene. 'That just wasn't done in those days,' Russell says. 'You didn't get a consultant to override another consultant's opinion, but he made them look at her and say, "Oh actually, she's just had morphine, she'll be fine" – and she was. What a birth!'

Nor was that the end of the Davies' troubles. 'And then …! They handed me over to her, and they said, "Congratulations, this is your son" – no wonder I'm gay, I was separated from my mother for two days! They handed me over – this is the honest truth – they handed me over to her and they said, "This is your son. He's got a club foot."'

It's not a diagnosis that's easy to take seriously in the presence of the adult Davies, who is an imposing 6'6". 'Look at me!' he says. 'Have I got a club foot? She's in the bed and they're going, "It's fine, we can give him physiotherapy, there are shoes…" As if the family hadn't been weeping their guts up anyway! So the mad woman is lying in bed with this baby going, "He hasn't got a club foot, he's got a heel! He's got a heel!" And they're going, "Yes, Mrs Davies, it's fine, it's fine, absolutely." And I went to fucking physiotherapy for two years! As a little toddler I went to club foot physiotherapy, being manipulated all over the place, and after two years they go, "Um – actually…" We would be millionaires now, millionaires!'

Unsurprisingly, Davies' mother kept the whole experience secret from him until he was much older. 'They didn't tell me this story until I was 27 years old as it was genuinely just a terrible trauma for her. They wouldn't even talk about it. It was on the night her mother died that she got drunk and told me this story. So that was my science fiction birth…'

Davies' earliest childhood memories are similarly charged with drama. He can just about recall that, at the age of two, he was dangled upside down and slapped by a stranger. On a visit to his grandmother's pub, The Cornish Mount (situated down a Swansea alley rejoicing in the name Salubrious Passage), he'd bitten into a glass and one of the pub regulars began without ado to get the broken pieces out of his mouth. Then, at the age of three and a half – to be precise, on Saturday 29 October 1966 – he watched in awe as one of his TV heroes transformed his physical appearance. More prosaically, actor William Hartnell had elected to leave the main role in the hit BBC show *Doctor Who* and Patrick Troughton replaced him. A young Russell Davies was an entranced witness to the occasion in front of a television set in a Swansea living room. The lifelong love affair between the boy and the medium had already begun.

'To be honest, I grew up watching everything,' Davies says. 'The marvellous thing about my parents was that they never switched the TV off. Not in a sort of liberal way: it's like, back in the sixties, which is so long ago, television had more authority than it has now. And it's a marvellous thing that it's lost its authority, but I mean they felt like they couldn't turn it off. If it was on it was on, and it went to Closedown and then you switched it off and you went to bed. It was like this sort of temple in the corner of the room. So they never ever stopped me watching anything, even when there were plays with sex and *I, Claudius* and things like that. They weren't being liberal, saying, "You must watch this." It was like they thought if it was on, you had to watch it. I work in television because I love television, and still, to this day, I watch everything. Name a programme, I've seen it!'

Surprisingly, though, he has no memory of watching one of the key moments of televised history from his childhood, namely the Apollo 11 Moon landing on 21 July 1969. 'Do you know, I don't. Isn't that weird?' Davies says. 'I don't remember the impact of it at all. People talk about looking at the moon that night and thinking, "Ooh, there's people up there." I don't remember that. And I was six, so it's within memory time. I can remember watching take-offs, and all that sort of stuff. I remember having to go to bed while Apollos were launching downstairs, and sneaking down the stairs. But I don't remember the landing! Whether I was asleep … I'm *sure* I must have watched it. I just don't remember it. It probably wasn't as good as that week's *Doctor Who*!'

Davies seems to have enjoyed a happy childhood. Aside from television, he became fascinated with drawing, a self-confessed 'ferocious cartoonist' as well as an avid reader of comics of all shapes and sizes, from Marvel to *Asterix* and Charles Schultz's *Peanuts*. 'I used to draw a lot, and I was into Marvel Comics massively,' Davies says. 'They used to reprint them in black and white versions: I remember them coming out as *Marvel Weekly* or something. I loved those.' On the subject of his family life, Davies told the *Guardian*'s Stuart Jeffries, 'Do you know Kingsley Amis' *The Old Devils*? My parents were just like that. Or rather, just like the TV adaptation.'

Davies attended the local Tycoch Primary School in Sketty, just a short walk from the family home by Hendrefoilan Avenue. It was to be a curiously formative time. 'As a writer, I always think you're like a kid who never grows up,' he suggests. 'When we were eight, we'd all run around the yard being Nazis or Daleks or cowboys. I was a squaw … We'd all run around doing things like that, and it's like, some people stop and grow up and be sensible, and some people actually keep on doing it. It's the same sort of process I go through now as you go through when you're eight.'

He has since confessed to being 'gobby' at Tycoch, so much so that he came in for unfounded accusations of bullying. His attitude changed, though, when he went on to the local secondary school, namely the vast Olchfa Comprehensive by Sketty Park. 'When I was 11, I went to this huge comprehensive school with 2300 people, which was a cattle market, just a ridiculous size. They don't make them that big any more. You were just thrown in as a tiny little kid with 2300 people and I was sort of a little solitary soul. I still am! I used to walk around in this little dream world, full of *Doctor Who* stories in my head, and my own sort of stories.'

During Davies' first year at Olchfa, the main school buildings were out of bounds. There was, at the time, much concern across the country about a certain type of cement which was causing public buildings to collapse. As this was being addressed, classes were being held in temporary Portacabins while Olchfa was wreathed in tape and wire. Davies' imagination was well and truly fired, and for his own amusement he'd make up tales 'that something mysterious and spooky and sci-fi-ish was going on in the school and they were hiding secrets from us in there.'

It was a formative point in Davies' life, for several reasons. By now, he'd pretty much arrived at the conclusion that he was gay, though he didn't fully come out until a few years later. 'It was always there,' he told BBC Radio Wales' Phil George. 'It takes you a long time to put the word on it, but I actually think from around about 11 or 12, I think I knew then. And … you just keep quiet about it. I mean, the world has changed so much now. Isn't it brilliant? I don't look back on it with any angst at all. None whatsoever.' The knowledge may have contributed to his introversion but it certainly didn't stop him from making firm new friends, including two, Tracy and Bobby, who would become lifelong pals. Nevertheless, he's admitted, on reflection, that 'I didn't like school much.'

Davies was clearly a very bright pupil, though, and a voracious reader. 'I was quite pretentious,' he confesses, 'reading *Sons and Lovers* at the age of 11 and things like that. My English teacher thought I was so marvellous, but I was bored to tears by it and couldn't tell her. I'm still bored to tears by it now at this age. But yeah, I was quite bookish, a bit of a swot.' Not that all his reading matter was so consciously highbrow. One favourite novel was *The Crystal Mouse* by American suspense author Babs H Deal, and in later life he reflected that it had impressed him so greatly that 'I can see it echoing in everything I write.'

The Crystal Mouse concerns the ageing Sara Hillstrom, who has recently lost her husband Howard and lives in uneasy isolation in a towering Florida condominium. On the face of it, it's not a novel that would obviously appeal to a young reader. It's an atmospheric, meditative, often haunted little book. For much of the tale, Hillstrom is entirely alone, musing on her bleak, companion-free future and the ultimate futility of existence. Since Davies was himself something of an introverted loner, as well as being an intelligent, voracious reader, *The Crystal Mouse* clearly struck a chord with him. Indeed, echoes of Sara can be detected in the isolated main characters of his later TV writing, as we shall see.

One perennial schoolboy pastime, sport, didn't hold much interest for Davies. Of course, his father Vivian had an impressive rugby career behind him. Once his playing days were over, Vivian had remained involved as Swansea's fixture secretary, and then club chairman for five seasons. Later, he acted as club president and subsequently became a life patron. Vivian's own father Trevor had also played for Swansea and been club chairman, so the family was virtually a rugby-playing dynasty.

Russell Davies, himself a strapping boy on his way to being 6'6", certainly wouldn't have looked out of place in the scrum, but simply didn't care for the sport.

'Everyone, especially, like, Games teachers in school, expected me to be a rugby player,' he told Phil George. 'I'm a big old fella, you know! And I was so the opposite of a rugby player. And he was completely fantastic, my father. I was about 11 and I was getting a bit hassled at school about it – by the teachers, I have to say. But my own fault as well because I was always missing the lessons and wandering off to the library … And he drove me home from school and he pulled up the car and he said, "I am not putting any of that pressure on you. I don't care." He said, "Obviously you like reading and you like drawing. I'm happy for you to do that." So was my mother as well, but she didn't need to say it. My dad needed to say it, I think! That was so fantastic.'

Instead, Davies found himself gravitating towards performance. In 1974, when Britain's local authorities were restructured, the West Glamorgan Education Authority came into being. Acting as drama advisor for West Glamorgan was one Godfrey Evans, who set up a new youth theatre programme within the region, with which Davies got involved. As Evans recalls, 'There were open-access drama centres meeting every Friday evening in two areas in the county and Russell became a member of one of them.' The hub of Evans' youth theatre programme became the West Glamorgan Youth Theatre (WGYT), which he established in 1975. To become a member of the company, young people attending local drama centres were required to audition. So it was that Davies auditioned for the WGYT, was offered a place, and became actively involved as a member.

His first production with the company was a non-speaking part in Euripides' *The Bacchae* in January 1977, closely followed by one of the smaller 'mechanical' roles in *A Midsummer Night's Dream* that July. Over the period of more than seven years that he spent with WGYT, Davies went on to appear in a whole variety of major productions, including performances as Fortinbras in *Hamlet* and Yasha in Chekhov's *The Cherry Orchard*. 'It wasn't just swanning about pretending to be a tree,' Davies later told the *Daily Telegraph*. 'It was massively disciplined.' In particular, Godfrey Evans worked hard to instil a professional attitude into members of the company.

'God, he would kill you if you were late,' Davies remembers, 'and I still carry a lot of that stuff with me. Never late!'

Evidently Davies was a well-liked member of the theatre company. 'Russell was one of the very able, talented, intelligent, funny, loyal members of the Youth Theatre, and he was very popular with all the other students,' Evans says. 'The age range of the Youth Theatre would be from around about 14 years to 20, 21 at any one point in time. Because a lot of the Youth Theatre's work was and is focused on residential work, and the rehearsals were almost exclusively at the authority's residential centre for the creative arts, it meant that the young people were living together for a period of time. That meant that there was a lot of work to be done socially. It wasn't only rehearsals. The students had free time, and we as a staff team had established a studio social committee, which Russell was involved in very effectively for a number of years. He was a total all-rounder.'

In particular, Davies struck up a friendship with actress Rhian Morgan, a (marginally older) fellow WGYT member. For three months, the pair even went out together. The relationship never became particularly intense, and in practice it seems only to have helped define Davies' sexual identity. Not that it ended unpleasantly: many years later, Davies and Morgan were to work together in a professional capacity.

Elsewhere in the England of 1977, the cultural squall of punk was gripping the nation's youth. But it didn't make much of an impact in Swansea, it seems. According to Davies, 'A lot of us just carried on going to school in Nature Treks, listening to Baccara, untouched by bin bags and safety pins.' Instead, he carried on pursuing his cartooning ambitions, drawing almost constantly. Godfrey Evans remembers, 'During his time with the Youth Theatre, he was always doodling in rehearsals and came up with some wonderful cartoon images of the various productions that he was rehearsing with us.'

1977 was also the year that saw the launch of *2000AD*, a weekly British SF comic that ran several serialised adventure strips at one time, the most famous of which featured futuristic law enforcer Judge Dredd. *2000AD* proved to be a key moment in the history of British comics. It gave exposure to a whole new generation of UK-based writers and artists who would go on to do major work. Perhaps most importantly, it provided a professional springboard for writer Alan Moore, who later wrote *Watchmen* and *V for Vendetta*. Perhaps unsurprisingly – the publication could have been formulated with him in mind – Davies became a firm fan of *2000AD*.

The boy's other key interests fed into his artistic pursuits, too. 'I did *Doctor Who* comic strips,' Davies says. 'If I could find those now they'd be worth a fortune! 'Return of the Robots of Death' – marching by Big Ben! You think, 'How did they get to Big Ben?' I remember spending weeks trying to find a photo of Big Ben, trying to draw it and get them marching past.'

Clearly Davies was full of untapped creative energy. He contributed regular cartoon strips to Olchfa's official school magazine. For a period during his mid-teens he even wrote a new three-page, superhero-type adventure comic every week, and distributed the results around the entire school. 'Kids these days would be dealing in drugs – I was dealing in cartoons,' he told the *Independent*'s Cathy Prior. 'I lived for that. Every Sunday, for a couple of years, I'd do the latest adventure ... So much detail and so many gags! Cliffhangers as well! Rattling great big daft adventure stories!' Even Olchfa's teachers, who often found themselves caricatured within, were full of praise for Davies' hand-made comics.

At 15, with school-leaving age approaching, Davies began to weigh up his options. In order to pursue a career as a working artist, he'd need to be qualified in subjects such as graphics and anatomy, so he considered applying to his local art college. However, Olchfa's Careers Teacher talked him out of the move. Davies is colour-blind, and it was feared that this might prove a major hurdle in such a field. Looking back, Davies feels this advice was 'probably nonsense', but at the time it seriously derailed his hopes. (Ironically, the colour-blind American artist Tim Sale is now, thanks to his involvement with the US TV show *Heroes*, one of the most visible comics artists of the day.) Davies continued to draw for fun, but shifted his academic ambitions towards another of his key interests, namely English Literature.

Not all Davies' classroom activities were entirely above-board. With his regular English teacher away on jury service, he wrote a short story as an assignment for the supply teacher, neglecting to mention that the result was actually, word for word, fantasy author Ray Bradbury's unsettling tale *The Emissary*. Impressed, the supply teacher had the story published in the school magazine, and eventually entered in a national short story competition, before the deception was rumbled to Davies' toe-curling shame.

At the time, the Davies family TV was pouring out a torrent of treasures. The advent of colour broadcasts seemed to have the household even more spellbound than before. 'It was always on,' Davies recalls. 'I used to come home from school and watch television, soaking in everything.' The 1970s were a heyday for British television drama, and Davies grew up keenly aware of the fact. *Doctor Who* itself was enjoying one of its most popular phases, with Tom Baker fully installed as the Fourth Doctor. Audience figures regularly topped the ten million mark, and Davies speaks with special fondness about such *Doctor Who* stories as *'The Ark in Space'* (first shown in early 1975) and *'The Talons of Weng Chiang'* (early 1977). Walking home from school, he'd daydream about turning a corner and spotting the TARDIS. Decades hence, the TARDIS would indeed land in South Wales, and Davies would be right there when it did.

His mother Barbara, a fan of science fiction drama, became his *Doctor Who* viewing companion. He remembers his sisters being keen viewers of the big television soaps, and as a result he couldn't help but be exposed to them. *Coronation Street*, unarguably the king of British soaps at the time, became a particular favourite. In fact, the show was instrumental in the very first stirrings of his fascination with TV scriptwriting. 'There were two episodes of *Coronation Street* a week then,' Davies says. 'I'm so old! Two, can you imagine! And when there were just two you could notice differences between them.'

It was a golden age for TV drama, and the teenage Davies steeped himself in it. There were groundbreaking BBC serials such as *I, Claudius* (1976) and Dennis Potter's *Pennies from Heaven* (1978), both of which made a major impact on him. Over on ITV, acclaimed drama *The Naked Civil Servant* (1975), about the travails of the openly gay Quentin Crisp, impressed Davies greatly; he's suggested the piece 'means a lot personally' to him. *Rock Follies* (1976) and its sequel *Rock Follies of '77*, music-inflected dramas about the fictional female rock group The Little Ladies, were two other favourites, while *Beasts* (1976) and *Quatermass* (1979), two original series written for the ITV network by legendary scriptwriter Nigel Kneale, were required viewing in the Davies household. In short, television was a key, constant part of Davies' youth.

Meanwhile, his school career continued to blossom. In 1979, having completed his O-levels, he elected to stay on at the sixth form at Olchfa Comprehensive, and was even installed as the school's Head Boy for the duration. Quite aside from studying for his A-levels, he also took on the challenge of Oxbridge examinations in the hope of winning a place at one of England's most prestigious universities.

These academic commitments didn't dent Davies' involvement with West Glamorgan Youth Theatre, though: far from it. Instead, he broadened his scope. 'Godfrey Evans, who's a brilliant man, got us writing,' Davies says. 'We'd be doing everything, you'd do dance, we'd do behind-the-scenes stuff. The one thing we were not doing was writing and he started us writing, anyone who wanted to. There'd be a group of four of us who wrote little plays and put them on. That was brilliant, absolutely brilliant.'

At first, WGYT's assortment of talented young writers worked together as a team on specific assignments. Notably, in two separate years, the company was commissioned to produce work incorporating dance and drama, in the Welsh language, for the National Eisteddfod of Wales. The first of these shows, *Pair Dadeni*, was performed as part of the Eisteddfod in 1980. It drew on elements of the Welsh myth cycle The Mabinogion: the title translates as 'Cauldron of Rebirth'. Typical of the young Davies, he took the opportunity to work his own preoccupations into the piece, appearing on stage in a hand-made superhero outfit, complete with Superman-style 'P' emblazoned on his chest. The second team-written show followed in the Eisteddfod of 1982. It was entitled 'Perthyn', a Welsh word meaning 'Belonging'. 'We just took the idea of what it meant to belong, as a teenager living in West Glamorgan in the early eighties,' Godfrey Evans explains. 'There was a lot of devised work of all types there. Scripted work, of which Russell did a lot of course, working in a team capacity.'

As part of Evans' company, Davies also met Princess Diana on her

inaugural tour of Wales, little more than a month after her wedding to Prince
Charles. A concert was given on 4 September 1981 in Swansea's Brangwyn
Hall, featuring a cavalcade of Youth Orchestras and Choirs. As part of
Swansea Youth Arts Company's performance of Vaughan Williams' *Job*,
Davies appeared as a dancer in the plum role of God. During an interval,
Diana met a line-up of performers and, on reaching Davies, exclaimed,
'Oh, it's God! I saw you putting your glasses on for the curtain call.'
She lingered long enough to ask him what he planned to do with his life,
but he professed not to know. 'Dance, dance, dance!' she advised.

For the time being, Davies' future involved a move away from Wales.
Having completed his A-levels, he'd been accepted by Worcester College
Oxford to study for an English Literature degree, and took up his place mere
weeks after the Brangwyn Hall performance.

Worcester, 'the pretty one with the lake' as Davies puts it, is one of
Oxford's oldest, most venerable colleges, close to the centre of the town and
complete with very fetching grounds of 26 acres. First established in 1714,
it's made up of a tasteful blend of architectural styles, with new buildings
being constructed as recently as Davies' own time there. For some, attending
an Oxbridge college goes on to define their entire future and leaves an
indelible store of halcyon memories. In Davies' case, the experience seems
to have been far less significant. 'I had a very nice time: a lovely time.
I suppose those three years were a good three years to grow up in. But I
absolutely could have skipped it,' he says. 'The funny thing is, in my whole
television career, not once have I been asked for my qualifications. Not once.
Never ever. And I think, "Well, that's what it's all for, isn't it?" I didn't even
like the study of English that much. I could do it, I was very good at exams,
and if I did like anything it was reading the books. What I did realise was
how much I like stories.'

Sure enough, Davies quickly came to appreciate which areas of English
Literature he liked best. 'I discovered that I only liked the narrative, actually,'
he told interviewer Phil George. 'Put me in front of a piece of poetry and I
was lost. I actually genuinely disliked studying it, and disliked reading it.'
His particular love was the 19th century novel, 'when I think narrative

was at its most powerful, its most story-driven. Dickens, in other words: that's top of the tree for me if you want to rate them.'

But naturally enough, on an English degree course, Davies was required to study the whole gamut of literature down the ages. 'I realised that you had to study poetry, 17th century novels, 20th century, 19th century. And I wasn't happy doing that. We had to do one term on the 19th century novel, and that was it! And I thought "Oh, Christ!" – then two and a half years of all the other stuff! So it was good to realise that. I hadn't realised that until I was confronted with it. But George Eliot … Virginia Woolf was not bad, but boring essentially… That's the only thing it really had me focused on, but I didn't know what I was focusing on that for. I had a nice three years, though. Didn't do me any harm! Well, I did English at Oxford University, now I hardly read a book. I've just read the latest Stephen King and I'm thinking "That's my literature for the year!" It's shameful how little I read now.'

It was an important period in other ways, though. He began to come out as gay, he says, 'slowly but sort of… obviously. Like, "What a surprise!"' He carried on with his creative endeavours, contributing comic strips and illustrations to celebrated Oxford student publications such as *Cherwell* and *Isis*. From afar, he managed to continue as an active member of Godfrey Evans' West Glamorgan Youth Theatre. What's more, in one crucial respect, he expanded his repertoire.

'At the Youth Theatre we focused on the rehearsal and performance of the play,' Evans explains. 'Set alongside that, though, we organised a series of classes which were running parallel with the rehearsals, so there would be classes in improvised drama and dance and singing and speech. We didn't set up specific creative writing classes, but out of the improvised pieces came some small-scale devised theatre pieces which required scripting. We saw that there were some youngsters, and Russell was one of them, who really clearly had a talent and an appetite for writing. And so what we did was set up, alongside the rehearsals of the main productions, a series of late-night performances which we asked some of our young members to write, and Russell was one of them.'

These were the circumstances, then, that saw the first public performance of a solo Russell Davies script. According to Evans, 'The Youth Theatre not merely asked the young writers to write something but gave the productions of those short pieces for late-night shows the same production values we would to the main production that was being rehearsed. So they were properly lit and costumed and designed. They happened to be perhaps half an hour in length. That would be the only difference, really, but they were given proper rehearsal time.'

The first such piece that Davies wrote was entitled *Box*. Memories of this milestone have since grown hazy. By Davies' own recollection he was 15 at the time, which would place it around 1977. On the other hand WGYT leader Evans dates it to 'about 1982. That was a piece which, as lots of Russell's pieces do, just starts and lulls you into a sense of security, and into one direction, and then spring some surprises on you and take you into a direction you didn't think you'd go. It was a piece which focused on the box in the corner of the room, the television set, and how it could influence and interact with the people who lived in the room. It was a mixture, as virtually all of Russell's pieces are, of humour and wit and very serious, dark elements, too. So that I think was his first piece.'

It's immediately striking that Davies' public writing debut centres on television. He loved the medium, and would of course go on to write extensively for it. But very often, his future writing would feature television, too, like a recurring motif – even a character. Davies followed *Box* with another short piece for a late-night WGYT showcase, and named it *In Her Element*. 'It's difficult to describe,' Evans says, 'because like all good performable pieces they need to be seen. But he was taking the idea of inanimate objects becoming animate. Now that sounds rather trite, but you can imagine with somebody like Russell taking that idea and developing it, it worked very well indeed.'

Evans stresses that this experience wasn't a case of pigeonholing Davies as an upcoming writer at the expense of all else. Rather, it was meant to add another string to his bow. 'Clearly his talent was emerging then, but it wasn't in the nature of the Youth Theatre to put people into a box saying, "You are going to be a creative writer,"' Evans says. 'We wanted to give the young people as broad a diet as possible.'

Davies himself remembers writing a third devised theatre piece for WGYT entitled *Hothouse*. "It was about the employees in an advertising office," he says. "Obviously something I knew a lot about at 16. But it was all office politics, with a tyrant of a woman in charge, and everyone plotting her downfall. Very Alan Bennett, I'd just read his play called *A Visit From Miss Protheroe*. Steal from the best!"

On balance, Davies' spell amid the celebrated dreaming spires of Oxford appears less significant than his ongoing involvement with WGYT. During the summers straddling his final year at Worcester College, he appeared in two major WGYT productions. In the July 1983 production of Arthur Miller's *The Crucible*, he appeared as Reverend Hale. 'He was a very capable young actor and that's a very, very demanding role,' Evans argues. 'His height added to the presence that the character demanded, alongside his acting ability.'

Then, shortly before graduating from Oxford, Davies starred as Lysander in WGYT's August 1984 staging of *A Midsummer Night's Dream*, having progressed from his small role in the previous 1977 production. Godfrey Evans remembers the 1984 version with enormous affection. 'We were very fortunate in having, with Russell, three other young performers, who had been with the company for some years and who knew each other very well, playing the lovers. The ability, as exemplified by Russell's, was so phenomenal that it was just a joy to rehearse with them. I can remember sitting in on rehearsals and starting them off and saying, "Right, this is the set that we've got. Now then, we all know one another well enough for you to be able to evolve the comic scenes just out of the context of the script and the structure of the set." It was just wonderful, absolutely wonderful!'

This was to be Davies' swansong for WGYT, though. By now he'd turned 21, the upper age limit for members of the group. After more than seven years with Godfrey Evans' company, he was finally obliged to move on. On reflection more than 20 years later, Evans feels sure that the writer whose work was to become familiar to millions was already fully formed during his time as part of the Youth Theatre. 'Oh, absolutely, yes, very much so!' he says. 'The same qualities are there. That marvellous sense of humour, the wit, the wonderful command of language that he's always had. Oh, he's absolutely the same Russell Davies.'

It's the perennial quandary facing every student upon graduation: 'Well, what now?' By the autumn of 1984, Davies was living at his family home in Swansea again, but without a job, much less a career. As such, he was on the dole. 'I so didn't have a clue what I wanted to do,' he says on reflection. 'I sort of thought I wanted to work in television. I didn't even think 'drama', because I wasn't writing then. I applied for all of those BBC training courses, and got turned down twice. But I wasn't really bothered. I was just hanging about. I was literally like a slacker!'

However, he did take the opportunity to announce to his parents that he was gay. As far as his strategy was concerned, he later bequeathed it to one of his own characters. In Davies' 2001 serial *Bob & Rose*, the eponymous Bob Gossage recounts his own experience of coming out to his parents as follows: 'I was 21. We were having tea and we were talking about cars. I took this sentence and I just kept going, like a rollercoaster. I turned it from cars, to all sorts of cars, to all sorts of people, to all sorts of men. Nice men and tall men and straight men and gay men - coz that's me. I'm gay.' On the DVD commentary for the scene, Davies remarks, 'I like that speech because that's what it felt like when I came out, like that. When he says it was like a rollercoaster… I did exactly that – start a sentence [and just keep going].' Much like Bob Gossage, Davies would have been 21 at the time.

The revelation seems not to have left his parents too crestfallen or surprised, though. 'Like they didn't know!' Davies told interviewer Mark Lawson. 'You forget that when you're a teenager they're actually watching you every hour of your life. Of course they know… No one was surprised, let's put it that way.'

In time, though, Davies' mother was keen, as mothers always are, to motivate him, and spotted an opening that might appeal to him. 'I didn't have any idea, but I did love the theatre, so my mother, bless her, said, "Look, go and do this course" – a Theatre Studies course at Cardiff University. It no longer exists now, and it was the most brilliant course. It took, like, 15 students a year and gave them a theatre.'

Cardiff's Sherman Theatre boasted a smaller studio theatre, the 200-seater Sherman Arena, upon which the Theatre Studies students were let loose. 'It had like ten slots in a year where you would put on plays for the public,' Davies says. 'There'd be a budget, and proper management. It was slightly half am-dram, half-professional. You could pay a certain amount to professional actors to come in and be in plays. We'd do that, but you couldn't afford a whole cast like that, so they had a pool of actors, and fellow students as well, who'd be in stuff, and you'd just put on plays! You'd have classes in stagecraft, and lighting, and design. You all did everything in each other's plays. You'd be the butler with three lines or something, and you also got the chance to work on the main stage, the big main stage theatre. It was brilliant.'

He was duly awarded a diploma in Theatre Studies. Nevertheless, in career terms, Davies admits he was 'treading water'. After completing the course, he was back on the dole, directionless. 'I did love theatre, and I thought that I'd probably direct or something like that,' he says. 'I just wandered along not knowing what I wanted to do, really. Actually, I was drawing all the time.' He fell into doing work for the Sherman Theatre's publicity department, picking up scattered commissions for illustrations and occasional spots of directing, signing on all the while. 'I was happy with that. Weird, isn't it? You look back and think "God!"'

Despite the passion he had for the medium at the time, nowadays Davies feels estranged from the theatre. 'I absolutely loved it. I loved the smell of them, the 'backstage-ness' of them. And you can't drag me into a theatre now. It's like, all or nothing! I go to the theatre once a year and then I'm bored. Or it's brilliant, and I'm jealous. I get asked to write stage plays and things like that and I don't think I'd know how to bring people on and off stage.'

One day during 1985, an actress friend from the Sherman happened to mention to Davies that a part-time job was going within the Children's Department at BBC Wales for a graphic artist. At the time, Davies admits, 'I was desperately short of money. I was overdrawn. And this woman said, "A friend of mine's a producer at BBC Wales and he needs someone to do a couple of days' work for *Why Don't You?*, that kids' show. Go for an interview."' Intrigued, Davies applied for the job, and was duly invited along to BBC Wales' Broadcasting House in Llandaff, just outside Cardiff city centre. 'I went for an interview and they said. "You'd be paid £50 a day." It was like a fortune! It was five days' work and I sat there thinking, "Oh my God!"'

Little did he suspect that his future career path was beginning, in a haphazard sort of way, to coalesce.

T IS FOR TELEVISION

TWO:
GIVE US A CLUE

Even by his own admission, most of the developments in Davies' early career in television relied heavily on chance, and he was very aware of 'just making it all up at the time, as you go along.' Apparently insignificant events led to fantastic opportunities, but rarely in an obvious or straightforward manner. In this haphazard way his early work in children's television was to sow the seeds for his subsequent career as first a producer and then, eventually, a writer.

Following his interview at BBC Wales and the offer of a job, Davies' time in the graphics department took the form of one-day contracts for specific pieces of work, and in this capacity he worked for producer Dave Evans on various projects throughout 1985 and 1986. These included illustrating Welsh *Jackanory*-type children's stories such as *Y Robin Goch*, and similar graphics tasks for long-running children's magazine programme *Why Don't You?* The latter was the BBC's hardy repository for jokes, crafts and recipes, broadcast during the school holidays with an ever-changing cast of child presenters. It was produced, in turn, by three of the Corporation's regional bases – Belfast, Bristol and Cardiff. Each time Cardiff's turn came around, it fell to Dave Evans to pull the shows together. Evans, Davies recalls, 'was a lovely producer at BBC Wales. He'd go to the bar and have a drink, and sort of fall asleep in the afternoon. He was a bit old-school BBC in that sense. Lovely man. He gave me my first job, so I love him.'

While he enjoyed this opportunity to build on his interest in drawing, Davies remained convinced that his colour-blindness would be a restraining factor on any full-blown career in graphics or design. In practical terms, at such a handsome daily rate of pay, he could afford to pick up around three days of such work every months, and fill the rest of his time with publicity work for the Sherman Theatre, or else seeking out freelance illustration work. Nevertheless, he began to feel sure that television was where his interests lay, even if his intended role within the medium was less clear. 'I got that job for five days' work,' he says, 'and I'm not kidding you, I set foot in that studio at BBC Wales, Studio C1 – which is still there and it smells the same – and that was it! It was like coming home!'

Speaking of his time as an artist, Davies now asserts that 'What I was actually doing was writing. I thought I was drawing all this time: I thought I was going to be some sort of artist. And I would have been very happy being a Marvel Comics artist. I love that sort of stuff. But I was actually writing. Because I could draw I was fooling myself, but I was constructing a narrative, dreaming up stories and dreaming up characters, things like that. It took me from about the age of 20 to 25 to work that out. For years and years and years, I thought I was drawing, but what I actually liked doing was the speech bubble.'

It wasn't just the story-telling side of television that piqued Davies' interest at this stage. With one foot in the door at BBC Wales, he began to make himself useful in all sorts of ways, and gained some wide-ranging experience of working behind the scenes in the medium that he'd always loved. On *Why Don't You?* he found himself working variously as a researcher, floor manager, and even a kind of unofficial director for the young cast, readying them for upcoming scenes.

He was keen to develop this when a new opportunity suddenly presented itself, quite by chance, during a discussion with producer Dave Evans. 'One day I happened to walk into the office, to get my expenses or something,' Davies recalls. 'It was the afternoon and he hadn't done the script. He was sitting there going, "I can't be bothered doing this. Do you want to earn a hundred quid?"' Davies, thinking of the money above all else, accepted the offer. So, that very afternoon, sitting in a spare office at BBC Wales, he wrote his first ever script for television.

Davies delivered the finished script to Evans, and awaited his verdict. Happily, it was an enthusiastic thumbs-up. 'Bless him, he liked it,' Davies recalls. 'I got a phone call that night saying, "Oh, you *can* write. This actually makes sense as a script. Do you want to write all five of them?" So I said yes, and that's how it began.' It was, as Davies is keen to point out, simply a case of being in the right place at the right time.

This big break, though, wasn't instantly life-changing. Davies didn't suddenly find himself working as a full-time scriptwriter. The experience was undoubtedly useful, but in the event he continued to sign on the dole and find work at the Sherman Theatre between his intermittent stints on *Why Don't You?*

In attempting to broaden his range of freelance activities, he managed to sell some comic strip illustrations to the hugely fashionable *Blitz* magazine, albeit only over a couple of issues. Looking for more work of this kind Davies answered a job advertisement in the *Guardian* for a job writing and drawing comic strips for a new Sunday newspaper, due to launch later in 1986. To his surprise, he was invited to submit a sample of his work. 'It was a full-page football cartoon,' he remembers. 'Not a four-panel strip: a full page, in colour. They came to me and said, "Can you do footballers?" I said, "If you want footballers I'll do a page of footballers for you!" I sent them off … and they said, "You've got the job, come up and meet us."'

Davies was immediately suspicious: 'You don't just get a job on a national newspaper. Don't I have to belong to a graphics union or something?' And the feeling was only compounded when, on visiting the newspaper's premises to discuss the job, he discovered that the office was a very seedy affair, complete with rows of pornographic magazines on one wall. He was initially offered £150 a week for a full-page colour football strip. But it was not to be, as he remembers his almost immediate reservations about the newspaper itself. 'They had these dummy runs of the newspaper, they printed up my harmless footballing cartoon strip, and on every other page were naked women!'

He decided that this was not exactly his preferred position in the media and turned the engagement down. 'I just thought, "I can't have my family buying that newspaper." I could not have held my head up high. Also, I thought that the football strip would run for three weeks, and then they'll start asking for naked women in it. And I can't do that! I don't mean literally. I'm sure I could draw the naked female form. But I just couldn't live with myself. How moral was I? Now I'd be in there in a flash!' The editor in question was Dave Sullivan and the newspaper, eventually launched on 14 September 1986, was the infamously news-light and breast-heavy *Sunday Sport*.

Davies had no great career game-plan and seemingly had no particular direction or aspiration when, nearly 20 years before he took on the mantle of *Doctor Who* writer and Executive Producer, a *Guardian* piece about another British television institution caught his eye. It would lead, almost, to more permanent work in television. William Smethurst, then the new producer of flagging but institutionalised ITV soap opera *Crossroads*, launched an appeal for new writers to breathe fresh life into the programme. At around this time there were several attempts to revamp the show in an attempt to confound memories of the often shambolic programme's history. Peter Fiddick's article, published on 12 January 1987, read:

> To some readers of this page, indeed, he [Smethurst] has a
> proposition: don't just watch this revolution – write for it.
> You will have to watch it first. And he does not want part-time
> amateurs: the eight or so writers of *Crossroads* between them
> feed four 18-minute episodes a week during the production
> period, and earn their r-and-r breaks. But the money is good,
> he finds there are regular television writers who still won't
> stoop to pick it up, a couple of the team are having babies, so
> the new *Crossroad* motel has vacancies. The rules are simple:
> 'Watch *Crossroads*, as it is now, for a bit, then write an episode
> with 15 scenes and 10 of the characters, and send it in.' (That's:
> W Smethurst, Central Independent Television, Central House,
> Broad Street, Birmingham B1 2JP.)

And that is exactly what Davies did. 'I sent it off to him and I'm not sure how badly *Crossroads* was run because I got the job! I went up and visited them. They wanted another shadow script off me with proper storylines, and I got shown round the set, all that sort of stuff.' But just two days after this visit the future of the Midlands soap took a sudden turn for the worse. As Fiddick wrote in the *Guardian* on 6 July:

> Well, this page did try to help. But our 1987 New Year Appeal –
> for new writers to help breathe new life into *Crossroads* – came
> too late. Last Thursday evening, as rehearsals ended, and with
> the yuppified glories of the re-styled roadhouse still to have their
> impact on the loyal viewers, the axe was wielded: the soap shall die.

As was also highlighted later in the same article, it was to be a 'lingering death', with already signed contracts ensuring that the soap stayed on air until 1988. However, Davies' services were no longer required. Given the extensive press coverage of the long-running show's cancellation it was, as he puts it, 'the most public sacking in the world.'

This was not to be Davies' final contact with the soap opera in question, however. A poorly received new vision of life at the Crossroads Hotel (née Motel) was later seen in a revival of the soap opera launched in 2001, with Davies' friend Tony Wood in place as producer. At that point, Davies once again found himself with an offer of work on the series. This time, though, his increased profile meant that he had the luxury of turning it down. 'Tony Wood said, "Just come and do three months at *Crossroads*, come and have a laugh," and I thought, "I would have." But I couldn't do it. I just couldn't do it now – my agent would kill me! It's a very snotty industry. A lot of people would say, "What are you doing that for?" – which is wrong, but there you go.'

It's certainly tempting to wonder if Davies could have reinvigorated *Crossroads* considering that, years later, he would re-establish a similarly rickety programme as a television institution. Davies would have been required to radically reinvent a cheaply made daytime soap opera at a time when viewers simply didn't seem to be interested – and ITV's concurrent new soap opera, *Night and Day*, had fallen by the wayside for similar reasons. Davies' proposed spell at *Crossroads* could possibly have worked, though, as we'll see, he has had mixed success with soap operas. As it was, the revived *Crossroads* failed to find an audience and was promptly axed.

Back in 1987, though, there was to be one last career twist before Davies settled into more comfortable behind-the-scenes television roles. He happened to meet *Why Don't You?* line producer Peter Charlton, who suggested that Davies could take a rather more public role within Children's BBC; that of a presenter on long-running pre-school series *Play School*. According to Davies, Charlton 'said to me, "You'd be good on camera, come and do an audition." And I just thought, "What a laugh! I'll go and do that."' As a result of the audition (at which, armed with a flip-chart, he both drew and told Roald Dahl's *Dirty Beasts* tale, *The Anteater*), Davies got the go-ahead to present the TV show proper.

Such a switch of careers would not have been particularly straightforward, though, as he wasn't a member of actor's union Equity, generally a prerequisite for paid performance work at the time. Equity were unconvinced that Davies should have special dispensation. But such was the weight of confidence behind him that it was argued his drawing skills made him a special case. After months of negotiation, a complex system was devised whereby Davies would be allowed to appear on *Play School* a limited number of times over a six-month period in order to qualify for an Equity card.

So it was that, along with *Play School* regular Chloë Ashcroft, Davies co-presented an edition of the 23-year-old children's show on Monday 1 June 1987 in his special capacity as a storytelling illustrator. Initially, it seemed an attractive proposition. 'It was so nice. There were proper rehearsals,' he says. 'They were at BBC North Acton. [The 1987 *Doctor Who* story] 'Paradise Towers' was in there, rehearsing at the time. I'd sit in the canteen and think, "Oooh, it's Sylvester McCoy!" I felt like I was part of it all because they were rehearsing.' But when the point came for the actual recording of the show, his feelings were less assured; indeed, Davies literally shudders at the memory. 'I'm not kidding you, the moment it finished I said, "No, I'm not doing that again." It felt absolutely wrong.' He adds, however, that 'They were lovely people, really, really nice, I had a nice time, it was quite fun.'

The BBC powers-that-be declared themselves well satisfied with Davies' appearance, and the offer was there for him to make a series of return engagements. But it was not an experience he wished to repeat. Davies was a young man with a golden opportunity, but for him it was the wrong one. 'I literally walked out of BBC Television Centre,' he says. 'How glamorous can you get! But I remember walking out of there thinking, "I am not doing that. I am not doing that to earn money." They weren't pleased because they'd gone to such a lot of effort to get me an Equity card and fix up all the meetings, and I just said, "I've had enough thanks." But just instinct says that's the wrong thing for you to be doing.'

Davies' subsequent highly assured career path seems to bear out his innate understanding of what would or would not be right for him. Not all of his projects may have been critically acclaimed or universally popular, but Davies himself rarely hints at any sense of regret. When given complete control over his work, the result is always confident and striking, even if it isn't an unqualified success. But Davies rarely expresses negative sentiments towards these projects, even when he accepts that they didn't turn out as well as they might have. In the case of *Play School*, bailing out was the only thing he could do to stop himself embarking on a career that he wouldn't be happy with.

His dalliance with presenting was never forgotten by his BBC contemporaries, however, especially when it came to the obligatory wrap party at the end of each production. 'Every fucking time someone would order up the *Play School* tape. They'd show the out-takes and stuff like that, and then they'd always cut to me going, "Hello, blah blah blah…" with my Kevin Keegan hair.'

The experience as a whole didn't particularly faze Davies, though. It was merely a brief side-step in his working life, but one that at least indicated what to avoid in future. His only other known appearance in front of the cameras at the time was when he donned a *Doctor Who* Cyberman costume for an edition of *Why Don't You?* – perhaps a classic case of bringing one's personal enthusiasms to work. '1987 was mad! I'd bump into people I knew in the street and they'd go, "What job are you up to now? Are you a cartoonist, on *Play School, Crossroads,* or what?" Mad…'

By 1988, Davies' career in television reached a crossroads – unrelated, on this occasion, to a Midlands motel. Over at BBC Manchester, in the latest development of a long and illustrious career in television, Ed Pugh was placed in charge of the regional children's department. Pugh's boss, Anna Home, informed him that *Why Don't You?* was to cease in its present form, as a show that was passed between the BBC regions. Instead, it would be produced from Manchester and Manchester alone.

In bringing this about, Pugh travelled over to BBC Wales to meet with Dave Evans and cast an eye over the final days of Cardiff's *Why Don't You?* team. 'I saw the studio, and met these two AFMs [assistant floor managers],' Pugh says. 'One was a girl who did the props, and the other was this rather tall bloke called Russell. I said to him, "So what's your role exactly?" He said, "Well, I sort of help the kids and I write and do this and do that. You know, lots of things." You could tell he was really good with the kids, getting good performances out of them, geeing them up just before they did a take and things like that, as opposed to just the floor manager saying, "Right, stand by studio."'

Pugh spent the following day getting a clearer impression of the way the team operated, and remained particularly impressed with young AFM Russell Davies. 'He seemed like a really clever, good bloke. In the bar, during the supper break or at the end of the day, I said to him, "So, what next then?" – thinking he'd be going off somewhere. He said, "This is the end of the run. I'm back on the dole tomorrow!" Pugh promptly offered him an alternative: to move with *Why Don't You?* to Manchester on a six-month contract. Davies was quick to accept.

It was a landmark moment. By his own account, Davies fully expected to be left high and dry on the departure of *Why Don't You?* from BBC Wales. His present contract had three months left to run, but, with no show to make, he assumed he'd be paid off. Instead, he took up Ed Pugh's offer and, at the age of 25, upped sticks and moved from Swansea to Manchester. 'You could tell that he was someone who was, even then, ambitious,' remembers Pugh, 'and he just had something about him.'

The move coincided with Kirstie Fisher taking the helm as producer of *Why Don't You?*, having previously worked on the children's news programme *Newsround*. Fisher and Davies soon became good friends. A strong ice-breaker, perhaps, was the revelation that Kirstie's father was scriptwriter David Fisher, who'd been responsible for a total of five *Doctor Who* stories between 1978 and 1980. Together, Kirstie and Davies made a show that he still seems proud of today.

Davies soon found himself working on several programmes for the BBC Manchester Children's department. He wrote and produced some sketches for Saturday morning summer filler series *On the Waterfront*, for which, most memorably, he wrote comic voiceovers to accompany extracts from the French television serial *The Flashing Blade*. In all, he took on many and varied roles while working in the department, and considers it to have been a good experience.

'In my time I did documentaries, dramas, children's sketch shows, comedy sketches, you do everything,' he remembers. 'And I got experience actually working in the department as like an assistant producer. I worked on film, I worked on OBs [Outside Broadcasts], I went to dubbing sessions. You get sent to the edit with no idea what an edit is! You get thrown into an old-fashioned, two-inch tape, two-machine edit. And God help the editor because he was used to this constant stream of children's workers walking in going, "I don't know what to do!" And they teach you what to do. By the end of a month, I knew how to do a two-machine edit. So its cheapness, and its high volume, and its capacity to cover anything is a brilliant place to get started.'

But there was more than just technical expertise to be learnt from his time in the department. He reminisces that, as far as scripting was concerned, 'In Children's you could get away with anything. You could write absolutely anything, and they're such a clever audience they'll go with you onto anything.'

As a whole, the Children's department at BBC Manchester became something of a powerhouse, endeavouring to deliver something special. 'There was a good spirit there,' Pugh says. 'We all had a kind of slight maverick feel. We wanted to try and do things that were a little adventurous and be different from what London was offering up.'

Davies continued to deploy his particular talents by creating original *Why Don't You?* fact packs, which were sent out on request to young viewers. One such viewer was Clayton Hickman, who, in adult life, would go on to edit the official *Doctor Who Magazine*. Writing in the introduction to the graphic novel *The Flood*, Hickman pointed out that these *Why Don't You?* packs were 'full of ideas and recipes and jokes and beautifully illustrated, in comic strip style throughout – the mad adventures of an egg and a plastic cup and a potato battling an evil paperclip.' Ed Pugh remembers them well. 'I've still got copies. Russell did all the writing, and all the little figures and things like that. It's extraordinary! You know you kind of sometimes hate people who are talented in lots of different respects… ? But no! – he was very clever.'

At the same time, Davies made occasional forays beyond the confines of the department, notably undertaking an internal BBC course for budding directors at Elstree in March 1989. He dabbled in writing for an older audience by providing a scattering of sketch material for *Def II*, Janet Street-Porter's painfully trendy youth magazine slot on BBC2. He even managed to have a jaunt abroad, as he accompanied presenter Keith Chegwin on a trip to Norway for the BBC Manchester show *Chegwin Checks Out... Politics.* Clearly Davies had earned his spurs, and proved himself a capable man of many talents. Ed Pugh decided the time was right to entrust him with a new challenge, one which involved greater responsibility. Pugh had pitched the idea for a new Saturday morning show to his superiors, one that would revolve around several different serials and one-off skits being loosely linked each week, with the diversity of the programme being the real selling point. He had earmarked Davies for the role of producer from the beginning. 'In my head was the thought, "Let's give it to Russell to look after." Lock, stock and barrel, to be the producer,' says Pugh. 'He thought I was mad when I told him! He said, "You're joking!" I said, "No, I think you'll be very good."'

If ever there was a programme that would seem unsuited to critical deconstruction, the result, *Breakfast Serials,* would be it. It was an obviously cheap and quickly made children's show that was broadcast at a time, 8.00 am, when so few people were watching television at all that it would soon have no original programming made for it. It consisted of a number of ongoing tales, episodes of which ran in each weekly instalment – not unlike the structure of traditional British comics, from *The Beano* and *The Dandy* to *2000AD*. The whole wide variety of tales was performed by a revolving cast of four. The result felt silly and inconsequential but, nevertheless, was entertaining. Sometimes this was by virtue of its sheer audacity rather than as a result of any refined wit or tightly paced drama. Not that this should necessarily be blamed for the series' lack of success. Some programmes are simply scheduled and produced in such a way that they can never achieve mass appeal.

Modern interest in the programme is the result of our knowledge of what was to come from Davies' career, as we can trace some of his trademarks back to this very early period. If there is one outstanding aspect of his writing (and, indeed, his apparent attitude towards the programme as a whole), then it comes from the incredible boldness of the production coupled with its often very funny tendency to explore the ridiculous.

Breakfast Serials was a programme that used, as its central linking theme, three rather odd puppets, namely a talking tomato, tin can and teapot – cousins, perhaps, of the talking potato, plastic cup and egg from those *Why Don't You?* fact sheets. Of course, puppets are a mainstay of children's television. That, in itself, is nothing exceptional. However, in the writing of their characters, the trio exhibited a confidence and a level of wit that scarcely bothered to accommodate the young audience. The programme was full of silly sketches and jokes that presumably amused Davies most of all, with the audience as something of a secondary consideration.

That is not to say that the programme was a failure. It was actually hugely watchable and often amusing, but the jokes tended to be of the non-sequitur variety. As Davies later said, it was very clearly written for students rather than children. It would be understandable if the young viewers were just plain baffled while older viewers sniggered at the casual introduction of an argument about *Howard's Way*, or an entire conversation between the three usually inanimate hosts about the rules of *Give Us a Clue*. 'Is that the one where they put their finger on their nose if someone gets the answer right?' asks Teapot. 'That's right,' replies Tomato. 'With Michael Parkinson, and before that Michael Aspel. They only let people called Michael do it. Next year it's going to be Princess Michael of Kent.'

The programme was littered with such pop culture references. As is often pointed out, fictional characters on television generally fail to refer to the medium on which they are appearing. Here, though, Davies went all-out to show off his love for the more mundane aspects of television broadcasting. Despite such quips providing a moment of amusement for the parts of the audience who shared Davies' love, elsewhere the humour rarely strayed from the obvious. Nevertheless, the concept of a pithy talking tin can discussing the time she used to work on *Button Moon* playing the rocket (except for the space shots, naturally performed by a stunt double) was particularly appealing for an older audience with a taste for the arch. It's easy to imagine the great joy of a wandering viewer discovering this programme by chance. Certainly, Davies himself was not the only person to appreciate the final product.

'I was its only viewer, I think,' says Gareth Roberts, later to work with

Davies on *Springhill* and *Doctor Who* among other series. This claim is largely echoed by Davies' memories of the poor ratings. 'It went out at 8 o'clock in the morning and it got 70,000 viewers!' he laughs. 'I might have gone round their houses and told them what'd happened! And it would have been cheaper!' Roberts may have been one of the few watching the show, but he relished it greatly: 'I remember noting the writer's name because it was so funny – it seemed to be aimed directly at me, even though I was 22!'

There was certainly a lot of student humour in the series – a *Land of the Giants* spoof revolved around its 'miniature' protagonists simply crouching down as they wander through the countryside – but there were also moments of drama that foreshadow some of Davies' later Children's BBC work. 'Runner', one of the recurring mini-serials spread throughout the series, was certainly a precursor of *Dark Season* in many respects, with its mysterious villains clad in sunglasses and black clothing, roaming middle-class streets.

There were several writers working on *Breakfast Serials* and this particular strand was originally written by Dominic MacDonald but was then heavily reworked by Davies. In truth, it lacked the humour and warmth of his later efforts. This was inevitably a result of it being sandwiched between so many lighter elements in the show, but it addressed the balance a little too drastically. Davies later acknowledged that it was possibly too dark for the time slot and envisaged audience, something that Ed Pugh, the head of Children's BBC in Manchester, agrees with: 'There were bits where I went, "Oh my God! Are we sure we know what we're doing?" So I showed it to Anna [Home, head of Children's BBC at the time] who was always a very understanding boss. I don't think we'd get away with it at all now. It was quite frightening – I think a bit more frightening than *Doctor Who* could be at times. It's probably quite a good healthy thing to be frightened, at times. There was nothing really horrifying about it, but it was probably pushing it, barrier-wise.'

Certainly Davies had been 'pushing it' more generally in his work at Children's BBC, in his role as, at this point, a relatively junior producer. He was not taking a soft option with his work, but creating a programme that genuinely marked itself out as being at least distinctive, although not for philanthropic reasons. This was simply the avenue that most appealed. There were elements that recurred in his later work, especially in the more dramatic serials, with the combination of the fantastic and the mundane.

This was becoming a key motif of Davies', but the emphasis on drama within his career was also emerging. He was a producer as well as a writer, but his work on *Breakfast Serials* indicated his interest in creating the stories themselves.

It's tempting to cite Davies' later children's serial *Dark Season* as the point that saw the emergence of his recognisable 'voice' as a writer, but many of the characteristics that were to come were already present and correct. The ambitious storytelling, plotted in broad strokes, echoes the comic strips which so interest him, with big stories being told in an emotional and engaging manner, with a healthy vein of humour. There are also elements of what may be called 'camp'.

Whole academic tracts have been written attempting to define that word. However one chooses to define it, though, *Breakfast Serials* had it in spades. Each episode concluded with a dimming of the studio lights as a disco soundtrack started up and multi-coloured lighting bounced off the set and props. So it is that the first episode ended with a red tomato, yellow teapot and blue tin can miming to Middle of the Road's hit single *Chirpy Chirpy Cheep Cheep (Where's Your Momma Gone)*. Asked if this was his touch, Davies responds, 'Of course it was!' Indeed, it has the correct mixture of campness, humour and unabashed ridiculousness to match much of his lighter work. *Breakfast Serials* was not quite a postmodern masterpiece but it unequivocally featured Davies' voice as a writer. His style was not quite fully formed, but there were definite signifiers as to where his writing career would be headed.

In all, Davies' rather abrupt move to Manchester seems to have been a resounding success. In personal terms, it was ideal. 'I was in my early 20s and still coming out really,' Davies told journalist Wayne Clews many years later. 'I hate to bring it down to something gay but Cardiff had one gay club and Manchester had something like four. That doesn't sound a lot but it made the place four times better in my eyes and that was part of my decision to stay. Within a few years, Canal Street really began to take off.'

Soon Manchester's large, thriving gay community was centred on the city centre Canal Street area, a neat 'gay space' made up of bars, pubs and clubs. Davies threw himself into this life with aplomb. Later, he'd reflect that, during this period, he'd commonly wake up after a night out not knowing exactly what part of South Manchester he found himself in. Less amusingly, during 1990 Davies wound up in hospital for some weeks with an acute case of appendicitis. For company he had little more than a Maeve Binchy novel, which, to his dismay, he hated.

Meanwhile, as far as his career was concerned, Davies had worked his way up the *Why Don't You?* hierarchy to become the producer of the show. The previous incumbent, Kirstie Fisher, had moved to explore new horizons in Australia. Davies not only took her old job but also went on to buy her house, and found himself settled on the outskirts of Manchester city centre, where he remains today. The new job came with its own frustrations – almost every 'make' suggested by the child audience was in fact the same recipe for chocolate Rice Krispie cakes – but such matters started to become less important to the show that he was now moulding. *Why Don't You?* had changed relatively little since its 1973 launch, still being a magazine show presented by children, centred around suggestions for things to make and do, with the familiar theme tune encouraging the audience to 'switch off your TV set and do something less boring instead.'

Under Davies' leadership, the programme moved away from this style and began to be centred more on drama, with the gang of child presenters finding themselves in various scrapes. Many of these adventures centred on popular Welsh 'inventor' character Ben Slade, whose crazy contraptions would inevitably cause chaos. As to whether there was any consternation within the department about the altering of a popular and long-running format, it's clear that there were two main reasons why the changes were permitted. The first was that the series was based at BBC Manchester. Even though they were not permitted to produce their own children's drama, few seemed to notice the programme's actual content. 'You did fly under the radar in Manchester, that's why it was a brilliant place to work,' says Davies. 'They didn't really pay much attention to what was going on – it was all stopgap programmes, the programmes that no one else wanted to make. It meant that you had enormous freedom, and literally got away with everything.'

Head of Children's Anna Home did notice, but did not chastise Davies for it, even if she was less than keen on the character of Ben. 'She wanted him gone,' he remembers. 'Anna Home hated him! She said, "The one thing that doesn't work is that boy." And I just ignored it! What a cheeky thing.' As was so often to be the case throughout his career, battles with figures of authority inevitably led to Davies eventually getting his own way. But this time he could be forgiven by Home, as not only was Davies enjoying his work on the series, but it was having an extremely positive effect on the ratings, which he claims more than tripled from 900,000 viewers to 2.9 million.

Of the producers under his care, Pugh cites Davies as 'one of the more rebellious ones' and certainly his parting shot to the production was to mark out his future intentions. Although Pugh points out that they simply could not create a full 25-minute drama each week, for his final episode Davies was allowed to dispense with the 'makes' altogether and instead scripted a full 25 minutes of drama. That's not to say that it was 25 minutes of hard-hitting plot. Instead it was very much in keeping with the frivolous nature of the programme, but it was nevertheless a radical departure when compared to the show just a few years earlier. This was a development that was certainly to Davies' taste, and he cites this as 'such a creative time,' not something that producers of light entertainment programmes would generally consider a key aspect of their day to day jobs.

'It was like a drama come the end, so the very last episode I did, they all became trapped in the café, and there was a supercomputer in the basement that tried to kill them! The *Why Don't You?* gang! And a sheep saved them all.' Such a crazy plot speaks volumes for what may be best described as the general tone of insanity in Davies' writing during this time, where comedy and drama are muddled into a single entity for much of his work. But, with a handful of exceptions, most of his future scripting would continue to integrate the two genres, with lighter moments and witty dialogue jostling with more dramatic sequences.

However, his budding writing career in Children's BBC was to be brought to a premature end. This was not down to any changes in the department itself, but rather Davies' own attitude. He had decided that he wanted to leave. The reason for his departure can be traced back to the transmission of the first episode of *Breakfast Serials* in 1990, serving as it did to highlight for him the direction in which he did not want his career to progress.

'I stopped working for Children's because I thought I was wrong for Children's,' he bluntly states, before pointing out the exact moment that he realised his career path would take him in a different direction. 'After the first episode of *Breakfast Serials*, my friend Sally phoned me up and said, "Do you realise you've just broadcast a joke about the juvenilia of Emily Brontë at eight o'clock in the morning?" and I thought, "Yeah, I did, didn't I?" * There was a part of me that was writing for students, which was allowed to a certain extent in Children's, because, frankly, it got a bigger audience in. But actually it took me till *Breakfast Serials* to realise that was what I really liked writing, and that I was wrong for Children's. I left the BBC with no job to go to. I just thought, "I'm in the wrong place, so I should go and find other work."' Not for the first or last time, Davies turned his back on a job simply as a result of gut instinct.

However, this lack of willingness to write down to a children's audience was to be one of the impetuses for Davies to seek work in different areas of television, even if this was not to be an immediate move. Indeed, his next project was to be his biggest yet, but with direct links to his producing past.

---

* When ruminating on her plans for the day, Tin Can says, "I myself was about to attend a brief lecture on the juvenilia of Emily Brontë, but that may not be to the tastes of one and all."

THREE:
MARVELLOUS, I'M A CLICHÉ!

Back at the dawn of the nineties, Davies had been living alone in a basic bedsit on Ladybarn Lane in South Manchester's Fallowfield area, where he'd pass the time mulling over new ideas for stories, initially for *Why Don't You?* 'I'd sit in that little room and think of Loch Ness, and monsters, and stuff like that,' he says. 'I can actually remember where I thought of things. It was a good place to live. It was so dull in there, all I could do was think, really.'

One particular dramatic excursion in *Why Don't You?* resulted in Davies considering an idea for a new adventure serial. 'We did one episode where they all went off to Loch Ness. A load of nonsense – it wasn't even Loch Ness, it was some lake. And they have an adventure and they potter about, and I remember being in the bath once and thinking, actually, if you did take all of the recipes and puzzles out of that you could do a story about a gang of kids. Like things I used to watch when I was young. Two days later, in my head was *Dark Season*.'

Davies wrote up the first episode of the adventure in script form, his first full drama piece. However, with typical Davies chutzpah, the serial was not submitted and commissioned in the usual manner. Before he left the Children's department, the script was submitted to Anna Home, then head of Children's BBC, via the internal post, with a glowing covering letter from his boss Ed Pugh, in the hope of avoiding the new writers' slush pile. Simultaneously, Pugh submitted a pilot script for *Sloggers*, a children's drama about a cricket club written by one-time darts commentator Sid Waddell. It was impossible for any drama to be made in Manchester due to the way in which Children's BBC then operated, with all drama series having to be made by the London department. The script was the first episode of what was hoped to be a six-part serial initially entitled *The Adventuresome Three*, using members of the *Why Don't You?* gang in a pure drama setting.

Davies' rather cheeky gambit worked. Home read and liked the script. What she didn't like, though, was the inclusion of the *Why Don't You?* gang. More especially, her open dislike of the character of inventor Ben Slade, who was central to Davies' script, was a major sticking point. According to

Davies, 'The very first plan was to take Ben and that little *Why Don't You?* gang and tell *Dark Season* that way, with that gang – but then Anna Home said, "I can't *stand* that boy!"' Consequently, the idea was reworked with an entirely new cast of characters, and the title was changed to *Dark Season*. 'That was really the proper start of my career,' argues Davies. 'That was actually when I knew what I wanted to do.'

But getting the programme made was not as straightforward a process as it could have been. The script was also shown to Granada, who expressed an interest in making it for the rival Children's ITV. Davies remembers meeting Granada's lead script editor Tony Wood to discuss the project. 'He wanted to commission it, but he wanted to commission it as a six-part story, just that first story, and I said no, it's two three-parters. He said, "ITV wouldn't like that," so I said, "Oh, fine."' The upshot was that Davies passed on the offer from Granada.

Davies knew that this matter was also potentially an issue for the BBC as he had deliberately not informed them of his unusual structure before delivery of the scripts. But his insistence that he would not alter his plans for the serial even when a commission was imminent demonstrates an important change of focus at this point. Suddenly, Davies was writing for himself, rather than simply writing to fill the time and earn a wage. He was now focused on writing projects that he had initiated. From here on, with just a handful of exceptions, he would continue to do so.

His refusal to kowtow to the requests of Granada did not endear him to the company, though. 'I got called in to Granada to be told off by David Liddiment,' Davies admits. 'I worship that man now, having worked for him, but at the time he was a complete stranger. He was telling me off, but I just sort of sat there going, "I don't work for you, you can't tell me off!" It was like being told off by a complete stranger. I thought I was barred at Granada.' As we shall see, this proved not to be the case. Nor was the serial in question derailed by this daunting experience.

'That was quite funny, because he'd done a naughty deal,' Ed Pugh recalls. 'He'd tried to sell it to Granada and they were keen on optioning it. I said, "What have you done that for?", because at that stage I'd put it in to the BBC. We hadn't heard from Anna [Home] and I had to tell her that he'd put it in at Granada. I said, "The silly boy's done this. So, I'm not holding you to it, but are you interested?" And she optioned it then, and went ahead with it.' In a stroke of luck, performer Tony Robinson had decided to take a year off from his popular Children's BBC comedy show *Maid Marian and her Merry Men*. The slot, and indeed the budget, that had been earmarked for it had to be redeployed to another project. So it was that Anna Home decided to take a chance with *Dark Season*, assigning Colin Cant, who had a wealth of experience in children's drama, to direct it.

At least part of the success of *Dark Season* and its counterpart *Century Falls* can be put down to their distinctiveness when compared to the rest of the schedules. This is true both in general terms and more particularly by comparison to other children's programmes. In 1991, there was simply nothing else of this type on television. As is often the case, Davies wrote a serial that was modern in tone but had an oddly timeless feel to it. Tellingly, in its wake, more programming of a fantasy adventure stamp would follow, not least Children's BBC's own *The Demon Headmaster*, of which Davies was very aware. 'That never quite worked,' he argues. 'It wasn't scary enough, was it? It wasn't real enough. I remember at the time thinking, "I wish I was writing *The Demon Headmaster*." I'd have had a good time with that.'

Any writer of fiction dreads being asked where they get their ideas from, but *Dark Season* has a more easily traceable genesis than most productions. Parallels have often been drawn between the serial and *Doctor Who*. For Davies, though, it was simply a conglomeration of various science fiction and adventure programmes of a similar ilk that had been prevalent during his youth. Indeed, the first inklings of *Dark Season* came about while he was dreaming up fantastical stories as a schoolboy at Olchfa. 'In my head I was very much in a sort of science fiction land. I walked around inventing all this stuff thinking, "What if there was a secret laboratory underneath the school?" And then, so many years later, you get to actually write that.'

First shown on BBC1 from November 1991, *Dark Season* revolved around a standard British secondary school and, more particularly, three of the students: Marcie, Reet and Thomas. Notably, Reet provided an early TV role for young actress Kate Winslet, shortly to find international fame as Rose in James Cameron's blockbuster *Titanic*. At first, the 'adventuresome three' find themselves implicated in a fiendish plot spearheaded by the mysterious Mr Eldritch, who donates a computer to each of the school's pupils in order to facilitate his quest for world domination. These first three episodes concentrate on the cynical but enlightened Marcie trying to alert adults to Eldritch's plan, while endeavouring to stop him. In a nifty resolution, computer expert Professor Polszinsky is revealed not to be the man living next door to Marcie, but rather his wife.

At this juncture, the serial appears to have wrapped after just three episodes. But this was just the prelude to the second half, where our heroes encounter a new villain. This is the turban-wearing Miss Pendragon, played by Jacqueline Pearce, best known as Servalan from *Blake's 7*. She instructs her blonde followers to assist her in finding, and eventually becoming, the 'Behemoth', as part of an archaeological dig on school grounds. In the climactic moments of Part Five, Pendragon crashes through the school's stage from below, strapped to a large mechanical chair, with green lasers darting all around the hall, bellowing in a mechanically treated voice, 'I am Behemoth!'

Dark Season bears more than a passing similarity to the later *Doctor Who* episode 'School Reunion', written by Toby Whithouse but with the school setting suggested by Davies. In its initial outline form, even the 2005 *Doctor Who* episode 'The Unquiet Dead' concerned a medium, a Miss Pendragon, and her troublesome Ectoplasm Machine. But these are future parallels; there were few overt similarities between Davies' serial and the *Doctor Who* of old.

A contemporary issue of *Doctor Who Magazine* put its tongue in its cheek when it printed Marcie's oft-quoted line, delivered as she finds herself crawling through a ventilation shaft – 'Marvellous, I'm a cliché!' – and asked its readers to identify the story. But such comparisons were more than likely drawn because the long-running science fiction series had been off air since 1989 and had not been replaced by anything of a similar bent. While Marcie and her two 'companions' may echo the traditional *Doctor Who* set-up, Marcie's alleged 'Doctor-ish' persona is no more than a plot device. She has a degree of omniscience, knowing from the very beginning that there is something deeply suspicious about Eldritch. So often, TV audiences are forced to watch the unfolding of a mystery where they are more clued in than the principal characters. In Marcie's case, that's easily disposed of by having a main character who thinks along the same lines as the viewer, who knows that there is an adventure unfolding. As Marcie says herself when asked why she's so knowledgeable, 'I watch a lot of TV.' (Certainly Davies' own television obsession was already much in evidence. The very first shot of *Dark Season* shows two characters, Eldritch and Osley, peering intently at a screen – albeit a computer monitor.)

In fact, considering later developments, it's more interesting to turn the question on its head and see how the new series of *Doctor Who* feeds off some of the plotting and structure, not to mention tone, of the Children's BBC serial. At Part Five's cliffhanger, just as Miss Pendragon makes her final, dramatic entrance through the school stage, Mr Eldritch strides into the assembly hall. Such a structure would be used again for the first two series of Davies' *Doctor Who*, with the Daleks and Cybermen reappearing in the penultimate episodes having previously been defeated. Certainly the pace of *Dark Season*, assisted by the aforementioned use of Marcie's inquisitive character, is reminiscent of the breakneck speed with which Davies would later open the inaugural episodes of each new series of *Doctor Who*.

However, the characters in *Dark Season* aren't fleshed out over the course of the narrative in the manner of most of Davies' later creations. Perhaps as a result of the action-based drama and relatively brief running time of individual episodes, there is a lack of emotional resonance in *Dark Season* that is not in keeping with Davies' later work. The story is simple and strong, surrounded by witty dialogue and a degree of action. This is not necessarily the result of the programme being written for a younger audience, as there is more of an emphasis on characterisation in his follow-up serial *Century Falls* as well as the later *Doctor Who* spin-off *The Sarah Jane Adventures*. Instead, this seems to be a tonal decision. Although it is no less frenetic than some of his later dramas, there's no room here for the characters to breathe. Character motivation would be a key plot point of *Century Falls* but, here, it would just slow down the drama.

The adventure is fun and light, except for when the villains need to appear as a particular threat. There are no deep dark issues, no skeletons lurking in any lead character's closet. Instead, the origins of the piece in *Why Don't You?* can be most clearly seen in its breezy nature, and the serial is no less entertaining for this. Nevertheless, like the *Sarah Jane Adventures* 15 years later, *Dark Season* simply revolves around things that would interest children but may not necessarily have the same appeal for adults. There is enough sophistication and spectacle for broader appeal but this makes it no less enjoyable for its core audience.

When compared to the darkness of his next work for Children's BBC, *Dark Season* is often ostentatious, with Jacqueline Pearce's performance being a spectacularly, and satisfactorily, camp element of the production. In fact, although Pearce brings a great deal to the character, she was not the first choice for the role. Originally, Sheila Steafel, an actress familiar to British viewers since the 1960s, was cast in the part, but had to pull out due to sickness a week before filming began. In her stead, Pearce gives an unfettered performance, but she is far from *Dark Season*'s only camp element. Even before the first episode's opening credits, the sinister Eldritch has uttered the immortal line 'Nothing in the world can stop me now', giving some sense of the unsubtle nature of his villainy. This also marks him out as part of the same demented lineage as, for instance, *Doctor Who* villain Professor Zaroff, who shouted those self-same words in the 1967 story 'The Underwater Menace'.

By deploying such well-worn science fiction clichés, some aspects of the serial almost seem to be written in shorthand, with the presumption that viewers are savvy enough to understand the way that stories of this nature pan out. There is no attempt to disguise the evil nature of the villains. As Marcie says when she first sees Eldritch, 'And so it begins.'

As previously indicated, *Dark Season* stands out as being a programme unconcerned with the environment in which it was broadcast, as with many of Davies' later productions. It ignores the then increasing trend towards realism rather than fantasy and is situated firmly in a fantasy idea of a secondary school in the United Kingdom, with the children not wearing uniforms and a rather reduced level of authority from the teachers. Not that these were instigated by Davies. 'I have to say, I did not put those children in those costumes!' he says. 'I thought, "Ooh, why were they all wearing pastels?" What was all that about?'

But while *Dark Season* was a rare excursion into science fiction for the BBC at this time, it was equally a rare example of Davies writing something that he had no influence on beyond the scripting stage. This extends to his preconceptions of the aesthetics of the production. Davies was fortunate that his creation would benefit from the healthy budget allotted to *Maid Marian and her Merry Men*, whose production and broadcast slot it was occupying. The production of science fiction at the BBC did not have a history of being visually impressive, with Davies' expectations lowered further when he considered the relatively low production values of other productions within the department.

'I literally just handed it over in those days,' he says, 'and I remember not even knowing what sort of budget it would have. I remember about the time in those years there were the cheaper science fiction dramas. I'd see *Watt on Earth*, and they'd just take CSO stars and sparks as the effects.' In fact, although the budget was respectable, the grounding of the programme in real locations, as with many of his later *Doctor Who* scripts, would enable the money to stretch further than usual.

Not all the locations could be easily constructed or adapted, though. 'I remember reading the scripts and thinking, the Behemoth in its chamber, that's going to be like a glittery panel against a studio wall,' Davies recalls. 'And then one of the best moments of my life, my whole career, was when I went and they were filming one of those Behemoth things in Ealing, and I thought, "Oh, it's probably just a space out the back." I turned up at lunchtime, the set was deserted, and I walked on to that set – which is still, to this day, one of the most impressive sets I've ever seen. That chair really lifts up with a 60-foot crane above it!' The Behemoth's chamber remains impressive even now, nearly 20 years later, and the overall appearance of the serial certainly lifts it above the level of some of the cheaper Children's BBC dramas. This has helped ensure that, costumes aside, the serial has dated very little.

Although Davies had no direct influence over any of these other aspects of the serial once he had handed over his scripts, this doesn't mean that the end product was a watered-down version. Indeed, though he had already established an authorial 'voice' of sorts through his work on other shows for the department, this was to be the first fully realised example of his writing. Without seeing the earlier, admittedly minor, items on his CV such as *Breakfast Serials*, it could be imagined that he simply arrived on Children's BBC's doorstep with the scripts of *Dark Season*, boasting a fully developed and completely distinctive writing style. In fact, of course, his style developed over time, with *Dark Season* being the culmination of his work in this period, setting the tone for what was to come.

Many of the recurring elements are there, including the witty dialogue and casual references to television and other aspects of popular culture, as first glimpsed on *Breakfast Serials*. When a child character returns to school bathed in an eerie glow, Thomas comments that it sounds like she 'hit the Readybrek too hard,' in reference to the familiar adverts for that product. There's also the slow emergence of one of the central motifs of much of Davies' work, the juxtaposition of the mundane with the fantastic. Although the characterisation isn't particularly strong in the lead roles, especially when it comes to the rather nondescript Thomas and Reet, there is nevertheless a sense of the series being grounded in the 'real world' yet not having to fall into line with all-out realism. In fact, it does Davies' dialogue a disservice to imply that these references to popular culture act only to amuse the audience. Instead, they allow characters to talk like real people.

It's clear that *Dark Season* was a turning point for Davies. It cemented his wish to write fiction, and demonstrated that he was capable of it. He acknowledges it as his first properly written dramatic script. His own first viewing of the serial, with a proper writing credit, was a formative experience, and he still remembers his feelings on seeing the opening titles on transmission. Whereas he had been sure that *Play School* was not for him after just one day, he was convinced of the opposite here. 'I'm not kidding you, everything made sense,' he says. 'I just sat there and went, "That's what I want to do." I got the greatest kick out of it … It felt absolutely right. At the time I was mainly producing and directing. But seeing that credit made my mind up. I decided, "Actually, that's what I've got to pursue in life."'

Seeing his name on the credits of *Dark Season* was a turning point in other ways, too. For the first time, he was credited as 'Russell T Davies'. The extra initial was simply a practical requirement, to differentiate himself from the media personality of the same name, best known as a Radio 4 broadcaster and editor of the bestselling *Kenneth Williams Diaries*. 'Everyone goes, "Oh, you edited the *Kenneth Williams Diaries*." No I did not! People genuinely think I did that,' grumbles our Davies.

So it was that the change was made but, in the event, it was done in some haste. 'As they were doing the credits for *Dark Season*, I always knew there had been that other Russell Davies. Literally, [director] Colin Cant was in the edit that day and said, "What do you want?" And I was in the office, sitting there, going, "Hmmm. Russell S Davies? Russell M Davies?" But I chose the T.' He had no middle initial of his own to use – or rather, he'd always been known by his own given middle name of Russell. That 'T' – which he'd later dismiss as 'daft, invented, artificial-as-snow' – wouldn't seem objectionable given its necessity, but he evidently feels no attachment to it, particularly its niggling echo of *Star Trek*'s James T Kirk. 'I hate that T! I'd never introduce myself as Russell T Davies. It's not me!'

Even before *Dark Season* had been transmitted, Davies had agreed to write a novelisation of the tale for BBC Books. It is, in fact, one of only two books that he's ever written. In Davies' own estimation it's a shameless aping of the style of Stephen King, but nevertheless it's an engaging read which adds some welcome detail and colour to the serial, although for the most part it follows the plot pretty closely. The climax of the novelisation, which ends rather more ambiguously that its television forebear, sees the entire school collapsing in on itself following the defeat of Pendragon and Eldritch. That's followed by a brief epilogue which outlines the future of the main characters, including that of Pendragon's accomplice Luke, who had been unmasked as an actor. In a trademark Davies touch, Luke finds himself being cast in *EastEnders* and featuring on the cover of *Just Seventeen* magazine. Always one to highlight everyday minutiae, Davies writes that Luke 'was smiling, which gave him a double chin.'

The novelisation ends, somewhat tantalisingly, on what seems to be a promise of a further adventure, as Davies mentions a new arrival on the high street. 'A neon sign named it *Valhalla*: it was an amusement arcade, a glittering hall of state-of-the-art electronic games. That morning, three children decided to skip school ... but that's another story.' In Norse mythology, Valhalla is the name of a heaven-like place for warriors who experienced glorious deaths. But no *Dark Season* sequel ever came to pass. Children's BBC's *Maid Marian*, whose very absence had allowed Davies' serial to be commissioned, returned as normal the following year; exit *Dark Season.*

Many years later, though, the *Sarah Jane Adventures* story 'Warriors of Kudlak' would feature two young characters playing the Combat 3000 laser gun game at a newly opened venue in the high street. Along with many others who had played the game they go missing; the greatest players are being recruited to an alien race's army to fight a war that is revealed to be non-existent. Just possibly, then, some elements of the story were conceived back in the days of *Dark Season.*

In Davies' imagination, there existed a theoretical second run of *Dark Season* that followed the same pattern as the first. The three initial episodes would have been set in the video gaming arcade, and the second mini-story would have involved psychic twins at a private school, eventually leading to the re-emergence of the villainous Eldritch. In 1993, a subsequent, much altered variant on the 'psychic twins' idea became Davies' second Children's BBC drama, *Century Falls*. 'They're very different stories, but they all mix into one really,' he suggests. 'They only really separate as you tell the stories. I sort of think of it as one big world, where they could all bump into each other. I honestly believe that.' At this, Davies roars with laughter. 'Sad, isn't it?'

Actually, it's difficult to imagine any of the characters from his previous forays into children's writing fitting into *Century Falls*. This new serial was a much more serious, even sombre, affair than anything he had written to that point. While aspects of the premise were just as fantastical as those seen in *Dark Season*, the tone was wildly different.

Century Falls had an unusual gestation. Colin Cant, the director of *Dark Season*, had been charged with making a BBC children's drama in which he had no faith. Instead, he asked Davies if he could write another serial that would better hold his interest. Drawing from his existing reservoir of ideas, Davies wrote a synopsis for *Century Falls* over a weekend, and Cant approved enthusiastically. The full scripts were written quickly, as Davies' scripts often are. Even more than its predecessor, it sits oddly within the environment of children's broadcasting at that time.

The tale involves Tess Hunter, an overweight teenage girl, moving to the remote village of Century Falls with her mother. The village seems to have a mysterious past, with the locals claiming that no child had been born there for 40 years. Tess teams up with two other teenagers who live at the local manor house, Cairy and Ben Naismith, the latter of whom seems to have psychic powers somehow linked to the waterfall after which the village is named. A series of flashbacks indicates that some sort of disaster took place, and a village seance indicates that ancient deity Century is somehow trying to 'fuse' with Tess's mother's unborn child.

Century Falls is tonally dark in a way that few of Davies' other dramas have been. It's almost unrelenting in its grim treatment of what is, at heart, a fantastical premise. Davies acknowledges that the tone probably wasn't right for the intended audience, even though it was shown in the later 5.00 pm slot. 'I should have put a talking dog in there, or something,' he jokingly suggests. 'I was just learning, and you sort of get off on the dark stuff. When you're young you think dark is good, dark is drama and light is just comedy. And comedy is not as deep and therefore not as real, not as true, and not as valid a way of earning a living.'

This is a tidy summation of what seems to be the underlying rationale behind *Century Falls*. Davies appears to have felt he should be producing work that was less whimsical and more sober if he were ever to escape from writing for children. This resulted in a serial that tries very hard to be taken seriously and, to its credit, often succeeds. It's unrepresentative of his authorial voice in general, but it does demonstrate the diversity of his style.

The quest for seriousness in *Century Falls* means that humour is sparse to the point of being non-existent, while the fast pace of the largely action-based *Dark Season* is eschewed in favour of a convoluted plot that's often difficult to follow. Nevertheless, it's little wonder that grown-up viewers of Davies' work seem to generally prefer *Century Falls*, with its implied adult themes and sometimes rather horrific tone. For older viewers there's also a likely nostalgic evocation of the HTV children's serials of the 1970s. Most especially, there are similarities to the 1977 drama *Children of the Stones*, which had clearly influenced Davies, aspects of the basic premise being very similar. The resemblance was even more marked in embryonic draft form, at which stage Davies' serial focussed on one Professor Llewellyn and his study of an ancient stone circle. However, the central concept of strangers arriving in a remote village that harbours dark secrets has long been a mainstay of horror and fantasy literature.

Century Falls bears little resemblance to Davies' other work, even his later adult output. There's no sense of mischief or fun, and very little sense of spectacle, which Davies acknowledges when discussing its sombre tone. 'I'm not saying that I don't think kids could stand that, but I also think you switch on your telly to enjoy yourself a bit more, even if the subject matter's very dark,' he says. 'It's not like *The Second Coming*, which is very fast and spectacular in places.' The piece in question was to deal with intense subject matter of its own – the return of the Son of God.

Certainly the plot of *Century Falls* feels restricted by being tied to so few locations within just one tiny village – represented on screen by Langthwaite in North Yorkshire – although the claustrophobic feel does add plenty of atmosphere. Even though Tess is supposed to be the audience's main identification point, she comes across as self-obsessed and dull. Conceptually Tess should be an interesting character, and certainly an atypical one for a lead protagonist. She is neither resilient nor heroic, and is seemingly a victim of bullying. She's not an aspirational figure, being even less self-assured than an average person of her age, as she struggles to make friends and hides her comfort eating with a prickly attitude. While *Dark Season*'s Marcie had an equally troubled set of social skills, she gleaned respect from those around her by displays of daring and intelligence. Tess rarely demonstrates any exceptional qualities. However, Marcie had also been something of a caricature at times, a larger than life figure drawn in broad strokes, ideal for children's television. By contrast, Tess is almost too real and too pathetic to inspire warmth or affection.

She does, however, conform to the role of the outsider, a recurring theme in Davies' work that had already manifested itself to an extent through Marcie but was made more explicit here. It's tempting to attribute the recurrence of this type in Davies' work to the feelings of isolation often felt by young gay men, and presumably experienced by Davies with his self-described 'solitary soul'. But this is a broader theme that can be recognised by many children as they struggle to fit in to what they perceive as the accepted norm.

Tess fails to prefigure characters such as Willow in *Buffy the Vampire Slayer*, who overcome their initially introverted state to become world-saving heroines. Davies remembers that he did not have a specific aim in terms of representation when it came to her character, although the very use of the word 'fat' caused a reaction. 'There was a review in the *Daily Mail* saying, "How brave of the BBC to show something that defies the Thought Police." I got praise from the *Daily Mail*! But you don't write it that way, you don't think, "I'll be brave and write something no one else is writing," it just fits in the story, really, that she should be an outsider. I really wanted to do a scene with her mother turning round and saying, "No, actually, you're fat," and challenging it, instead of going, "Actually, she's marvellous" all the way through.'

Conceptually *Century Falls* is certainly the stronger of Davies' pair of Children's BBC dramas, but as a piece of television for a young audience it's ultimately less satisfying. It does, however, benefit from some strong set pieces, such as the burning of the old temple (a rare foray into spectacle), and is effectively atmospheric. Much of this can be put down to Colin Cant's excellent direction, alongside the brooding story itself. But while the serial as a whole is mysterious, it sometimes lacks a central drive or focus. The drama is anything but high-octane, being somewhat mellow and subdued in its treatment of characters reacting to extraordinary events. This subtlety, and the serial's lack of easy answers, may account for why the story is sometimes hard to follow, as it sometimes relies upon the audience's reading, and subsequent remembrance, of a character's true motivations. However, at least part of this problem can be put down to the fact that unusually extensive editing was required to keep the final episodes within the allotted running time.

Perhaps the most revealing aspect of the serial is the extent to which it demonstrates how the most identifiable aspect of Davies' work is generally not his plotting, or even the characters, but the texture of the dialogue. Normally, it is the words that Davies puts into the mouths of his creations that is the most recognisable aspect of his work. In just about every other Davies script, conversations between characters are naturalistic and informal. They may be wittier than many of us could hope to be; they may be discussing anything from the apocalypse on a Liverpool council estate to an army of Daleks flying through the skies of London. But the tone is distinct. In Davies' work the narrative often seems to be a secondary consideration to the enjoyment of simply seeing these characters on screen, interacting with each other in a very real way. *Century Falls* discards much of this informality in favour of more standard dialogue between characters. The characters can be stilted in their communication, often sounding as if they would have been more at home in *Children of the Stones* itself.

Coming from someone who would so often resisted Received Pronunciation in his later casting choices, it's odd to see Davies' characters speak in this manner, and while the narrative itself is unaffected it does serve to emphasise how much Davies' subsequent work relies on this one aspect for its distinctiveness. At this relatively early stage in his career he was consciously attempting to write in a manner that was not his natural style, in order to prove his credentials as a serious writer. Over the next five years he would come to change his perception of how drama should be treated, but this one serial remains an insight into his initial observations.

Davies accepts that there was a change in his style between the two serials for Children's BBC. 'It's funny that, when you look at *Century Falls* and *Dark Season*, *Dark Season*'s much truer to the way I write,' he observes. 'Before I started thinking about all of this, before I started analysing "What am I doing, what am I writing, why am I writing it?", I just sat there and wrote. I've taken a whole 15 years to come full circle and think, "Oh, *Dark Season* – that's what I write."' With reservations, he's rightly pleased with *Century Falls* too. 'I'd say it's too dark. It's convoluted as well. But I still love it!'

Davies did not write for the BBC's children's department again until the pilot episode of *The Sarah Jane Adventures* some 15 years later, although, as we'll see, he hadn't left children's television entirely. Nevertheless, in the aftermath of *Century Falls,* he did dream up the bare bones of a possible third Children's BBC serial that didn't even reach the scripting stage, which he provisionally entitled *The Heat of the Sun.* It was to be set in the near future, taking place over a period of six days between Boxing Day 1999 and the dawn of the new millennium. It seems that the story would have been even darker than *Century Falls*, and was a continuation of the psychic theme established in that serial. A plot to take over the world was fronted by a television show presented by a schoolboy who could predict the future. Other elements would have included a girl seeking out her missing brother in London under martial law, young street gangs run by a public school drop-out, an Asian man trying to kill his daughter, and the sinister, widespread disappearance of the homeless.

We can be reasonably clear then that, had it ever seen the light of day, *The Heat of the Sun* would have pushed his work even farther from *Dark Season*'s light-hearted adventures. Judging by the brief snippets that Davies remembers, it seems that this serial would have foreshadowed many of his later themes. The use of television as a component of his narrative recurs throughout his work, while the idea of a single figure of power foreshadowing the apocalypse is highly reminiscent of *The Second Coming* and even *Springhill.*

For these dramas on Children's BBC Davies had almost exclusively worked by himself. They were self-contained serials with no restrictions other than the basics of budget and timeslot. However, his career had moved him into a somewhat different environment, where he was often a member of a team working on a variety of projects over time. Some of these were long-running shows, while others would be brief forays into new programming. Though these programmes would have mixed success, the experience he gained over the next five years would be instrumental in his eventual placement as one of the foremost writers on British television.

T IS FOR TELEVISION

FOUR:
SINK OR SWIM

On the morning of 8 April 1991, Davies strode through the entrance of Granada Television on Quay Street just as the ITV franchisee celebrated the launch of what was to become one of its most popular and well-respected programmes. The previous night had marked the broadcast of the first episode of *Prime Suspect*. The police drama starred Helen Mirren and would influence all those that came after it, as well as winning a clutch of awards that included four BAFTAs for the first mini-series alone. The atmosphere throughout the Granada building was electric, and it was the perfect day to join the company. 'I remember walking into the building and the building was buzzing,' Davies says. 'The security guard was like, "Did you see that last night?" Even people in the canteen were going, "Wasn't that brilliant?" The whole place was buzzing with it, and you just thought, "What a brilliant place to be."'

Having left BBC Manchester, Davies was very briefly on the dole before being taken on as part of Granada's script-editing team by Tony Wood. Quite literally, this meant he was working only ten minutes' walk across Manchester from his previous employer. Although he'd made the break from the BBC in order to work on adult projects, the first key programme in his time with the new broadcaster would be another drama aimed at a youth audience. The hospital drama *Children's Ward* originated from a successful 1988 pilot and had gone on to be one of the strongest elements in the programming portfolio of Children's ITV.

Davies was an avowed fan of Granada's output, and felt sure he would benefit from working in such a stimulating working environment. 'Having given up Children's BBC I knew if I got in there I'd go and work on soaps and storylines. What I really wanted to do, though, was meet other writers, because in Children's all you ever met were comedy writers. I'd been script editor on *On the Waterfront*, and on a programme without a budget you didn't exactly meet [respected comedy writer] David Renwick. You met men who had twirly bowties and comedy squirty roses in their lapels, so I wasn't learning much from meeting them. I really, really wanted to meet other writers and see how they lived, see how they did it.'

Davies had never before socialised, or indeed worked, with other writers to the extent that he would at Granada. Though he would go on to principally write by himself, he's made a point of the fact that his time spent working with others helped him realise that writing could be his entire career – and even, more fundamentally, that writers were real people. But he was fortunate in that he was not only working with 'real' writers, but writers who would go on to have a notable pedigree in television drama.

In this he was guided by Tony Wood, then Granada's chief script editor and later to become producer of *Coronation Street*. 'He looked after me and introduced me to a million people,' Davies says. 'My first day's work at ITV, I was in an office with Paul Abbott and Kay Mellor, who just *run* television now! You don't see a week go by without something written by them. Two very lovely people, and I was in a room with *them*, working on a children's drama. That's how it started.' Coincidentally, there was at the time a new boss in place at Granada's Children's department: Davies' former mentor Ed Pugh.

Over the next few years at Granada Davies quickly rose up the ranks, although he did not achieve his short term aim of working on *Coronation Street* for some time. In 1992 he graduated from script editor to producer of *Children's Ward*. He continued to contribute scripts to the show while also writing *Century Falls* for the BBC and formulating his own ideas for potential series. Indeed, it was around this time that he first considered the project that was to have the longest gestation of any of his works, concerning the return of Jesus to modern-day Manchester. However, at the time he had not reached the stage in his career that would allow him to develop such a production; instead, his concern was the day to day running of the children's hospital series, which went from strength to strength under his leadership.

In seeking to develop his career as a writer, Davies undertook some freelancing work. Perhaps one of his more surprising, and arguably less imaginative, ventures would be his contribution of three episodes to the long-running *Chucklevision* comedy series, starring the eponymous Chuckle Brothers, Paul and Barry. Eschewing his usual positive attitude towards his past projects, mention of *Chucklevision* elicits a groan of despair. 'Anyone can write one *Chucklevision*,' Davies says. "'Ooh, they slip in a pool of water and a banana skin and they get a custard pie in the face." Second *Chucklevision*, you're like...' At this point, he mimes the melting of his brain. "'They slip on ... an apple core. They get ... an apple pie in the face..." Third *Chucklevision*, you are *bleeding from the eyes!* And you want to kill them, and have comedy anvils murder them, forever!'

There was, alas, no killing spree in any of Davies' contributions to *Chucklevision* in late 1992. Indeed, his three episodes are simply bog standard entries in a series that rarely offered anything else. Nevertheless, it's notable that the first of the three, 'A Lazy Day', revolves around the moustachioed brothers enjoying a favourite Davies pursuit: watching the telly. The classic premise of his second *Chucklevision*, 'Rich for a Day', might, at a push, be taken as foreshadowing *Mine All Mine* that would follow. 'Spooks and Gardens', as broadcast on Boxing Day morning 1992, has a Narnia-esque alternate world existing on the other side of a wardrobe – an unusual move for the series. The jokes in all three, however, were largely standard issue *Chucklevision*. 'It was terrible,' confesses Davies. 'I was so late with my third *Chucklevision* script that it was hand-written on A4 lined paper!' The experience was not without its rewards, however. 'I still get, to this day, five quid because it's just been shown in Hong Kong. Because it's slapstick – it's a universal language! Chuckle is universal.'

While he would later adopt the mantra of 'no boring issues' for his writing of *Queer as Folk*, Davies' time at *Children's Ward* allowed him to tackle some controversial topics relevant to a young audience in modern Britain. A notable example was an edition broadcast in late 1993 that concerned a patient infected with HIV. Although Davies later pointed out that a storyline about HIV or AIDS is not necessarily a gay one, it was an issue that was nevertheless closely connected to gay men in the minds of many members of the public.

The patient concerned, teenage boy Richard Higgs, was infected through a blood transfusion. While the programme explicitly dissociates Higgs from any suggestion that he is homosexual, Davies nevertheless used the opportunity to preach liberalism. 'You must be a poof if you've got AIDS,' accuses the ward's token bully, fellow patient Jason Lloyd. 'I'm not gay, and I haven't got AIDS – I'm HIV Positive,' replies a level-headed Richard. 'But just for the sake of an argument let's say I was homosexual. Would it matter? What difference would it make?' When Jason claims that Richard would 'fancy me, wouldn't you?', Richard mocks his behaviour. 'There's not a boy, girl, man or woman alive who could possibly fancy you. Look around. Where's this queue of people dying to ask you out? They don't exist, Jason, because you're stupid, you're bigoted and you don't matter one little bit.'

If that sounds like the episode was an unequivocal attempt at educating its audience rather than entertaining them, then that would be an unfair impression. This was not what US shows would call 'a very special episode', where a serious issue is addressed in an otherwise lightweight show, in order for the lead characters to learn something from their experience. While the above description highlights the most interesting aspects of the episode in relation to Davies' development as a writer, the speech takes up a very small portion of the episode, which elsewhere includes an amusing set piece where a learner driver finds herself initiating a car chase in the middle of her driving test. While many other characters refer to Richard's illness, it's not always in a manner that highlights it as a serious theme. 'He's going to be a lorry driver,' says one character of him. 'That woman says he's got HGV.'

Puns aside, the focus of the episode is generally on the reactions to his illness rather than on Richard himself. But Davies was trying to push the barriers of the series and develop themes that could be difficult to tackle. Many series, especially those for children, can find themselves stuck in something of a rut, churning out undistinctive and obvious plots that do little to broaden the scope of the series, but continue to be acceptable viewing for the programme's audience.

Nevertheless, it's unusual for Davies to tackle an issue head on in this manner. In the future he would usually make a point for liberalism by introducing characters who might be unappealing to a *Daily Mail* reading audience, only to ignore the obvious debating points that they present and allow them to function as characters rather than issues. The number of gay characters who are casually introduced in *Doctor Who*, for example, is indicative of this. However, this was the first time that Davies had written something that directly referenced homosexuality, and he would continue to write gay characters and plotlines for many of the other shows he was to be involved with at Granada.

Davies stayed on as producer of *Children's Ward* until 1994, but continued to write for the series after he had left. His most important contribution would be the hundredth episode of the series, screened in October 1996. By now the title of the show had been shortened to the snappier *The Ward*, while the opening title sequence had been transformed into a montage reminiscent of *ER*. Both changes indicate an attempt to dispense with the traditional tenets of slightly patronising story-telling in children's drama. Instead, the series had become a drama that happened to feature children in its lead roles. The series had continued to tackle serious issues, often explained in a way that would educate its predominantly young audience. For the hundredth episode Davies decided not to write a traditional celebratory script, instead using the milestone as a platform to highlight what was then a new threat.

The internet had just started to become known to the mainstream populace when Davies wrote this episode, one that would warn children and parents alike about the potential dangers of the new technology. Scott Morris is about 11 years old and is sitting in front of his computer in his bedroom, talking to another boy, Josh, in an *X Files* chatroom. Josh has the first issue of a magazine that he'll sell to Scott for ten pounds. 'Where shall we meet?' Scott asks. As the reply is typed on Josh's machine the camera pulls out to reveal that the person at the other end is not another young boy, but a man in his mid-thirties.

Parental fears of predators on the internet are frequently expressed in modern current affairs programmes, but we shouldn't underestimate exactly how naïve people were about the internet back in 1996. From the outset the crux of the plot is made clear to the viewer; the audience is initially encouraged to think that Josh is another child, only for this assumption to be proved false. This is the key lesson for the children, and parents, watching. The subject matter could have been handled differently, perhaps with a friend teasing Josh online by using a false name in the chat room. This would have made the point of anonymity behind the participants' usernames while avoiding the subject matter of implied paedophilia or other abuse. Nevertheless, this less controversial option wasn't the one taken.

Scott is not a stupid boy, and does not conform to the traditional role of the child in a public safety film, where dangerously inadvisable behaviour brings the protagonist to grief. He has his misgivings, but the temptation of the magazine is too much. Ten pounds for a magazine 'worth forty' is seemingly irresistible, while the meeting is to be in a public place. When he turns up in a park to be met by the man (never identified by name, even in the credits), Scott is even less sure, not completely convinced by his claim that 'Josh sent me.' The man seems to be normal and charming, gentle even. But Scott becomes uneasy and gives chase, only for them both to be involved in a traffic accident. They make it to hospital but, before Scott is able to tell his story, the man escapes.

Later, Scott's mother points out the dangers to him, while he is asked to describe his attacker. 'Just a man,' he says, 'like any other man.' The final scene has a blond boy, even younger than Scott, at the same meeting place. This time, when the man approaches offering to show him where he has the desired comic, the child goes with him. The camera pulls back to show them walking away until we lose sight of them as the credits roll to the sound of children playing in a park.

Davies insists that he is still 'very proud' of this script, and rightly so. It may sound a little unsubtle, even melodramatic, when taken out of context, but the handling of the plotline within the programme is effective and rather shocking. The denouement is undoubtedly the most controversial aspect and is clearly designed to shock children into taking the subject matter seriously. The casting of an 'average' looking man as the villain of the piece was a bold move that contributes to its success. The episode won a Children's BAFTA for Best Drama, and was a deserving recipient for not only its mature handling of a difficult issue but the overall confidence of the piece, including its use of humour and characterisation, both strengths of the series as a whole.

In looking at this episode of *The Ward*, we've just skipped several years along the timeline of his career. Indeed, in the meantime, he'd made a vitally important decision. Despite being in demand as a producer at Granada, Davies longed to concentrate on scriptwriting. Over the previous few years, he'd carefully saved up £40,000 – by his reckoning, enough to keep his head above water for up to three years without an income. And so, much to the surprise of his colleagues, he quit his producing contracts and sought work as a freelance writer. As a stroke of pure luck, he was, by his own recollection, offered a job on a new Granada soap called *Revelations* the very day he embarked on the writer's path. In effect, for the next few years he switched from working at Granada as a producer and script editor to working for the company purely as a script-writer.

While he did indeed continue to write for *Children's Ward* over this period, by 1996 he had worked on several shows besides. His time at Granada had incorporated various behind the scenes roles, with the programmes themselves spanning several genres. For a time in 1993 he worked as a storyliner on daytime soap opera *Families*, created by Kay Mellor and launched in 1990 but by then nearing the end of its run. The programme's original concept was that it would mirror the typically dramatic lives of two linked families on opposite sides of the globe.

By the time of Davies' appointment the Australian angle had been dropped, making for a more conventional soap opera. However, in common with his later forays into the genre with *Revelations* and *Springhill*, the programme tried to be more controversial and less homely than *Coronation Street* in particular. Despite the late afternoon timeslot, it touched on more controversial issues than Granada's flagship show. But it did not perform well in the ratings, although this was at least partially due to the fact that it was not a networked programme and so was shown at different times in different ITV regions. Davies' job involved initial brainstorming and creation of plot elements as well as the mechanics of breaking down the various plots episode by episode. He has since claimed that he enjoyed his time storylining at Granada 'almost as much' as the process of writing his own scripts for the shows, and furthermore that he was extremely good at it. But his best work in this regard was still to come.

Davies insists he loves all television but the soap genre seems to particularly interest him, although he's had little contact with any of the long-running series. 'I love soap opera, and I worked as a storyliner on soaps for many years,' he says. 'But I was very lucky at the time because I always avoided the big ones. Granada used to make little daytime soap operas like *Families,* which were the cheapest, cheapest things in the world – thirty thousand quid for half an hour. That's how much they cost. But Kay Mellor used to work on these, Paul Abbot, Sally Wainwright, Jan McVerry; fantastic people used to work on these. Granada really did pull together good writers. Well, it did in those days. It doesn't do it so much now, because it doesn't have programmes like that. It doesn't have daytime soaps at which you can throw writers, and they sink or swim.'

A particular skill of Davies' has always been the ability to write to order. Faced with any list of requirements he can pull together a script quickly. This is clearly rooted in his time at Granada, and even though he is now in a situation where he does not have to write with such rapidity, he still does not prevaricate over redrafting his writing. But many people cannot write in this fashion. 'The list of people we sacked is horrifying,' he says, speaking of his time in soap operas. 'But if you couldn't do it, you couldn't do it. There was no time to muck about. And we had a brilliant time.'

Not all Davies' projects at Granada had legs. At one point he was involved in devising a soap opera called *Saxon House*, which in the event never made it off the drawing board. Another of his drama projects, *The Partnership*, about a firm of lawyers, made it to pilot script stage, but progressed no further. He was also charged with researching the phenomenon of boy bands for a proposed drama series on the subject. The series never happened, but Davies got as far as spending a day at the offices of Simon Cowell, then an upcoming figure in the British record industry. Cowell, Davies reflected many years later, was far nicer company than his reputation might suggest.

Before he built on his experience at *Families* and moved on to a series of his own creation, one of Davies' side projects was a script for a programme that would be seen by a primetime audience. While this would be performed by such high-profile celebrities as Joanna Lumley, Liz Smith and Jerry Hall, the programme was not an original drama or comedy. Rather, Davies wrote the opening episode of the fourth series of mystery gameshow *Cluedo*, based upon the Waddington board game. Each programme opened with a short film that depicted the background to a murder. The victim always performed an action or made a revelation that would cause a considerable problem to the residents and visitors currently in Arlington Grange, only for them to be found dead shortly afterwards. The rest of the programme featured two celebrity teams attempting to identify the true murderer by interrogating the suspects in the studio.

The programme had always been a somewhat muddled, cheap, almost amateur affair that relied heavily on the charisma of the performers playing the roles of the game's suspects. It also required the audience to completely ignore the cross-questioning from the celebrity contestants if they wished their apparently random deductions to be at all satisfying.

Davies' contribution, 'Finders Keepers', was not especially strong and, most surprisingly, lacks his usual sense of humour or any indication that it understands its own ridiculousness. The plot, such as it was, revolved around the discovery of an ancient artefact in a local farmer's field. Although it was once owned by the church, the farmer not only wished to sell the item for his own profit but wished to use it as a blackmail tool because its discovery exposed secrets of the history of Arlington Grange and the Peacock family. Coupled with an overbearing style of presentation from Richard Madeley, it is not an especially successful half hour of television. *Cluedo* was a show that relied on a format that seemed strong on paper but was then produced ineffectively, and this episode is as indicative of the programme's flaws as any other.

During his time at Granada, Davies managed to fit in a fair amount of moonlighting. Aside from writing *Century Falls* and instalments of *Chucklevision* for Children's BBC, he contributed script material to *Do the Right Thing*, a primetime BBC panel show hosted by Terry Wogan. Not so very different from *Cluedo*, it was based on the popular Brazilian format *Voce Decide* – 'You Decide' – and presented moral dilemmas in the form of melodramatic mini-dramas. The guest panelists, comedian Frank Skinner being a regular, were then required to debate the relevant issues and decide the outcome, thereby determining which pre-filmed conclusion should be shown. Not perhaps the most significant or prestigious entry on Davies' CV – individual writers weren't even credited on the show – *Do the Right Thing* was produced by Manchester production company Action Time, who were based in offices just a few minutes' walk from Granada's Quay Street headquarters. It was a particularly tricky format to write for, but since Davies demonstrated that he had the knack, he found that his services were repeatedly in demand.

There is no need to politely understate how badly received Davies' next project was, as no one seems to have a good word to say about it, least of all those involved in the production. *The House of Windsor* was a sitcom that ran for a single six-episode series in the spring of 1994. Davies had nothing to do with its inception or the overall running of the programme. He was drafted in to write some new scripts at short notice; this remains the only out-and-out adult sitcom that he has ever worked on. 'It wasn't my show and every other writer walked off it because it was so terrible,' Davies points out. 'Transmitted weekly, so the actors were dying on the floor. It was the most classic television scenario. People crying and scripts being thrown across rooms and things like that. It was marvellous, I loved it. And writers literally walked out, so I was drafted in because I was the only person who could put up with that. I wrote the second one; I wrote it in a weekend, and then it was made and transmitted. It was terrible.'

It certainly is. Even by the generally low standards of ITV sitcoms, *The House of Windsor* is shamefully bad. It's no surprise that director Graeme Harper, with whom Davies would later collaborate on *Doctor Who*, later said that they did not so much work on the production as 'mutually survive' it. The 'sit' involves events taking place at the residence of the Royal Family. The main characters are 'below stairs', including the serving staff and the press office, trying to spin news items in the Royals' favour. The 'com', such as it is, consists of jokes that would disgrace even the worst 1970s British sex comedy. 'Oh, I recognise that phrase,' says camp footman Danny as he looks at a car magazine. 'Flip me over and make like a piston.' The audience roars with laughter. It's to the show's advantage that the members of the cast have a strong pedigree, with lead characters played by Warren Clarke, Leslie Phillips and Barry Howard, but not even the most talented performer could elevate such weak material.

The reaction to the programme was fiercely negative and Davies decided to take action in order to minimise the effects on his career. 'It went out under my name and the review in the *Observer* said the next week, "Russell T Davies obviously read a script from the 1973 book of comedy"! We were still making the next week's, and I just thought, "I cannot have another episode go out," because it wasn't my fault and it wasn't my show.' In such dire straits, Davies elected to write a later episode of the show under a pseudonym, Leo Vaughn, although it doesn't seem to have made it to the credits of any of the finished episodes. 'Leo Vaughn! It's like a porn star isn't it? The moral is, you wouldn't believe how well that sold. Hong Kong, Paraguay, all sorts of places, and the royalties went on for years. And of course, I never got any of Leo Vaughn's. No one ever filled in the little bit of paperwork saying "Leo Vaughn is actually Russell T Davies." Bastards. I was ripped off in the end. However, it's blood money, I don't want it! Terrible.'

The year 1994 would see Davies devising an adult series of his own for the first time, another move away from children's television, to which he would rarely return after this point. Working with Tony Wood and writer Brian B Thompson, he created the late-night soap opera *Revelations*. Unseen in all but a handful of ITV regions, the show had limited success but ran for two series. The series was an early example of Davies' fixation with the church; here it was the organisational structure of religion and the effects on its followers as opposed to God. Not that this was a serious critique of the machinations of organised religion at the turn of the millennium. Instead, *Revelations* concentrated on the wife of a priest, Jessica Rattigan, and her family.* They were a wealthy but dysfunctional group of characters who philander, cheat and murder their way through the two series.

Revelations rewarded dedicated viewing but undoubtedly had its fair share of weak points, especially early in the run. The opening episode, something especially difficult to write for soap operas, is particularly poor. Most problematic is the poor acting on display and something of a lack of pace. The dialogue is unusually clichéd and devoid of wit for Davies, and while the

*Another Revelations family were the Tylers, the first of many occasions when Davies used the name. 'I just like it,' he explains. 'It's the T with the Y. They just feel comfortable. There's not Tyler in the family or anything, no boyfriends called Tyler. I've probably used it to death now. Rose is so iconic, she's such a huge Tyler, that it would be hard using it again now. She's killed all the Tylers, single-handedly!'

series would become progressively more camp as it developed, there is little to entertain here. However, the dialogue was intended to be more grandiose than that traditionally used in soap operas, even if no one seems to have told the director or actors. Instead, the dialogue is hammy but without anything to indicate that this is a self-referential wink at the tele-novella tradition upon which it was based.

'That's exactly what we used to say about it. It was so cheap, cheaper than any other soap – you could barely go outdoors, and you had tiny sets – so all they could do was talk,' Davies says, explaining the reasons for the style of the programme. 'So the talk became extraordinarily florid. If they'd talked and spoken in the sort of normal demotic language of soaps, you couldn't have done that for half an hour because there would have been nothing happening on the screen. So it became like a melodrama, partly like a Victorian melodrama, and partly like in South America, they do these TV novellas which are very hyped-up, very emotional. Like big grand opera, on the screen. Which is fantastic to write, actually.'

It is unfortunate, then, that so little of this comes across on screen. Perhaps this was because the series was not operatic *enough* in many respects, instead seeming simply melodramatic at many times. While they have been described as camp, the shows don't go for this to any extent that differentiates it from a standard soap opera. For example, the opening titles are clearly attempting to be glamorous and dramatic, in the style of *Dynasty* or *Dallas*, as champagne corks pop and women disrobe. Seemingly presented without any sense of irony, it falls flat and simply seems ridiculous. Davies is also writing against type for one of the few times in his career, with his authorial voice diluted. He had done this before with some success in *Century Falls*, but this and his later attempt in *The Grand* worked less well.

'Personally I think it's very good to have written that stuff to get it out of your system,' he says of the grand style of *Revelations*. 'If I wrote like that now I'd be chucked out of the room. It's one of those rules of soap opera that everyone says what they're thinking, all the time, there's no hidden emotions. People sitting going, "I love you, I love you!" That's how soap is written. This was like… times that by ten! So that it was huge – "I will love you, I will kill myself!" It was that big and operatic and mad. And it was brilliant to write. We had such fun on it.'

But in the midst of the big stories of death and drug addiction was a revelation on a smaller scale. Half of one of the episodes was dedicated to a scene where a female vicar, played by Sue Holderness, comes out as a lesbian. It was a two-hander with Carol Nimmens and was the first time Davies had properly handled a gay character and created a storyline accordingly. He still remembers it fondly. '*Revelations* is a knockabout soap, and it was a 15-minute scene beautifully acted. It was like one of those pieces of real studio theatre. A tiny set, smaller than this kitchen and just the two of them in it, and dialogue, pure dialogue for 15 minutes with a slow coming out. That was the first thing I ever did [about homosexuality] and then once I'd done that there was no stopping me.'

But it wasn't a conscious decision to do a big issue-based storyline. Davies was more practical in his approach, realising that he simply had to find sufficient stories of a bold enough nature to keep the series going. 'That was dictated partly by the sort of pressure-cooker nature of the stories. It had to keep topping itself, and you had a bishop with a mistress, and then he murdered the mistress, and then... I think he probably dressed up as the mistress, or something like that! So inevitably with a sort of scenario like that one of the sons is going to turn out to be gay. When they introduced women to the church, I was thinking, "Yes! We can do a lesbian vicar!"'

So Davies was not attempting to make a socio-political point by outing her as gay. 'It wasn't controversy for controversy's sake,' he insists. 'It was the nature of a show like that. You had to sort of pull all this material in and make it work as dialogue, as a two-hander. You're never going to get the visuals. Visuals don't have to be a car chase, visuals can be a woman sitting at a table, thinking. And if that's beautifully shot and beautifully lit, that's a gorgeous bit of story. So you reach for those sorts of stories. Everything's a story, and you can't be precious about it. There are no taboos on anything, I think.'

Ultimately there is much that does not work in *Revelations*, but it was at least an attempt to do something a little more interesting with the soap opera genre. It does not sit comfortably with Davies' later career, but it did act as something of a watershed in his professional life. He was settled in adult television and had broadened his skills at scripting and production in order to encompass both programmes of his creation and life as a jobbing writer. But he feels that some good material can be found in *Revelations*. 'Cath Hayes wrote a scene in which a wife confronts her husband's mistress, that's the sort of scenario that crops up quite often, that sort of adultery confrontation type scene. It's still the best version of that scene I have ever seen, with just sizzling dialogue. And it was shot in ten minutes and broadcast to three people and there's such good stuff in those cheap things. I love it. If someone said to me, come and invent a soap opera I'd be so tempted, I really would … They won't now!'

Not only did this period at Granada help to develop the scripting side of Davies' career, it also increased his focus on scripting and storylining responsibilities rather than the overall jurisdiction of being a producer. When a new contract for this role was offered in 1994 he declined, having saved enough money to ensure he could continue writing instead. By the next year he had joined the broadcaster's script-writing team, but in the meantime he assisted fellow writer Paul Cornell in a bid by Sandra Hastie at Richmond Films to pitch a new soap opera to Channel Four for an early evening slot. While they were to become friends and work together on *Doctor Who*, they did not know each other well at this point.

Davies' influence on the project, titled *RU*, was mainly in helping with the mechanics of putting a story outline together. 'We were pitching for the slot that was eventually taken by *Hollyoaks*,' remembers Cornell. 'Another show created by Steven Moffat's dad Bill, like *Press Gang* had been. Bill wrote the original pitch; I wrote three out of the four episodes, Russell wrote the other and storylined 20 episodes' worth of plot. And that's where I first met him.'

Davies did not feel very confident about the production as a whole and had little involvement, but it led to a meeting with the man who would eventually succeed him as Executive Producer of *Doctor Who* over a decade later. 'That's how I first met Steven Moffat,' says Davies, 'and Paul Cornell, who must have called us beforehand – writer's world, sort of thing. I just came in and wrote one episode for them. They didn't have any storylining experience and I'd done a lot of that. I never thought it'd work, to be honest, because it was about students, although *Hollyoaks* has sort of become about students now. You wouldn't launch a soap saying it's about students, because who gives a fuck about students? Sorry, but who cares? Workshy bastards!' he laughs. 'Very nice ideas in it. To be honest, though, I think the Mersey TV deal was stitched up from the word go, and it was always going to go to Phil Redmond.'

Cornell and Davies were both able to advance their careers as a result of their meeting. Davies introduced Cornell to the producer of *Children's Ward*, where he then worked, while Cornell put Davies in touch with Rebecca Levene of Virgin Publishing. The imprint had been running a series of original novels based on *Doctor Who* during its extended sabbatical from television. The resulting book, released in October 1996, was *Damaged Goods*, a well-received entry in the series that will be examined in more depth in a later chapter.

It nearly played a part in his time at Granada, however. 'I was working with the lovely Catriona MacKenzie at the time, and said I was writing it so she read it.' One of the subplots that particularly interested the executive, leading Granada to take out an option on the idea, revolved around a woman, Eva Jericho, who was unable to have a child of her own, paying for one of another woman's twins. But the child battles illness for its entire life, and so Jericho returns years later and demands the other twin instead.

The proposed title for the Granada drama was *The Mother War*. 'I just said, oh, you can take that out. And I still think you can do it one way, just the mother and the twins story, especially now there's all those ITV two-part thrillers.' Another element of the plot was that Jericho had suffered a series of miscarriages, leaving her infertile. It is later revealed that her obsession with becoming a mother was exacerbated by a foetus that had failed to develop correctly and had calcified. Said foetus was now 'whispering' to her. It seems likely that the more supernatural elements of the subplot would not have been present in *The Mother War*, although Davies points out that 'Nowadays you could probably put those psychic powers back in and you'd get away with it.'

The science behind the calcification had been researched by Paul Abbott for an episode of *Casualty* that was rewritten to the extent that he had his name taken off it. This explains the note of thanks to Abbott in the book. But although Granada optioned the idea for future development, it was not to be, mainly because Davies became caught up in other projects. 'I just never ever had time, never had a meeting about it. Their rights have probably expired by now.'

Although Davies had graduated to working on series in which he had a heavy involvement, there was soon to be an exception. Paul Abbott and Davies became firm friends during their time at Granada, even bonding over plans for strike action amongst the station's writers. When Abbott devised a new drama for ITV, *Touching Evil*, the first series' six episodes were divided up between Abbott (five episodes) and Davies (one). Davies' episode was the first instalment of a two-parter, 'What Amatheus Wants', screened in spring 1997. It's most useful now as an example of how Davies was able to adapt his writing to fit into someone else's series.

The drama revolves around the use of technology, in this case computers connected to the internet, and has therefore aged very badly. Many of the sequences are simply laughable in their use of internet technology, but even disregarding this the thriller element is not particularly strong either. It is completely unrecognisable as a piece of writing from Davies, evidence enough that, even at this point in his career, he was still writing to order on occasion. Indeed, two of his last projects at Granada would showcase this diversity. One would be an example of his natural 'voice', while the other would be his first attempt to write for mainstream prime-time programming at the expense of some of the strongest elements of his writing.

FIVE:
SURELY SOME REVELATION IS AT HAND...

Naturally, not every show that Davies has worked on assumes equal prominence in his career. Some, such as *Chucklevision* and *Touching Evil*, deserve little more than a mention, as they certainly don't represent significant leaps in the development of his writing. Similarly, the programmes that receive the most analysis tend to be those that best captured the public imagination or were critically lauded as television that stood out from their contemporaries. *Queer as Folk* and *Doctor Who* are the most prominent examples of this. But there is a programme with which Davies was heavily involved that tried just as hard to push the boundaries of television drama. The soap opera *Springhill*, which ran for two series from 1996-7, was not a high-profile flop. Its failure to find an audience did not result in sneering reports regarding its falling ratings. Rather, it simply went unnoticed by the average TV viewer.

In retrospect, the most striking element of *Springhill* is not the finished show itself but the pedigree of those working on it. To have a programme co-created by Paul Abbott and Frank Cottrell Boyce, which also heavily involved Davies and featured writers such as Sally Wainwright, would now be exceptional even for a prime-time programme with a high budget. Back in 1996, though, Abbott and Davies, in particular, were only on the cusp of breaking through as TV heavyweights. Together they worked on Davies' next foray into soap opera, only this time the audience and the aims were to be a little different.

Though produced by Granada, the programme was initially run on the satellite channel Sky One before being screened by Channel Four, pencilled in for an early evening weekday slot. The budget was low, just £30,000 per half-hour episode, but this did not mean that the programme would be limited in the stories that it wanted to tell. Far from it; *Springhill* was the tale of a potential apocalypse taking place on a Liverpool council estate.

The plot of *Springhill* does not lend itself to a brief synopsis, being somewhat convoluted, but the programme centred on the Freeman family and the arrival of a figure from their past, Eva Morrigan. Liz and Jack Freeman are the parents to five teenage children, but it soon transpires that Eva is the natural birth mother of three of them. The first series, of 26 episodes, largely focuses on the battle between the two mothers over the children, with Liz finally seeming to win back the love of her family by becoming pregnant and vowing to move as far away from Eva as possible.

At the end of this first set of episodes Liz goes into labour and is taken to hospital by Eva. The family hears no word for several hours until Eva calls them from a public telephone, insisting that Liz is fine and is sleeping, the baby having been safely delivered. As the family breathes a sigh of relief, the camera pulls out from the close-up of Eva by the telephone to show that she is calling not from the hospital, but a phone-box in the middle of moorland. She steps outside and picks up a baby at her feet, bundling it into the car as she drives off, Liz nowhere to be seen. As the car races away, Eva reads from the W B Yeats poem 'The Stolen Child' in a voiceover.[*]

In many respects such a synopsis does the series a disservice. It gives an indication that the programme was a traditionally domestic affair with the tried and tested soap opera lynchpins of familial squabbles. In some respects that's true, but there were many other elements of *Springhill* which held rather more interest. The first episode, for example, centres on the funeral of the children's granddad, Liz's father. While *Revelations* opened with a wedding, *Springhill* opens with a death: somewhat indicative of the different approaches of the two programmes. Not as indicative, however, as the fact that, despite being dead, the grandfather of the Freemans' children finds himself deep in conversation with John Paul, the youngest of the brood. John Paul treats this nonchalantly, distracted more by his grandfather's plea for him to lend him a bit of money.

These supernatural elements crop up throughout the series, and the trend only escalates as the series continues (most especially in its second year), but it's rarely treated as anything particularly unusual. Indeed, the supernatural

---

[*] This poem was to feature later in Davies' *Doctor Who* novel *Damaged Goods*, an episode of *The Grand* and the *Torchwood* episode '*Small Worlds*', written by P J Hammond but added at Davies' suggestion. 'No special significance, though,' he says. 'It just suits melodramatic plots about kids!'

and religion are treated in exactly the same manner, both central to the plot and the characters' motivations and just as real or fake as each other. Religion, more specifically the Catholic Church, does not come out of the series particularly well. Father McGinley is the local priest and friend of the family, with Liz and her pious son John Paul being the keenest on the church. In John Paul's case, this results in constant claims of God's eventual retribution and absolute power. Liz's love for the church manifests itself more literally, as she drunkenly sleeps with Father McGinley, who may even be the father of the child she is carrying at the end of the series.

Liz was still missing at the start of the second series, which was set some months later. The focus for this series would be the arrival of a baby, Gabriel, who may be Liz's child. Also prominent was the new character of Marian, a housekeeper for the Freemans who would take her religious zeal to extremes by the end of the series. Meanwhile, Eva was more explicitly seen as a character possessing some sort of supernatural ability, and may not even be human, depending on interpretation. Although the series had generally allowed its audience to see apparently supernatural events as either coincidences or hallucinations, this was less true in the later episodes. While this may have resulted in a less subtle production, it did allow the programme to become more explicitly fantastical. Davies wrote several episodes across both series, and storylined many of the major plot lines. As a result his style of writing and characterisation are prominent throughout.

Frank Cottrell Boyce agrees that Davies influenced the series to a similar extent to its co-creators. 'We had different agendas,' he remembers. 'The supernatural element either came from Russell or was greatly amplified and brilliantly exploited by him. I think Russell grabbed hold of the supernatural touch and invented a whole epistemology to go with it, the way he does. He was only supposed to be writing a few episodes but Paul got busy and Russell was a force of nature.' Cottrell Boyce also has no doubts that Davies' own interests and personality fuelled his work on the series. 'He seemed to be able to pull all aspects of himself into it,' he says. 'There's gay Russell, there's Russell the TV fanatic and there's Russell the science fiction and horror fan. He put all of himself into it and probably does that with everything he does.'

Certainly there are elements of the series which Davies was to later modify and re-use for other projects. Most obvious was the idea that the arrival of Liz's baby, Gabriel, could be the second coming of Christ – or else, the coming of the Antichrist – which had something in common with a similar theme in his *Doctor Who* novel *Damaged Goods*. 'I storylined a lot of the first series and I chipped in with a lot of ideas for the second,' Davies clarifies. 'That second series was mad. I was told off. I got called in by Carolyn Reynolds because I decided it was all about the Antichrist.' Such a bold decision confirms Cottrell Boyce's observation that 'We were both full of beans, writing for the first time away from the constrictions of soap and, at the same time, with soap's guarantee of broadcast and all the energy and hurry that brings.'

Indeed, there is a sense when watching *Springhill* that those who were writing for it were having a great time, paying little regard to what may be conventionally considered popular or obvious for such a programme. The plot line revolving around the baby Gabriel is a case in point. By television convention, we are led to believe that Eva and Marian, the two women who squabble over his wellbeing most frequently, are evil and good respectively. There is little subtlety here, as Davies points out: 'All they could afford to do to show that [Marian] was an angel was a white mac!' And so it is that 'evil' Eva wears a black coat for most of her appearances, while the apparently angelic Marian invariably dresses mumsily, the aforementioned mac often making an appearance.

However, while Eva is clearly portrayed as a devil-like figure, her battles with the pious Marian reach fever pitch when it is discovered that Marian plans to secretly baptise the baby Gabriel. In a confrontation within the church, Marian, who generally operates as the series' metaphor for blind religious extremism, is revealed to have killed her husband and daughter in a house fire when she found them in bed together. Clearly this was unexpectedly heavy stuff for an early evening time slot.

The run of episodes ends on an undoubtedly brave and, depending on interpretation, seemingly atheistic note. As with *The Second Coming* four years later, there is little doubt that *Springhill* really does depict a battle of supernatural forces which some characters interpret as 'God' and 'the Devil'. But the series does not allow for this demarcation to be so straightforward, especially as it reaches its conclusion. Throughout, religion has been portrayed with some disdain, not least because of the hints of fundamentalism or even a suggestion of a cultish attraction to the Catholic Church. However, the series' final episodes seem to indicate that in the universe of *Springhill* it isn't God who will win the final battle, if He exists at all.

After she has dispensed with Marian, Eva is finally welcomed back by the family, who had slowly turned against her since the disappearance of Liz. The person who had initially seemed to be the villain of the piece has saved the Freemans from an altogether more sinister figure. 'It's ironic, really, that you had to turn to me,' says Eva to John Paul. 'Has your God forsaken you?' Indeed, John Paul is the only person to remain unconvinced that Eva should be welcomed back, having maintained for some time that she killed Liz. So, away from the others, he asks Eva a direct question. 'I need to know if you killed my mother,' he says, 'and if you did, and have got away with it, then it means God is dead.' After a beat, Eva smiles a little: 'You've always known. Liz understood in the end. She accepted it. She was even happy, safe in the arms of her maker. She told me, "God knows His own."'

The final episode concludes with John Paul running over moorland, possibly where his mother was killed, his faith broken as he screams for her with tears running down his face. Wherever Eva drew her powers from seemed to have little link to God, as the Freemans knew from their faith. At one point she goes into the church and runs her hand through some holy water. 'Did you think it would burn?' she asks.

If this makes *Springhill* sound melodramatic then that's probably a fair assessment, but there was also a considerable amount of humour running through the series. This is particularly strong in Davies' episodes where the comedy is often subtle and generally based around characters' mundane obsessions (notably eldest daughter Sue's monologue regarding her love of an Argos shoe rack), or else a swift dismissal of attempts to spout melodramatic dialogue.

One of Davies' most notable contributions would be his influence on the final episode itself, which takes place after Eva's revelation to John Paul.

The first half of the episode takes place years in the future, with Marian in an old people's home despite looking the same as she ever has ('I'm not old!' she protests), confronted by a future that, from her perspective, is hideously liberal. John Paul is a drug dealer, Sue is living with her lesbian lover, Father McGinley is preaching about the advantages of premarital sex on television while the other Freeman daughter, Trish, has a family made up of children from different races. Eva, however, looks exactly the same and has taken up residence with her new lover – the grown-up Gabriel.

The concept of the episode was partially Davies', and it is the last gasp of a series that could only tolerate such a self-indulgent mix of excesses had it been a complete success or doomed to failure. For *Springhill*, it was the latter. 'I remember Russell, [producer] Paul Marquess, Frank Cottrell Boyce and I having a crazy storylining session for that last episode,' recalls Phil Collinson, script editor on the series and later to be producer of *Doctor Who*. 'It was barmy and I spent the whole meeting telling them that. Thankfully they ignored me and I think a great episode came out of it.' Davies remembers the same discussion. 'That last episode! That's insane. Phil always tells this story that me, Paul Marquess and Frank sat there and came up with that. I've always liked Phil from this moment on. He was a very young junior script editor and he sat there and went, "I think you're all mad, and I can't follow it!" We ignored him. And he was right, you know.'

For the second half of the finale, which took place in the present day once more, Marian locks herself in a bedroom with Gabriel. 'He can look after himself,' assures Eva, as the baby transforms into his adult form as seen in the flash-forward earlier in the episode. The adult Gabriel then strangles Marian before reverting back to being a young child. 'I wanted that baby from *Sapphire and Steel*,' states Davies, referring to a suddenly ageing baby in the early 1980s ITV series. 'I was sat there going, "What if the baby aged 20 years, murdered her and regressed back to a baby so they'd never find the murderer. But the fingerprints would be the same!"'

Gareth Roberts, who worked as a script editor on the series, admired the ambition of the production, but implies that the series' aims were not always clear even to those working on it. 'As it was developed I began to understand what it was about,' he remembers, 'a huge Manichean struggle between good and evil that just happened to be set on a Liverpool housing estate. But the final episode was a big surprise to us all – we kind of left the storyline blank, and then Frank Cottrell Boyce revealed that the whole series had been about the coming of the Antichrist!' That such a revelation was almost peripheral to much of the programme speaks volumes about the number of ways that the series could be interpreted. Indeed, if Gabriel is anything of significance at all, then it is not clear whether he should be considered a force for good or evil. He could be the Antichrist, Jesus or simply a normal child. Springhill eschews any standard definition of 'good' and 'bad' for its characters, allowing a degree of ambiguity that makes for rewarding viewing.

One of the most endearing aspects of *Springhill* was that none of those involved in the production felt remotely reined in. 'We were just barmy,' chuckles Davies. 'No one was stopping us! Mad. Brilliant though. What a laugh!' Little consideration was given to what a general audience might enjoy or what was currently popular elsewhere in television, as Gareth Roberts confirms. 'It was a mad programme by the standards of the day – this is the height of mid-90s TV social realism, remember. [The action-adventure series] *Bugs* was considered daring!' Paul Cornell, who also script edited and wrote some episodes, is less sure about the effectiveness of the series' overall style. 'It had a very specific tone of voice,' he says. 'It was very tough to match. And Russell just wouldn't let it become *Father Ted*, which it was straining on the leash to be!'

It would be unfair to give the impression that *Springhill* was solely centred on supernatural occurrences and religious obsession. For the majority of the time the programme's plots revolved around more traditional soap opera concerns. Trish seduces her teacher, Jack temporarily leaves his wife for Eva, and eldest son Nick has a problem with performing sexually which leads to an escalating set of circumstances and the eventual suicide of his fiancée. And so on. Indeed, without Davies the programme could have been a rather different affair, as the original outline had more in common with a later Paul Abbott creation. 'It started with myself and Paul writing what I now realise was a dry run for *Shameless*,' says Cottrell Boyce. 'As far as I remember it started with me talking to Paul about a play, *Easter*, about someone watching a house.'

The August Strindberg play revolves around a family who, in common with the Freemans, have many issues to resolve and secrets in their past. While the mother in *Easter* lives in fear of the family's creditors one day coming to devastate her family, so Liz Freeman was dreading the re-emergence of Eva Morrigan. A similar dynamic within the family, including a pious child, is certainly reflected in *Springhill*, as is the overall theme of death and resurrection. 'About a day later, Paul had produced this 30-page document about it,' continues Cottrell Boyce. 'He wrote something very like *Shameless* – full of energy and surprise – and I filled in the gaps. I think I was more interested in storytelling than content, if you know what I mean.'

Probably the best remembered plot line from the series, and certainly the most significant for Davies' developing career, had nothing to do with the supernatural elements that would make the show so distinctive. The second series saw the development of a friendship between teenager Anthony Freeman and his girlfriend's brother David, which eventually turns romantic. After weeks of a slow realisation on both sides, the two boys find themselves alone together after a particularly abnormal day in the Freeman house. They seem to be moving in to kiss as David stands up and throws his drink against the wall in frustration. What looked to be a tender moment is transformed into one of anger as David starts to rant about the situation. 'Well, what are you going to do?' he asks. 'They're all out, kid's asleep. I told you that on purpose, you know I did. It's just us. So are you staying?' Anthony is scared; 'I think I'll go home.'

But David keeps making his point and, as with Davies' handling of HIV in *Children's Ward*, he speaks not so much as a character but as a Davies mouthpiece. 'We're 16, 17, 18 years old, we're wasting all that time, thinking, "Not yet, don't commit yourself." They're all around you, men and women. The whole wide world is men and women. I've become such an expert I could go on *Mastermind*,' he says, Anthony listening silently as David stands over him.

Just as *Revelations* dedicated the entire second half of one episode to a character coming out, this scene is, similarly, not intercut with any of the other plot lines running concurrently. It is one simple, striking event that results in a dilemma for Anthony. 'I've seen it but felt none of it,' continues David. 'I'm leading the life of a 12-year-old girl. Those girls, they've got magazines because they're full of men, and they watch Australian soaps because they're full of men. It's not my life, it's second-hand and I'm sick of it. Come to bed with me.'

At one point David points out that young gay men do not get the same opportunities at 'making mistakes' in fumbling early relationships. It is a touching monologue, and Gareth Roberts remembers it well. 'Russell's finest hour on *Springhill* was a beautiful, *beautiful* speech from one of the gay teens, who was played by Sam Hudson,' he remembers. 'I can near enough remember it by heart. It was about gay men missing out on the bread-and-butter experiences of teenage life, all the huge trivial things like being stood up, getting drunk and snogging the wrong person at daft house parties, etc. "We should be making those mistakes," he said. That was magnificent.'

It is certainly remarkable, all the more so because Anthony was easily the most likeable of the entire Freeman clan and had always been so strongly played by Kevin Knapmann. The performances from Knapmann and Hudson elevate a scene that needed a lightness of touch to create one of the absolute highlights of the series, and indeed one of the highlights of Davies' writing of gay men. At the end of the episode David has gone to his bedroom, leaving Anthony to decide whether he is going to leave the house or join him. Anthony follows him up the stairs.

Davies was only able to contribute two episodes to the second series of *Springhill* as he had by then committed to another series, *The Grand*. But he ensured that he was available to write the material dealing with the emergence of the relationship between David and Anthony. 'We just had a whale of a time,' he says. '"Bring him out of the closet, bring it on!" We'd already had lesbian vicars in *Revelations*. What a laugh! I had a lot of say in it, I got a say in the storylines and that, and I only had time for two episodes in order to bring him out of the closet.'

While the storyline is well handled – and ultimately results in that rarest of soap happenings, a happy relationship by the time of the series' finale – it suffers a little when it shies away from being quite as bold as it implies it will be. Sex is mainly discussed in euphemistic terms, but this is no different to the handling of heterosexual relationships in most soap operas. However, it is disappointing that, even after Anthony has stood up in front of his family to profess his love for David, the two are unable to do anything more than hug each other.

It now seems bizarre that as recently as 1997 a decision was made by someone (possibly not on the production team) that a programme designed for an early evening time slot would not tolerate a single kiss between gay men. Similarly, a great deal is made of Anthony turning 18 shortly before the plot develops, presumably so as to ignore any issues of under-age sex, but this comes across as rather unsubtle. It also immediately moves the story away from being about gay people of school age and those old enough to be able to declare their independence from their family should they so wish.

Although it ran for two series, *Springhill* failed to find an audience willing to embrace it. Certainly when measured by audience ratings and Channel Four's treatment of the programme, it can only be considered a failure. Commissioned as a co-production between the channel and Sky One, it was broadcast on the latter before being screened in an early evening slot on the former. It did not stay there long, however, and was not only moved out of prime time but out of the way of almost the entire potential audience. Eventually, it saw out its run in triple-bills of episodes in the early hours. Perhaps tellingly, Frank Cottrell Boyce wasn't even aware of the show's strange broadcasting pattern. 'To be honest,' he says, 'I didn't know it was on Channel Four. I thought it was just on Sky.'

Though far from being a 'hit' programme, was *Springhill* a success in its own right? 'I loved the balls and the strangeness of it, the way it clashed with the banal and everyday,' says Gareth Roberts, highlighting the strongest aspects of the series. 'It developed a small but devoted student following. Yes it was cheap, yes it was barking mad, but it was inventive and unusual and a lot of the writing was remarkably good. You had Russell, Frank, Paul Abbott, Jan McVerry – of course it was!' However, Phil Collinson acknowledges that it never reached the heights hoped for. 'I don't know that I'd call *Springhill* a success,' he says. 'I think it was far too off the wall to hit a mass audience. But I loved working on it and learnt an awful lot about making TV.'

Paul Cornell was less impressed with the overall product. 'The thing about *Springhill* is that any individual episode description is always much more interesting! It's never as good as it sounds,' he claims. 'I think, if anything, it's overrated. But Russell's bits are really good.' Davies himself still remembers the series fondly, while acknowledging its inconsistency of tone and the limitations of its very small budget. 'It was a bit mad. The first series was genuinely evil in places. I'm really proud of a lot of stuff in the first one. It's insane, that second series.'

Had it been more of a success then *Springhill* could have been the *Twin Peaks* of the British television landscape. Students' theses could discuss the treatment of religion, its approach to the supernatural, the ultimate question of what is 'good' and 'bad' in television storytelling. But it is also a culmination of Davies' well-honed scripting skills up to this point. The series shows off the strongest aspects of his writing, joyously revelling in the ridiculous and fantastic vying with the mundane. It is funny and sharp, fast-paced with a hint of spectacle. In itself *Springhill* is one of the programmes that best shows off an unadulterated Davies product. That it should be such a contrast to the often leaden production that followed was an unfortunate, but essential, part of his eventual transformation into one of the biggest writers in television today.

Whatever the quality of the end result, *Springhill*'s writing team clearly relished their comradely working relationship during this period. On Paul Abbott's encouragement, Davies even became involved in a brief Granada writers' strike. For the most part, though, an air of contentment appears to have reigned. According to Cottrell Boyce, 'the unusual quality that Russell and Paul [Marquess] shared was that they were very comfortable in the building, the building being [Granada headquarters] Quay Street. Most British TV writers are essentially amateurs. TV drama is a cottage industry. Writers can't wait to get home, to the pub. Russell and Paul were both part of the life of Quay Street – they knew everyone, they took on producing roles, they found little corners to work in. That's very unusual in Britain. But it is exactly the way that great American TV writers operate – they work in the room, they have hyphens and all that. Russell and Paul worked on *Springhill* and other shows as though it were *The Sopranos* or something. I feel very privileged to have met them. They made me raise my game.'

Before he moved on to his next project, Davies was continuing to offer his services to *Coronation Street*, as he had ever since his arrival at Granada. 'I used to go and knock on the door of *Coronation Street* and say, please let me write for it. Because I love it. I genuinely love that programme, for all its faults.' But despite his experience, he was not taken on board. 'It was like the Royal Family in those days,' he claims. '"We'll deign to approach you one day." I do think I was lucky. If they'd said yes, I would still be there now, because I absolutely love it. I'd be there, a grumpy old man, sitting there thinking up stories for Deirdre.'

He was never to make it as a script writer on the show itself, but did spend some time in 1997 as a storyliner – albeit just a fortnight's work, providing holiday cover for another writer. He also wrote, over a period of just three days, the video special *Viva Las Vegas*, starring key characters Jack and Vera Duckworth. Davies clearly had a whale of a time writing it, especially in the sequences that reference the show's rich past. A farcical 90 minutes opens with an *Alas Smith and Jones*-type dialogue between Jack and Vera, and the comedy continues throughout. Despite writing for such well-established characters, Davies manages to inject his own voice into the proceedings. Unlike most dramas *Coronation Street* has always revelled in making its characters sound as real as possible, including references to real-life events and popular culture, or references to events that would normally not merit a mention. It seems plausible that Davies' adoration of the show led to his own adoption of this welcome stylistic quirk.

The special features direct references to, or spoofs of, programmes ranging from *Dynasty* to *Animal Hospital*. That's not to mention the closing re-enactment of the famous Cinzano Bianco advert starring Leornard Rossiter and Joan Collins, the latter of whom makes a cameo appearance. Unashamedly silly and lightweight, the video is great fun, even if it's bogged down by the inclusion of the cardboard cutout characters of Fiona and Maxine from the *Street*. And even here Davies continued his inclusion of gay characters, with the revelation that ex-regular Ray Langton was now married to a man – a twist that was ignored when he later reappeared in the show proper!

Once Davies had earned his spurs by writing his own primetime show in the form of *The Grand*, the *Coronation Street* team finally invited him on board, but he demurred. He does not regret his decision. 'I'd just got a taste of what you could do outside that world, and thank God I went and did that,' he says. 'I'm not slagging off soaps as a bad place to work, because more people watch them than anything I've done. And when they're good, they're absolutely brilliant. But I'm very glad that, just at the right time, I sort of went another way.'

Today, Davies appears to have got *Coronation Street* out of his system. In theory, if he were to be asked to go and run the soap, he insists he'd turn the offer down. 'No. I couldn't now,' he reckons. 'I'm so out of touch with it. Now I don't know how they make them. I'm sure that give me a week in there and I'd learn it but in my day you could actually take the story to more or less wherever you wanted to. You can't really now, you're much more of a slave to what's on location and what's in studio. I couldn't do that now because it's almost impossible to run a soap opera for beyond a fortnight in which you're interested in every story. And that's just the nature of them, that's just impossible to sustain, and I couldn't bear that now.'

Such concerns would be a million miles away from the relatively lavish budget given to Davies' next project. A glossy period production, *The Grand* was set up to be a big hitter for ITV in the ratings war. Perhaps unsurprisingly, given the profile of the production and Davies' relative lack of experience in major primetime programmes, he was not the channel's original choice. Another writer had devised the series and penned an opening episode for it. However, Granada was not confident that the scripts were strong enough to convince the ITV network to commission the show.

'I don't want to name [the original writer], but it was just terrible,' says Davies. 'It was one of those very odd situations. ITV wanted cheaper dramas at Friday nine o'clock, so Granada had spent about six months working on a hotel drama. Then, and it's amazing how often this happens, a month before they were due to pitch it to ITV they decided it was rubbish. And it was.'

This was far from an original Davies creation, then, with his eleventh-hour involvement echoing the hasty scripting of *The House of Windsor*. However, this time the series was to be more of a success, even if it failed to perform quite as well as may have been hoped for.

But with such a free hand there was potential for Davies to put as much or as little of his own voice into the series as a whole. He would eventually write all eight episodes of the first series, but, in the first instance, he was unwilling even to rework the pilot. 'There was a script,' he remembers, 'and they said to me, "Rewrite it." And I read it, and I thought it was rubbish and said I didn't have time. I was working on *Revelations* and my agent said, "No, he's too busy." Paul Abbott happened to be in the Granada offices at the time and heard this and, bless him, said, "No he isn't." He said, "I know how fast he can write, and I know he can write that for you in a week, and I know it will work, so don't phone his agent, go directly to him." And so they did, they came directly to me.'

Davies immediately knew how he wished to shape the series, given its likely time slot and status within the channel. 'I did get it, that it was a 9.00 pm drama. And I read what they prepared and I didn't like it at all, but I knew it could work. I just got it straight away. So I did write it in a week, [and] chucked out everything that they'd prepared.'

The end result was a series that centred on the Bannerman family and their struggles to run a quality Manchester hotel in the wake of the First World War. The list of characters could be from any melodrama of the last hundred years. The ineffectual husband who eventually snaps; the strong-minded wife who figures strongly in the overall balance of power; the black sheep of the family who returns to the family home and holds the key to their future success – all these and more figure as part of the Bannerman family. They would be complemented by a substantial supporting cast, largely staff within the hotel. A variety of maids and male serving staff who are kept in check by their cold-hearted superior Mrs Harvey (played by Christine Mackie) and tough-but-fair Mr Collins (Tim Healy); both, of course, are eventually revealed to have a softer side. Finally, there was the upper-class 'tart with a heart' prostitute Esme Harkness (Susan Hampshire), who lived in the hotel and also entertained her suitors there.*

With such a collection of people inhabiting the main location, *The Grand* could have been a camp farce, or a comedy drama, or even an ironic take on its own clichés. However, it was instead something of a stony-faced drama, initially at least. Fun and enjoyment was not on the agenda for either the characters or the audience. *The Grand* does not comfortably fit into our analysis of Davies' development of recurring narrative devices and motifs. While the experience strongly figures in his professional development, the series itself is bereft of many of the factors that signal his strong authorial voice.

The series opens with the hotel's accountant hiding a gun in readiness for his suicide later in the first episode. A party in the hotel, which showcased the series' setting and characters, follows this bleak first scene and is rather more representative of the tone of *The Grand*. Perhaps the best indication of the underlying pessimism and negativity running through much of the series is its treatment of maid Monica Jones, played by Jane Danson, who would later find fame as Leanne Battersby in *Coronation Street*. Initially there are many similarities between her character and Rose Tyler of *Doctor Who* nearly a decade later. Both are from underprivileged backgrounds and are working in jobs that offer little in the way of career aspirations, but both are also able to look beyond their current circumstances and aim for a different way of life.

'It's no good just wishing, it's got to burn,' says Esme to Monica. 'Oh and it does, it really does,' the maid replies. 'You can go up to the roof of this place and look down, and it can be midnight but there's all this light. You look across the city and there's light and people as far as the eye can see. You can see the curve of the world and feel it turn. And all I've got is that thin bed downstairs. Lights out at eleven and up at six – and that's not fair. There's a better life out there.'

A sense of wonder in everyday events and an appreciation of the beauty of the 'normal' world would become increasingly dominant in later productions, most obviously in *Doctor Who* and *The Second Coming*. When Stuart and

---

*An Esme Harkness had been one of the elderly inhabitants of Century Falls in Davies' 1993 Children's BBC serial. In time, Captain Jack Harkness, of *Doctor Who* and *Torchwood*, would follow. By Davies' own admission, the original Harkness, who inspired him to name all those who came after, was the sorceress Agatha Harkness, a recurring character in the Marvel team comic *The Fantastic Four*. Further proof, if by this stage it's still needed, that Davies' childhood enthusiasms can be detected throughout his work in adult life.

Vince go onto the hospital roof in the middle of the night during the first episode of *Queer as Folk* they essentially re-enact the scene just described. They look over Manchester at night and, mimicking the film *Titanic*, pronounce themselves 'king of the world'.

More obviously, Monica's speech is later echoed in the first episode of Davies' *Doctor Who*, as Christopher Eccleston's Doctor tries to explain to Billie Piper's Rose how his perspective of the universe is different to hers. 'I can feel it,' he tells her. 'The turn of the Earth, the ground beneath our feet, spinning at a thousand miles an hour, and the entire planet is hurtling around the sun at 67,000 miles an hour. And I can feel it. We're falling through space, you and me, clinging to the skin of this tiny little world, and if we let go … That's who I am.' This exuberance allows Rose to see the Doctor as her way out of a monotonous life, and she spends the next two series seeing the universe with him, her horizons expanded. By the time she is exiled to a parallel universe Rose is a changed woman; more confident in her own abilities and motivated to do much more than work as a shop assistant for the rest of her life.

By way of contrast, Monica Jones works her way above stairs by becoming the lover of a guest, James Cornell. But things take a nasty turn when Cornell's friend expects her to sleep with him also. Defending herself, she accidentally kills him. She is subsequently found guilty of murder and, in a harrowing sequence, is hanged. This turn of events underlines the difference between the optimism of *Doctor Who* and the pessimism of *The Grand*. The programme is regularly hard work for the viewer, and Davies acknowledges that it was often too dark.

'It was terrifying,' he says of the writing experience. 'It was nine o'clock and on film, and I was very much going in to it thinking, "Drama is tragedy," and every week someone different had the heart pulled out of them.' This is certainly true; the first series has a consistently bleak tone, and, although it has an underlying ongoing narrative, each episode would have its own stand-alone crisis. There are moments of humour but they are fleeting in these first eight episodes, and often feel out of place because the sporadic appearances of light comedy do not sit well with the overall sense of doom and gloom. Eight episodes meant eight different traumas for the staff of the hotel, from a son being executed for desertion through to a previously employed maid, now pregnant, pleading to be given somewhere to live and threatening to kill her unborn child.

When the series was released on DVD in North America the back cover proudly expressed the key elements of the series in a series of bullet points highlighting 'Murder/Adultery/Prostitution/Bankruptcy/Mystery'. Unsurprisingly, 'Humour' and 'Fun' were nowhere to be seen. While he acknowledges that the overall tone was not right for the first series, Davies seems to have found the writing process a cathartic one. 'It's a very good thing to have written because once you have written those suicides, those traumas, and genuinely written them, got to the heart of them, you actually feel free not to write them again. And to move on and think, life is about other things, it isn't always like that.' However, it's clear that he has some affection for the time he spent inflicting pain on his own characters. 'That execution is marvellous!' he smiles.

The second series of *The Grand* had a slightly extended run of ten episodes and largely kept the same cast and a broadly similar approach to the plotting. This time the tone was significantly lighter, although not exclusively so; indeed, the darker moments had more impact because they were less frequent, carrying more emotional weight by serving as a contrast. The greatest success of the second series was that there were strong character moments which didn't have to serve as either light relief or to indicate the latest disaster to affect the hotel. Instead, characters could develop in their own right without having to serve a dramatic purpose. 'In the second series, right in the last few episodes, it started to get funny,' says Davies. 'Sally, who phoned me up laughing about the juvenilia of Emily Brontë [in *Breakfast Serials*], she used to watch stuff and she said to me, "You have a laugh in real life, why can't it be like that?"' At the time Davies defended his plotting to her: 'I said, "It's drama, it's not like that. It's much more serious."' But this comment has affected his approach to writing ever since.

After *The Grand*, Davies' work becomes more consistent and easily identifiable. His strong authorial voice seems to be a result of him having a strong voice of his own. When speaking to Davies in person he tends to talk in a similar manner to his dialogue. He can be dramatic and honest while still dropping in-jokes between anecdotes. He thinks a lot but talks even more so that the pace of conversation never lets up. You can hear that same energy in his work, once he'd worked his way through the depressing end of the dramatic spectrum. From that point on, Davies' work sounds like he is having a great time. Somewhat ironically, after ten years in television, he moved back to the quick wit and high drama of *Dark Season*, albeit with added character depth.

Remembering his friend's questioning of his downcast approach to drama in *The Grand*, he says that 'It took two years for that comment to seep into my brain, and still to this day I think, "Oh, she's right." A casual comment over coffee. It wasn't a deep dark secret. But years it took for that to filter in, and I thought, "That's the most precise piece of criticism I've ever had, that's bang on." And literally in the last year of *The Grand*, in the second series, the other writers were all sacked. So I ended up writing them all; again, I had to write all of those in about a week each. I was just sort of giving up by that stage and so I started to have a laugh.'

Although Davies is not credited as writer on every episode of the second series, the workload was clearly far from ideal, with the welcome result that the drama of the week was no longer restricted to disasters and deaths. Instead, there was more variety, even if this was the result of expediency rather than any grand plan. 'There was no time to research the history of the First World War or suicides of ex-soldiers or stuff like that and so I just had a laugh. I remember sitting with Paul Marquess in Pizza Express, going, "I've got five days to write an episode. I haven't got a plot, what can I do?" And he goes, "Why don't you do that story from that old camp 1920s series [*Mapp and Lucia*]. I saw a marvellous episode of that once where Prunella Scales scandalised the entire village because she wore trousers!" I thought, "Oh, I'll have that!" So I had half an episode about that – an actress from *Revelations*, Carol Nimmens, walking into the hotel wearing trousers! I started to have a laugh with it. It was funny.'

Davies cites the eighth episode of the second series as the turning point for *The Grand*, but only two episodes were to follow it. He claims that 'In episode sixteen there's some of the funniest dialogue I've ever written. My boyfriend thinks it's the funniest thing I've ever written. All of the staff go for a day trip. Mrs Harvey says to [young maid] Lark Rothery, "Now you sit up front with me now, there'll be plenty to see. Open countryside, cows in the field – ever seen a cow?" And she goes, "Yes, Mrs Harvey." Mrs Harvey's offended, and she says, "Some folk've never seen a cow!" And I think that is so funny! My boyfriend's always going, "Some folk've never seen a cow!" No matter what I write, that's his favourite line! And it is me, having a laugh. I'm sitting there at like midnight and type, type, type, due in tomorrow. But actually you become yourself a bit more, you become freed and released and start to write properly.'

Another shift in Davies' writing style was to follow. 'Episode sixteen was where there was a huge change in me and lots happened in that episode – without me knowing it,' he says. But it was not just the introduction of comedy; by the end of the second series the programme had ceased to be a rather sterile imitation of previous period dramas such as *Upstairs, Downstairs*. Moreover, it no longer felt like an attempt to tick all the right boxes for a drama on ITV at 9.00 pm, but instead was taking on its own life.

'For a start the staff started being funny,' points out Davies, 'and then a man, a seaman, had to call off his engagement with his fiancée. She was called Christina Wyndham-Price – 'plot device'! Because she didn't have a character! She just walked in so he could get jealous. So there's a scene where he has to call off his engagement and I remember sitting there thinking that I've done that so many times, "I love you," "I don't love you," blah blah blah. I thought, that's not the way people talk. What if we could write this scene so that he never calls it off, it gets called off without either of them saying so, they both just know what is going on, which is a lot more intelligent way of writing. That was like a huge door in my head opening. Only Tony Wood noticed, and that's why Tony Wood's a marvellous writer because he did say, "That's different." That was huge. It just all started happening then.'

While far from being the strongest example of Davies' writing, *The Grand* is certainly entertaining after the sombre opening episodes, and was on an upward trajectory when it failed to be recommissioned for a third series. Davies had been aware of this likelihood while working on the second run of the programme, hence his willingness to stretch the format more and not play so safe. Put simply, he was injecting more of his own personality into the series.

The episode that most clearly signposted his future ambitions occurred midway through the second series. An exploration of a single character, the script concentrated on the hotel barman Clive and his secret homosexuality. The narrative uses a framing device of Clive visiting his ill father in an attempt to tell him the truth about his life. It is made clear that Clive has recently been promoted to porter, assistant to head porter Mr Collins, played by Tim Healy. However, it is clear from the opening that some event has caused him to be demoted to barman again. In flashback, the episode tells the story of the arrival at the hotel of flamboyant guest Mr Villiers. Villiers takes a shine to Clive, and forces him to confront his repressed sexuality when he discreetly invites him to his room.

The episode also includes Clive discovering the underground gay scene of the 1920s, while he desperately tries to convince himself that he is heterosexual. But eventually he gives in and goes to Villiers' room. After he discovers that Esme Harkness knows of this, Clive goes berserk and forces himself in to Villiers' room, where he is with another man, insisting that the police are called. Although he is initially fired for his actions, Mr Collins' intervention means that Clive is allowed to return to his previous job. At the episode's resolution it becomes clear that Clive is not really talking to his father, but has returned from his funeral and is acting out what he would have liked to have said.

The episode may often be downbeat, but on the whole it's affecting rather than depressing. Both the character and his situation feel real and the audience cannot help but be sympathetic. But the importance for Davies' career was in the writing of a whole hour of proper drama, not a soap opera, which dealt with a gay character. It was a successful venture, with the episode working well through the use of a central character who made the situation seem both touching and devastating. The gay storyline was not peripheral to the main action; it was not a subplot. Davies could not only make the 'issue' work as drama, but he could make it work more effectively than any other episode of the series. Not only had it been established that one of his strengths was the use of his own authorial voice in his writing, but he also seemed to write best when plotting topics that he was comfortable addressing. To combine the two would seem to be the natural next step.

In practice, Davies faced strong opposition from within Granada even to get the script made. There were no objections to the gay theme. Rather, the episode focused on one particular character, and deployed narrative devices such as flashbacks. Davies recalls Granada executives telling him, 'You can't do this. You've broken the format. This is too radical.' Feeling sure it was, as he says, 'the best thing I'd ever written,' Davies refused to back down. He had his agent arguing the case, and showed the script to his friend Paul Abbott, who reassured him of its quality. Eventually, having stood his ground, Granada conceded – most likely because it was too close to production to abandon it. Davies didn't regret it one bit. 'It was a huge breakthrough in terms of my writing,' he told BBC4 journalist Mark Lawson. 'It was massive. Suddenly, it was streets ahead of any other episode. It was just better drama … As they say, it was where I found my voice.'

When reflecting on *The Grand* overall, Davies suggests, 'It got commissioned with too little preparation time, I think. That haunted it all the way through, and in the very last episode I got it right. In the very last minutes, Susan Hampshire [as Esme Harkness] buys the hotel. *That's* the series. If we had a third series of that I would have finally got it right. It's 18 hours of television and you learn from it. You get to train on air. I make it sound like it's terrible, and it wasn't, but to actually learn on film, with a cast like that, is quite extraordinary. And not beneficial for ITV because it died a death in the ratings, but it did me the power of good. It's all hindsight with this sort of stuff. And if I hadn't written that I wouldn't have written *Queer as Folk* so clearly.'

And so it was that Davies left Granada to work on his own new project. He was leaving a high-profile drama on a major channel in order to write a drama for a late-night Channel Four slot. His writing was about to 'go gay', and as a result he would become one of the most influential and respected writers in the television industry.

SIX:
REALLY DOING IT!

'No boring issues' was Davies' private mantra when devising and writing his next project. Following his successful episode of *The Grand* dealing with Clive's homosexuality, he was simultaneously encouraged by colleagues to both write truer to himself and, as he has put it himself, 'go gay' with his writing. Not that he'd ever been shy of deploying gay characters, as we have seen. He even claims that Miss Pendragon in *Dark Season* was a lesbian, although later characters would be rather more overt in this regard.

This new venture would be something of a break in Davies' career, as he departed Granada and both devised and wrote his own series. Granada drama executives Catriona MacKenzie and Gub Neil had recently moved to Channel Four, and they encouraged Davies to write for the channel. They put him together with producer Nicola Shindler of Red Productions, whom he had first encountered at the Emmy Awards in New York, and with whom he would work repeatedly over the new few years. 'I knew about his work on *Families* and *The Grand*, and I'd enjoyed lots of the episodes,' Shindler says. 'I'd always heard that he was a very good person to work with. And I always felt from his early stuff that he had a lot more to say. So I was really keen to work with him, and they wanted him to do an idea, and they wanted me to do some ideas with them. So they said, "Why don't you two get together?" And I called him.'

Stealing a line from one of his own characters, Davies and Shindler got on so well that he later referred to her as his 'wife in a parallel universe.' Shindler laughs at the suggestion. 'We get on brilliantly and have very, very, *very* similar takes on things. And that's the key to working with someone really well, it's about your tastes. So I think that's what he means. I don't think he finds me in any way attractive!'

Formerly a drama producer who had first cut her teeth on the BBC's much acclaimed drama *Our Friends in the North*, Shindler established her independent Red Productions company in premises within Granada's Manchester headquarters. *Queer as Folk* was to be her outfit's inaugural commission.

For Davies, the new project was something of a valediction for a whole way of life. During his time at Granada he'd developed a hugely active and lively social life in and around Manchester. By his own account he rarely spent an evening at home. Instead he'd stay out with friends almost until dawn, day in, day out, clocking on at Granada after a scant few hours' sleep, feeling very much the worse for wear. Not that this arrangement was unproductive. As Davies tells it, he managed, for instance, to crack the tricky problem of the climax to the first series of *The Grand* while on a visit to the Canal Street club Cruz 101.

Then, one night early in September 1997, Davies had a calamitous, sobering experience at home with a guest, very nearly succumbing to his excesses. Of course, he survived, but he reflected that, had he died, the event would barely have registered as a blip in the world outside, which was reeling from the death of Princess Diana just days before. As a result Davies resolved to clean up his act, a slow process that he admits took years to fulfil. By the end of 1997 he was working on the series that became *Queer as Folk*, a vivid celebration of the hedonistic lifestyle that he was gently stepping back from.

The road to *Queer as Folk* wasn't entirely smooth though. Initially Catriona MacKenzie suggested that Davies write a drama about gay characters sharing a flat, in the vein of the hit *This Life*. Davies instinctively felt this idea, which he dismissively dubbed *That's My Muesli!*, wasn't the way to go. Instead he developed the saga of a core group of friends on Manchester's gay scene, less shackled to one single location. A potential title for the series was *The Other End of the Ballroom* – as in, 'I dance at the other end of the ballroom', a quaint, coy euphemism for homosexuality subsequently deployed by the Stuart character in *Queer as Folk 2*.

By February 1998 Davies had written a full draft of the series' first episode. It was evident to all that the script was too long, and working in close collaboration with Shindler and script editor Matt Jones, Davies revised it, and spliced it in two, forming the series' opening pair of episodes instead. The remaining episodes followed thick and fast, and in all Davies took around six months to write the full series. For a brief time the series went by the title *Queer as Fuck* (or *F**k)*, at the suggestion of an unknown Channel Four executive. Eventually though, the gentler, cheekier name *Queer as Folk* won out.

Writing the series proved to be a liberating experience for Davies, not merely in terms of the gay subject matter, though that was of course hugely significant. After years of writing drama contained within Granada studio sets, he now found he could given his imagination full rein, which lent his work a new verve and pace. 'No wonder the *Queer as Folk* characters kept running and driving and standing on rooftops,' Davies has since reflected. 'I was free!'

Queer as Folk follows the experiences of gay friends Stuart and Vince in Manchester, with the plot's main catalyst being the arrival of 15-year-old Nathan in their lives. The opening episode features a typical night out on Manchester's Canal Street for Vince and Stuart, with their group of friends. But when Stuart brings Nathan home it's just the start of the 15-year-old's obsession. However, they need to make a trip to the hospital between sex sessions when Stuart's friend Lisa informs him that her partner Romey has just given birth. Stuart is the biological father, but it's already clear from his cavalier behaviour that he's not ideal role-model material.

Following on from this, the initial eight-part series encompasses several different plots and introduces a raft of strongly drawn supporting characters. Most significant of all the story threads, however, is the underlying suggestion of an unresolved tension between Vince and Stuart. It's not necessarily sexual, but certainly indicates deeply held feelings between them. While there is a death and some serious discussion of the ramifications of more hedonistic lifestyles, for the most part the programme is simply fun. There is no HIV storyline for example, nor any heavy-handed discussion of safe sex (although Davies and Shindler have both insisted that all sex was to have been depicted as safe, even if it was not explicitly shown). And there are relatively few weeping relatives shown struggling to come to terms with a gay member of the family.

We shouldn't attribute this to any particular desire to depict gay men as characters in their own right who just happen to be homosexual. Representation was far from Davies' mind, as we shall see later. Rather, the stronger motive was Davies' own desire to simply write a drama that was entertaining and which touched on issues in his own life. As a gay man living in Manchester he drew on his own experiences and told the story that he wanted to tell, rather than worrying about its depiction of gay lives.

Queer as Folk is not yet old enough to be considered a time-capsule of gay drama. Society's attitudes towards gay lives haven't substantially changed since, and the lifestyles it depicts are just as prevalent ten years on. But it's no longer modern or new. At the time of the series' first transmission, between February and April 1999, it felt like it was part of a new wave of drama, including *This Life* and *Holding On*, which would herald a new form of adult storytelling on television. However, Davies has cited the popular ITV drama *Band of Gold*, a series about a group of prostitutes, as one of *Queer as Folk*'s most influential antecedents with its frank treatment of sexuality. Conversely, the contemporaneous rash of one-dimensional gay characters in British soaps, such as *EastEnders'* Tony and Simon, helped only to convince Davies that there must surely more sophisticated ways of dramatising gay lifestyles.

Nevertheless, the depiction of young adults on television seemed to be changing in the late 1990s. They were given more of a focus and treated more earnestly, while being fully rounded figures in their own right. There was more attention given to making characters 'real', with prominent personality flaws. The emphasis on the day-to-day lives and interests of urban professionals seemed to be the new fashion for drama. But the television landscape largely regressed after this point. Sometimes this would be in relatively minor, but still influential, ways. For instance, Davies has pointed out that much of the bad language used in *Queer as Folk* would be frowned upon today. That's not to say that there have been no groundbreaking or acclaimed dramas in the past ten years, merely that the path demonstrated by *Queer as Folk* and its contemporaries was not embraced as wholeheartedly as might be imagined.

Casting the three leads for the series would be crucial. Actor Christopher Eccleston was initially asked to read for the character of Stuart, but decided that he was too old for the part. Instead, he suggested Aiden Gillen, who went on to be cast in the role. Gillen and Craig Kelly, who was cast as Vince, would share top billing throughout *Queer as Folk*, but it was the third role of Nathan that would be most difficult to allocate. Davies had made special efforts to get Nathan's character right, even researching the experiences of young gay men through Manchester youth groups. After a great deal of searching it was felt that an actor older than the character might be suitable, and Charlie Hunnam, a relatively inexperienced actor just 18 years old at the time of filming, was deemed perfect for the role.

The only character whose casting seemed straightforward was that of over-the-top Alexander. The role was actually written for Davies' friend and former colleague Phil Collinson, who was also working as an actor at this time. 'I auditioned for the part,' confesses Collinson. 'Russell didn't tell me he'd based Alexander on me till much later, but he did call me and say, "There's a part in *Queer as Folk* that I'd love you to read for." By that point I'd been script editing for about a year and so I was in two minds whether to even go along. In the end I did and gave a truly terrible audition. Apparently Anthony Cotton came in afterwards and dazzled them and the rest, as they say, is history. I've become friends with Anthony as a result and we both see that audition as a defining moment in our lives.' In years to come, Anthony Cotton would make his mark in the mainstream as an ongoing star of Granada's *Coronation Street*, and even his own day-time chat show.

Davies continued to revise his scripts right up until filming, and even beyond. In particular he took several passes at the opening scenes of the first episode. Getting the tone of the piece right from the very first moments was clearly of critical importance. One abandoned variant cut straight to Stuart, Vince and Phil on a night out on Canal Street. Another introduced young Nathan and Donna at a standard-issue teenage party, only for Nathan to raid someone's coat for cash and promptly make a bolt for a bus to Canal Street. Indeed, this was the series' opening as shot, but the footage was abandoned at the editing stage, as the team didn't care for the misleading 'scary and tense' tone it created. 'It was like a thriller,' Davies has said. 'You expected Stuart to take Nathan home and murder him, like an episode of *Cracker*.' On the hoof, Davies created an entirely new, and more direct, opening, of which Shindler approved. Disliking the party sequence, she'd been urging her team,

'Cut it. Get on with it!'

On a budget in the region of £3 million, the series was shot on film in and around Manchester, with the most prominent location being the largest gay scene in the north of England, Canal Street. Of the two directors charged with bringing Davies' scripts to the screen, the first, Charles MacDougall, had received great acclaim for his work on Jimmy McGovern's powerful drama *Hillsborough*. The second director, Sarah Harding, had previously helmed many episodes of *The Grand*, not least the crucial 'barman Clive' episode. Channel Four experimented with an unusual duration for the series, requesting that all eight episodes be suitably for a forty-minute slot, intended to be screened at 10.00 pm. It was hoped that the move would allow drama to remain a prominent part of the schedule more often, even if the amount of material filmed was approximately equivalent to a six-part serial in an hour-long slot.

While the series was Davies' first modern drama for an adult audience, it continued to be built around themes that had been prevalent in his work. The unconventional family unit was seen once more, not only in the depiction of Vince's mother Hazel and her older gay lodger Bernard, but also in the fact that its family units weren't necessarily linked by blood ties. Fully functioning families are rare in Davies' work and are often ancillary to the plotline. There are exceptions, such as some of his work on soap operas and his later drama *Mine All Mine*, but in general he forms his own groups of characters that take on a family-like role.

Once more, this is in line with *This Life*, an acclaimed drama, first broadcast on BBC Two in 1996, which centred on the lives of young professionals living together in London. In *Queer as Folk*, even when the plot moves towards the formation of new romances or the dissolution of old ones, it always moves back to the central group of friends. Indeed, the first series concludes with Vince making this exact choice, between his boyfriend and going back to his old life dancing with Stuart in a club.

However, Vince's boyfriend Cameron points out to Stuart that it is hardly a typical family unit, especially considering Stuart's general shunning of his own relatives. 'What is it, a family?' he asks. 'Your own little make-believe family? You even have a baby just to finish it off. If you think that's a family, you're fucked.' Nevertheless, for the most part characters move back to their own 'family' of friends.

Inevitably the drama revolves around the three main characters, each of whom has absolutely distinct character traits. Vince, another Tyler to add to the list, is the *Doctor Who*-loving 'nice guy' who balances out the extremes of the other two. His working life at a supermarket may be uneventful but he doesn't hint at any particular set of aspirations for his career or life. His focus seems to be almost entirely on the time he spends with Stuart, a friend from school. There is a definite sense that this preoccupation has lasted throughout his life. As Hazel tells Stuart, 'Vince comes home, he says, there's this new boy at school, this Irish boy. I had weeks of it, Stuart this, Stuart that. Then weeks he didn't mention you at all. Like the two of you had a secret… Soon as I saw you, I thought, clever little bastard.'

Stuart Jones is successful, good-looking and well paid – not to mention highly sexed. He can seemingly bed any man and tends to be the focus of whichever group he is in. Somehow his arrogance and rudeness do not outweigh his charisma in the eyes of most of his friends. Strong-minded and opinionated, his Achilles heel is the fact that he is still not out to his parents. Finally, schoolboy Nathan Maloney is, to quote Davies, 'one of those irrational teenagers, and he's horrible in all sorts of ways, but you love him.' After being bedded by Stuart in the first episode Nathan becomes hooked on the gay scene but, even more than that, on Stuart himself.

Davies has since explained that *Queer as Folk* drew heavily on his own experiences in gay society, and that virtually every event in the drama happened to him personally, or else to a friend. As he confessed to the *Independent*, 'There are people who won't talk to me again after that. Vince does that speech about losing his virginity while watching *The Two Ronnies*. It's word for word what happened to an ex-boyfriend of mine'.

Nevertheless, the writer is wary of drawing any direct comparisons between himself and *Queer as Folk*'s core triumvirate. On the face of it, it's tempting to presume that, as a person, he's most like Vince, not least because the character is the most sympathetic and shares Davies' love of *Doctor Who*. But Davies insists the matter isn't so straightforward. '*Queer as Folk*

103

was very simple, an ordinary man split into three,' he explains. 'There was Vince, who feels a bit insecure, and non-sexual, and ordinary. There's Stuart – and frankly we've all had nights like Stuart, haven't we? Everyone says he's a bastard, blah blah blah. Oh, come on! Don't tell me you haven't had one night like that! Or thoughts like that, constantly, about people. And then Nathan, who was a twat, who was a teenager – as we all were.'

Davies refutes any suggestion that he specifically put aspects of his own character into each one, however. 'Because they are one man split into three, they're all me but at the same time I'm not saying it's autobiographical. It's much more complex than that. You change them, and they do that thing of having their own life, which always sounds ridiculous, really, but it's true.' He is pleased to point out that he is not alone in thinking this. 'I saw Harold Pinter saying it in an interview the other day, in the *Guardian*, and I thought, "Oh, thank God someoné posh says that, instead of just me bitching!" "Oh, my characters have a life of their own!" And you're there going, shut up. But they do slightly.'

Although the three lead roles command much of the on-screen action, the secondary characters are particularly strong. While the adventures of flamboyant Alexander and his friend Dane allow the series to occasionally venture into out-and-out comedy, they effectively operate separately from the main action. In the first series especially, Alexander and Stuart barely even speak to each other. Vince's mum Hazel, Stuart's sister Marie and Nathan's friend Donna ground each of the main characters, each possessing the rare gift of being able to make their friend or relative defer to them – at least on occasion.

In pondering what Davies was trying to say about the lives of his characters, perhaps most interesting to consider is Phil. He doesn't possess any particularly strong characteristics, instead being a rather nondescript member of the social circle. Well-liked but single, he is essentially a cipher until he brings a man called Harvey home one night. Encouraged to snort cocaine by his one-night-stand, Phil has a violent reaction to the drug and falls to the floor unconscious. Harvey panics and disappears without calling for an ambulance, taking a moment to steal from Phil's wallet on the way out. When Phil's mother calls Vince five days later his body has only just been found. The script makes the passage of time more explicit than the transmitted episode, bringing up captions for each of the days that pass after Phil's death. It specifies a series of fades to black followed by a caption showing the day, this happening for Monday to Thursday. After the day is shown, the picture mixes up to show Phil's lifeless body as we hear messages left on his answerphone.

Perhaps the eschewing of this approach in the finished episode is indicative of a feeling that it would be too unsubtle in its portrayal of the potentially solitary life of a single gay man. But Phil is not a strong or central enough character for the plot line to revolve around the loss of his character from the series. Instead, it focuses on how his friends and family deal with this reminder of their own mortality. In doing so this highlights the differences between the programme's depiction of the heterosexual world and of the lives of gay men in general, as well as more specific instances in relation to the main characters.

Even at the funeral Stuart remains sexually predatory, not even taking a break from checking out the other men during the service itself. Vince is genuinely upset, whereas Nathan nonchalantly shrugs the incident off. 'Didn't really know him,' he points out shortly after the funeral before being followed upstairs by Stuart for sex. Phil's mother, however, provides one of the rare instances where an issue is tackled by way of introspective dialogue. Davies was keen never to have Vince explicitly declare his love for Stuart in a self-pitying monologue, in the same manner he had avoided Christina Wyndham-Price and her fiancé outlining that they were to call off their engagement in an episode of *The Grand*. Here, however, the point is made clear. Would Phil's death have occurred had he been straight? The question has two facets; would a woman have encouraged him to take drugs in this manner, and would she have left him when he reacted badly?

There can be no answer, of course, and an argument could be made that the sex, or sexuality, of a person does not dictate their actions. But Phil's mum highlights the fact that the lives led by the gay characters do have consequences. They are not immune to the real world. Tellingly, her speech makes no discernible difference to them, and the way they continue to live their lives. In a sense the scene is less a statement about Phil's life than it is a comment on the mother's sense of futility, or even an inherent resentment. But Vince and, more especially, Stuart continue to act as they always have done, including drug taking and promiscuity.

Queer as Folk marked the first time that Davies would have an executive producer credit, one that he would retain for all his major projects subsequently. He has his own vision for the scripts that he writes beyond the printed page. Even if we overlook his day-to-day involvement in issues relating to overall production, his scripts certainly read very differently from many written for television. Quite apart from the naturalistic and often jokey dialogue, there is the question of 'stage directions'. They are written very clearly and without ambiguity, often specifying details that might normally be left to the director's or actors' discretion.

For example, the script for the last sequence of *Queer as Folk* describes Vince and Stuart's reconciliation in more prosaic form than simple general directions. It describes them as 'both leaping up onto the podium in the same second, as the music goes wild, into the chorus. And both start dancing, mental, happy, laughing. Spotlight slams down on them. They're looking like twats and not giving a toss. Run credits over this ... End on Vince and Stuart. A small and tiny world, but they're slap bang in the middle.'

'Directors say that. "Ooh, you're very visual,"' confirms Davies. 'I can't bear people who think that writing's just the dialogue. If you get a good picture on screen, they'll go "The dialogue was very good, the writer was very good, but the director was brilliant." [But] actually, *I* said "Put that camera on a cliff top and have two people standing there! That's what I said would look beautiful!"'

While Davies was happy with most aspects of the production, he reserves his most fulsome praise for the director of the first four episodes, Charles McDougall, although he is still extremely positive about the work of Sarah Harding, who directed the second half. He calls it 'the greatest collaboration' that he has had with any of his directors. 'He's a genius. That's no offence to other directors I've worked with. But he's absolutely rare. I mean, he's mad. And I think he's autistic, and strange. He's genuinely got that solipsism of autism. Which makes him a genius, actually. It's his devotion to the

camera, and his willingness to abandon the schedule and abandon the budget
– which drives producers mad – but he lifted those lines and those pictures
into something absolutely extraordinary.' Nevertheless, such devotion to the
product has its own pitfalls. 'You can't work like that a lot, because literally
budgets were broken. And schedules snapped in half, and contracts were
a nightmare, so you've got to say to him, it's collaborative. Every director
could be brilliant if they had all day every day to do one shot.'

Davies' approach to writing characters in scripts is more succinct.
'When I'm writing the stage directions, and someone walks in the room,
I absolutely limit myself to three adjectives about them,' Davies points out.
'I think scripts are terrible when it says, "Fred walks in the room. He's a
feisty kind of guy and he lived in South America for 20 years, and he now
smokes cigarettes, and he's a bit pissed off because his Mother's been on the
phone to him. And he's the sort of man who doesn't take fools gladly. And
nonetheless he has a vulnerable side to him." You read that a lot in scripts.
Oh, get out!' Personally, Davies prefers to allow his characters to develop
more naturally. 'Let the script tell you all that, and let the dialogue tell you
what sort of person he is. I would sort of say, "Fred walks in, he's 50, tired,
and depressed." Three. I always try and limit it to three. And that's it.'

Given the extent to which he exerts control over the development of his
material wherever possible, and also the way that he does not conform to
a strict plan in the way that he structures his plotting, it could be assumed
that Davies is possessive over his projects. Indicative of this may be the fact
that he wrote all ten episodes of the two series of *Queer as Folk*. Davies,
however, insists that this was not a result of a keenness to retain control.
In fact, episodes five and six of *Queer as Folk* were originally to be written
by another writer, Matthew Westwood, who now contributes to *Hollyoaks*
among other shows. Westwood completed scripts for the relevant episodes,
but Davies confesses, 'They just didn't work. But that often happens. Scripts
fall through and you end up writing them really quickly. Every show in the
world, that happens on. That's normal.'

In the event, the two episodes were written by Davies himself after he'd
finished the rest of the series, which goes some way to explaining why the
events they follow are generally away from the main action. There's some

furtherance of the plot of Vince and his prospective boyfriend, but the result is more a comedy set piece revolving around their first date than any kind of serious character development. The episodes work in their own right, scarcely touching on the series' ongoing narrative.

Shortly after the second episode of *Queer as Folk* aired, Davies and script editor Matt Jones took part in a web chat on the Channel Four website, where Jones made the point that 'We're not making representational drama, we're not interested in doing a worthy or political piece of drama. It's an authorial piece, and it comes from Russell's heart.' Sure enough, *Queer as Folk* finally afforded Davies' writing the opportunity to operate without restrictions of audience, genre or time slot. As a drama, *Queer as Folk* simply works very well indeed. It is probably the most successful mixture of comedy and drama as an entertaining whole in Davies' entire career and, until the revival of *Doctor Who,* it was the title with which his name was most readily identified.

Although the production strenuously resisted the notion, there is no avoiding the fact that many gay people felt *Queer as Folk* had some social responsibility. Especially when taken out of context, many of the events could be seen as providing ammunition for those antipathetic to the gay lifestyle. Indeed, in some quarters the notion still lingers that, upon *Queer as Folk*'s first transmission, the whole country was in uproar.

In interviews at the time, Davies confessed that he was surprised by the enraged reaction in certain circles. Certainly, there were some pungent responses. No fewer than 136 calls were made to the Channel Four switchboard following the first episode to complain about the content. Mary Whitehouse, British TV's infamous self-appointed watchdog, voiced her strong disapproval, despite having otherwise fallen into semi-retirement. Under unusual circumstances, back in Swansea, Davies' own parents were watching too. 'My dad lost his sight so my mum ... would describe what was on telly for him,' Davies told journalist Stuart Jeffries. 'God knows the words she used ... She said [to me], "This is porn," and I said, "Well, no it isn't."'

Channel Four's newly installed Strategy and Marketing Director, David Brook, had a field day. Huge *Queer as Folk* posters were displayed in public advertising spaces across the country, and a bold radio campaign was created by showing the drama to middle-aged women and taping their astonished reactions. In fact, though, the first episode's sex scenes, a source of much media attention, were barely more explicit than many of the racier dramas on British television around this time. The only element that marks out those scenes in *Queer as Folk* was the presence of two gay men and, perhaps more controversially, the age difference between them. Nathan, as a 15-year-old, was then three years under the age of consent for gay sex.

Indeed, the Sexual Offences Act 1999 was presented to the House of Lords on the day of the second episode's broadcast. This piece of legislation was intended to force the age of consent for gay men to be kept in line with heterosexuals. It was defeated in the Lords despite a Commons majority of 168 – it did not pass until the following year, when the Parliament Act was invoked. This forced the adoption of the measure despite the opposition in the upper house.

Given the debate at the time, surely Davies knew that the depiction of a sexually active gay 15-year-old would be controversial? Perhaps it was even included as a way to gain attention and pre-publicity? 'No, honestly. Honest to God,' Davies asserts. 'I remember we didn't see controversy. I think what I was thinking was, "That is what Channel Four does, and that's what it should do." I know Channel Four had just been making [the period drama] *Dance to the Music of Time*. There was very much a feeling of ... that is not what Channel Four should be doing. It shouldn't be period, it shouldn't be expensive. *Queer as Folk* was actually surprisingly cheap to make.'

Davies is unabashed in his opinion that Channel Four's drama output '*should* be wild. So you're already talking at that level right from the moment it was commissioned, it was meant to be that sort of show. It's not kicking the doors down for the public because, well, it's a small channel, and the drama on that channel doesn't have a history of being responded to – not since *Walter* really, you know.' *Walter* was the channel's inaugural drama on its opening night, which dealt with the struggle of a man with learning difficulties. It was quite unlike anything else on television to that point, and for many signalled the direction for Channel Four as a deliberately provocative broadcaster. 'Good opening night!' Davies says.

But what of Nathan's age? To make him 15 seems almost to play into the hands of the *Daily Mail* brigade, all of them desperate to find a reason to be outraged. 'If you made him 16 he could have left home,' Davies points out. 'You're not adult at 16, but dramatically you are. So he had to be 15. I could have made him 14, I wouldn't have cared. I think I tried to at one point. So all of that felt natural for Channel Four, you don't think it's going to be noticed that much, you think, "Oh, it's Channel Four, here we go again." There was a certain amount of that. And there wasn't that much press stories, it wasn't that big. It gets exaggerated actually. A lot of the newspapers ignored it. I was in London, like eight o'clock in the morning [of the first episode's transmission], so I got all the papers, all the previews. I think one newspaper mentioned it, and it wasn't mentioned in any of the others. There wasn't a great big campaign saying take it off the air.'

Perhaps thinking of the negative reactions from some long term fans regarding the new *Doctor Who* he is keen to emphasise that he does not care to listen to such criticism, simply because he questions its value or worth. 'It's really just a couple of nutters phoning in on radio stations. You might as well listen to people on the internet! It's like that anti-Daniel Craig Bond website. And you think, actually, that's ten nutters. It's always been the case, Mary Whitehouse and her 20 supporters, but it's getting worse. Set up a website criticising something, and the newspapers will publish it. "Programme Under Attack," "Actor Under Attack." It's not true.'

Nevertheless, after transmission of *Queer as Folk*'s third episode, there was one extraordinary reaction that no one had anticipated. The series had been sponsored by the beer company Becks, while the advert breaks themselves were populated by high-end products with glossy commercials attempting to tap into the 'pink pound'. However, it transpired that someone of importance at Becks had decided that *Queer as Folk* was not the sort of programme they should be associated with, and at this juncture, midway through the run, sponsorship was hurriedly withdrawn. 'We couldn't believe it!' says Shindler. 'It was absolutely unbelievable, that in this day and age that kind of thing could happen.' Shindler seems more amused than angry. 'It gave us a bit of good scandal I guess, which did no harm, and it didn't harm *us* financially, so it didn't worry me in that way. But it was quite astonishing.'

At the time the explanation was given that Becks had withdrawn from the sponsorship for purely economic reasons. 'That's what Channel Four had to say in the end,' Shindler continues. 'But they told us a story about Fraulein Becks, who was the daughter of Mr Becks. She was in a hotel in London and switched on and saw some of *Queer as Folk* with Becks sponsorship, and just went mad. Although it was actually Scottish and Newcastle Breweries, so it was all very complicated.' Davies, meanwhile, cheerfully condemns Becks as 'homophobic bastards'.

Perhaps unsurprisingly, the programme found itself criticised by some gay men and women who felt that it did not represent their lives. While reaction in the gay press and among gay men more generally was largely positive, this was certainly not universal. 'I remember actually on the morning of its launch I had to go on that fucking Ned Sherrin thing [*Loose Ends*] on Radio Four,' says Davies. 'There was an old gay man out to trap you. I walked into that trap, not seeing what was coming, but I got out of it. Very unpleasant.' Probably the most memorable example of this was on Channel Four's *Right to Reply*, a programme that featured discussion of recent television programmes. A gay member of the public and a representative from gay rights group Stonewall both criticised the programme for failing to properly represent the lives of gay men as they saw them.

Davies still maintains that it was not his job or intention to write a 'representational' drama, but understands why those who felt mis- or under-represented may be aggrieved. 'Because it's a minority,' he states. 'They're always looking to see themselves be represented. Most people had a brilliant time. Most people are out buying a soundtrack and liking the gags and fancying the boys and seeing a bit of arse and were very happy.' He grins. 'A million wanks, I like to think! On that Tuesday night, I looked out across the city...'

There does seem to have been some naïveté regarding the programme, however. Speaking of its scheduling, for example, Davies recalls that 'We honestly thought, when they said it would go out at 10.30, "We're like a programme about golf!" That's the truth of it, so actually when it gets mentioned in newspapers and people are talking about it, it's brilliant. Simply joyous, a great, great time. It was mad, but it was wonderful. That's what you made it for, to be seen.' While it was not a massive ratings success, *Queer as Folk* did well for its time slot. The first episode attracted 3.52 million viewers across both the original screening and the subsequent repeat, making it the eleventh most watched programme of the week on Channel Four. By the final episode it was maintaining a similar level, with 3.39 million viewers for a single screening.

Even in terms of mainstream press reaction, there was surprisingly little furore. The newly launched *Heat* magazine gave the series consistently good reviews and ran a couple of feature pieces throughout its run. It also drew attention to the early sex scenes, but in a manner that suggested surprise and a cheeky interest rather than disapproval. The *Radio Times*, unfailingly middle-class, simply warned that viewers who were 'averse to sex and bad language should be warned that this contain a lot of both.' For the first episode they were hardly fulsome in their praise, but seemed to prefer to ignore the series after this point rather than give it any added publicity by discrediting or championing it. 'Stuart is such an unsympathetic character that it's hard to relate to his dilemmas, and the overall feel of this opening episode is gloss without substance,' it concluded.

Understandably, Davies prefers to emphasise the extent to which he sensed that there was a positive reaction to the series from the audience at large. 'People talked about it everywhere,' he remembers. 'They talked about it in school. That's what I liked. And when you say people were talking about issues, I honestly don't think many people were standing around the water-cooler saying, "Well, what do you think about the age of consent?" They sit there going "Wasn't that a laugh?" or "Wasn't that cheeky?" I had a lady say, "I can't believe you got away with that." It gets described as a lot of controversy, but there was a lot of joy, actually. It sounds arrogant to talk about, but actually there was.

'I always remember there was a march to save the Oldham Coliseum on a Saturday morning and every actor went along, and I went along, and this was several weeks into the transmission of *Queer as Folk*. The actor who played Dane was there and the woman who was Stuart's secretary was there – and they're not big parts. They were mobbed by schoolchildren and, I am not kidding you, they had 30 12- and 13-year-old girls screaming and running past *Emmerdale* stars and getting their autograph! That's one of those times you stand there thinking, "This is going mad," but there were these kids watching it, there were 12-year-olds watching it, because it's naughty, because it's cheeky. But actually they were properly loving it because it was a great big laugh at the same time. And it was a very funny programme.'

The reactions, then, could be fairly described as 'mixed', and any negativity cooled considerably over the course of the series. By the time of the season finale the sex scenes were not the topic of discussion, nor were the big issues of gay representation on television. The interest was in the relationship between the three leads, and how it would be resolved. Given that the majority of *Queer as Folk* revolves around characters rather than sex scenes or any other potentially 'controversial' aspect, it raises the question of how differently the programme would have been received without them.

It's difficult to judge now, but there is certainly a possibility that the explicit nature of the first episode of *Queer as Folk* in particular may have hindered its wider appeal. Shindler has considered the possibility that there may have been a little too much sex in the first episode, and it may have been better spread more thinly across the early part of the series, but neither she nor Davies questions the inclusion of the scenes themselves. In an interview with *Heat* magazine before the second series, she pointed out that each of the scenes was 'dramatically justified', while Davies was keen to draw comparisons with other television in the same interview. 'The moment a 29-year-old man fucked a 15-year-old boy the story started,' he points out. 'Of course that's shocking. But what's shocking about a bit of sex compared to, say, the baby-eating in *I, Claudius*?'

With the passage of time it certainly seems that the half-hearted angst-ridden headlines in tabloid newspapers have been largely forgotten. 'When it's mentioned in the *Guardian* and stuff like that they don't say "the show in which a 15-year-old is fucked," they say "a show about gay men,"' Davies points out. 'So actually its concept has become the talked-about thing.' By the time of the second series, critic Boyd Hilton called it 'one of the most touching TV love stories of our times' in the ever-positive *Heat*, and the series certainly had a warm reception generally upon its return. But it did not come back in the form that was initially expected.

SEVEN:
ALL THE POOFS AND ALL THE DYKES AND ALL THE PEOPLE IN BETWEEN

The first series of *Queer as Folk* had established a bustling and entertaining world, of both characters and situation, that had captured the attention of its dedicated audience. Though the plot had the relationship between the three leads as its central focus, the supporting characters were clearly strong enough to carry storylines of their own. It was a very healthy basis for an ongoing series.

The writing of the fifth and six episodes, which were scripted out of order, is the strongest indication that the programme could have operated as a long-running show rather than as a self-contained serial. Although he ended up scripting each episode, Davies insists that there would not have been a problem with other writers being brought in for a second series. When he started work on outlining the plot for a new run of episodes he intended it to span more episodes than the first series, this time with a mixture of writers.

'I'm not precious about it,' he says. '*Doctor Who*'s a different thing, because it's a different adventure every week. It's like Paul Abbott does with *Shameless,* and stuff like that. It's nice working with other writers, and nice to run away from other writers at the same time. It's healthy, actually, to get more people in the mix. So I wouldn't have minded, because we were, for a good few months, talking about doing a proper second series of ten episodes. I would have never written all those, now I think of it. We must have been looking for other writers at the time. We were quite happily considering it. It happens. It would have been okay.'

For a brief time Davies was the apple of Channel Four's eye; they were keen for him to formulate a sequel, and possibly more. He has said of later projects, however – most notably *Bob & Rose* – that no story lasts for the length of time that most TV drama serials do. So *Queer as Folk 2* was never going to be simply more of the same. The first run did not need to be furthered; it needed to be resolved. After attempting to outline a ten-part second series, even getting as far as beginning the writing process, Davies found himself struggling to find a story he wanted to tell. Instead, after some discussion a decision was reached. 'We sat with the people from Channel Four, who were very bold and not pushy, and we all just said, "Actually, let's just tell a fantastic two-part story,"' says Nicola Shindler. 'That's what Russell really wanted to do, so that's what we all wanted to do.'

So it was that the proposed second series became a sequel of two parts, both of them to fit an hour-long timeslot rather than the first series' forty minutes. Most of the original cast members returned, with Donna being the only significant character missing due to scheduling conflicts with actress Carla Henry. In February 2000, a year after the first series had begun, *Queer as Folk 2* was broadcast.

The first series of *Queer as Folk* was hardly lacking in confidence, but its sequel felt even more comfortable with its story. Riding on the back of generally positive critical reaction from professionals and audience alike, it had little to prove. It was often even more outrageous than the first series had been, but also placed more emphasis on the series' major storyline, that of Stuart and Vince's apparent unrequited love. In the final episode of the first series Vince dumped his caring and safe new boyfriend Cameron in favour of his old life, partying with Stuart. The final realisation came about when Stuart prompted Vince to ask his new boyfriend to list the actors who had played *Doctor Who*, something that Stuart knew off-pat. The series could have ended there, effectively finishing as it opened. 'It's the greatest love story never told. Cameron, long after you're gone [Stuart] will still have Vince,' says Lisa to Vince's then-boyfriend. 'If it's any consolation, Vince can wait as long as he likes, that shag's never gonna happen.'

The question of whether or not that shag, or more, would ever happen is central to *Queer as Folk 2*. The 'McGuffin' to continue the story takes the form of the wedding of Vince's half sister. A weekend spent at a country retreat for the ceremony forces Vince and Stuart together, overlooked by Hazel and Alexander. The relationship between the latter pair is effectively set up for an eventually abandoned spin-off called *Misfits*, more of which later. But the emphasis on the story of Vince and Stuart's relationship is refreshing in itself. While in many ways this had been the basis for the first series, it had generally remained in the background, a plot that ticked away quietly and altered other stories but rarely came to the forefront. With the decision to wrap up the series, so the question of their relationship became central.

So central, in fact, that Nathan's role is rather diminished. This was originally the result of practical thinking; Davies had been unsure whether Charlie Hunnam in particular would return to the series now he was being touted in Hollywood. As a result, Nathan's plot, that of his 16th birthday, became largely superfluous to the rest of the story. It is not ineffective, however, and demonstrates that the character has matured. Thanks to a sexual intervention, he even manages to stop being in awe of Stuart. By the programme's resolution, he is leading the new generation of gay men inhabiting Canal Street.

The sequel culminates with Stuart's decision to leave Manchester, feeling that he is getting too old; he's also bored by the same nights out after over a decade on the local scene. But the driving issue of the plot is not Stuart leaving, but the question of whether or not Vince will try to join him. In a subplot devoted to Vince's attempt to get a promotion at work, he finally succeeds and finds himself working independently, trying to make the most of his life. But in the same way that he had abandoned Cameron in favour of Stuart in the first series, so the second episode of *Queer as Folk 2* features a tense, but over the top and ridiculous, chase sequence through the city carnival so that Vince can catch Stuart before he leaves, ostensibly for London. Prompted to make the decision by Hazel, Stuart and Vince meet on Canal Street – where else?

After dialogue in which Canal Street is both praised and condemned, Stuart crowns Nathan as the area's new king while day turns to night. He and Vince run into the jeep, which turns on its own axis as it speeds down Canal Street and then seems to explode in the distance. Perhaps this is a *Grease* homage, with the musical's flying car at its climax carrying the reconciled couple off to a new life. For *Queer as Folk*, this new life appears to be America. Somewhere in the Deep South (actually filmed in Spain), they operate as modern outlaws. They even force a local to retract a comment about 'faggots' at gunpoint. This is not the Stuart and Vince of old; in the closing credits it is claimed that they became 'legends'.

But is it a happy ending? Superficially it would seem so. It is certainly the only ending an audience would easily accept, and the only one that would really justify resolving the story at all. By showing the pair resolutely 'together', but with the exact nature of their relationship left open to interpretation, the series could end on a high without being too obvious in its resolution of the characters' stories. However, lost in the camp marvel of the speeding Jeep are some more pertinent questions about their destinies. Stuart has rejected Vince so many times, and their new-found relationship is so enigmatically presented, that it still feels like an unrequited love – a Davies motif. Perhaps the happiest outcome is merely that they are leaving behind the outside influences that had complicated the relationship between them. But a more straightforward conclusion may have been a disappointment; here, the audience is allowed to decide for themselves.

Queer as Folk 2's conclusion was not universally well received, some believing that the fantastical ending was too camp for the series. To an extent this is understandable, given that, despite being a series centred on gay men and their often camp lifestyles, the programme itself had never been inclined this way stylistically. But a final burst of exuberance can be forgiven when a series reaches its resolution, and in any case a fantastical car has nothing on the *Springhill* finale.

Queer as Folk provides evidence that Davies could write most effectively when free of constraints. The series is low on subtext and symbolism, making it a less obvious candidate for textual analysis. That is not to say it is a simplistic piece of television, simply that it does not overstate its own twists and turns. Most of all it is a joyous series with great energy, and tragedy used sparingly but effectively. It was the first time that Davies had successfully achieved a light-hearted serial that still made a dramatic impact on the viewer.

Davies has his own feelings about the positivity and optimism that dominates so much of his work. 'I think bleakness is easy to write,' he asserts. 'I'm not knocking those dramas that have done it, but it's what your sixth-former writes. It's partly that process I had to go through with

The Grand. It's like, done the tragedy: actually you can move on now.'

Considering his words carefully, he continues. 'The awful thing is, truly, I think life is terrible, and we just die. And everything you love and everything you own will be gone. *Everything* will be gone. This building, the whole city, everything will be gone, one day. Nothing lasts, and nothing is remembered in the end. And so, I think, not just in fiction, but in the living of your life, you might as well have a laugh. I don't think there's *any* afterlife. I don't think there's anything to come. I don't think there's anything *special* about us. Well, in individual moments there's something special, but there's no special *purpose* to us at all. I think, actually, the world is more fucking bleak than you can possibly get inside your head. But why go on about that? Since we all die in the end, why write a drama in which everyone dies in the end? That's going to happen anyway.'

Fiction, then, can offer an alternative. 'The artificial creation of a happy ending is a very brilliant thing,' Davies insists. 'It's not sentimental, it's not superficial. Your heart genuinely feels the strength of a happy ending. Because they don't exist, *anywhere* in life, *ever*. There is no couple who will be happy forever. One will die before the other. *Really* I think that. And then, in the shape of an hour's drama, by those end credits, you might as well aim for that, because what's the point in dwelling on the obvious?'

Davies' response to what he perceives as the 'bleakness' of real life is to make sure that he personally enjoys himself as much as possible, while his writing reflects this drive for personal happiness. 'I love having a laugh. That whole sense of humour that I started to find in *Queer as Folk*, that's where it really came out. They have a laugh at [Phil's] funeral there. And they're despicable at that funeral. But, I think that's very true: you go to a funeral, and you have a laugh. They're very, very funny occasions. You *always* end up having a laugh somehow – because it's a human defence system. It's a way of survival. Next day at work, you say while I was at the funeral *this* happened, and you just *tell* it, and you tell the story of your life, and the reason we do that is to shape it, because it's shapeless otherwise. It's *absolutely* fucking shapeless.'

He pauses for breath, whistles, then thumps the table, smiling. 'There we are! I really do think that, though. I could out-bleak all of 'em. Equally I think there's no point in raging against the fact that we all die and that's it, that's the end, and nothing lasts: why rage about it? It's like, because actually now, *right now*, we're having a good time! In everyday social intercourse, I have a laugh *all the time*! I have a hell of a laugh at work. I have a laugh with my friends. I have a laugh with my boyfriend. Me and my boyfriend sit and watch television and we laugh all night long! And we've been together for years! We have *such* a *laugh.* I really, actively, choose to do that, because that's a good way of living your life.'

So, after nearly a decade of writing and an initial movement away from his natural tone of voice, Davies struck his preferred balance of humour and drama. He showcased real characters, and a few caricatures, all of whom worked together as a coherent basis for a variety of stories. And it was a success, far beyond the level the viewing figures would indicate. It might sound hyperbolic to call *Queer as Folk* a cultural phenomenon. But the merchandise spawned by the series, including CDs, videos and books, is a sure indicator that, although its audience may not have been as large as for dramas on ITV or BBC1, it was a truly dedicated audience nevertheless. Additionally, the programme itself became synonymous with edgy modern television in the public vernacular, even if this association faded over time. In short, even though many did not see the series, many more knew of it: its reputation preceded it.

Although *Queer as Folk* had reached the end of its short life, there were still more stories from its universe that could be told. An assortment of new short fiction set in the *Queer as Folk* universe was scheduled to appear on a Channel Four website for the series, and was to have included original prose from Davies. Even more exciting, however, was the prospect of a full spin-off television series. Called *Misfits,* this was to focus on Hazel's boarding house and the waifs and strays from all walks of life who lodged with her. Aside from Hazel herself the series was intended to feature subsidiary *Queer as Folk* characters Alexander, Bernard and Des Stroud, the policeman to whom Hazel was married off in the end credits of *Queer as Folk 2*. Donna was also considered as a regular, with Nathan pencilled in for a brief cameo. They would be joined by a raft of new characters, with the most prominent initially being Des' son Mickey.

Envisaged as a late-night soap opera for Channel Four, Davies outlined the plot for 22 episodes. He set to work on writing the opening four scripts, of which he finished the first two. Other writers, including Davies' former *Springhill* colleague Paul Cornell, were brought in to contribute scripts of their own. Most exciting for die-hard *Queer as Folk* fans was the proposed return of Vince in the first four episodes, though Nicola Shindler suggests these plans were in a constant state of flux. For the most part, the early episodes concerned the lead-up to Hazel's wedding to Des, with the ceremony itself as the focus of the fourth episode.

According to Shindler, *Misfits*, by comparison to the show that spawned it, 'was very different, because it was all set in Hazel's house. It was about a group of people, some of whom you'd seen before but a lot of whom you hadn't, like her son and her policeman husband's son, who were both gay. It was set in the same world [as *Queer as Folk*] and it had some of the same characters, but it had a much more long-running set-up and more expansive feel.' Certainly there seemed to be a great deal of potential for the series, with no central storyline but a strong cast of characters to draw drama and comedy from.

In the script for the opening episode, as in *Queer as Folk 2*, Bernard and Alexander are living with Hazel, but their future following Hazel's imminent wedding is unclear. Certainly Alexander's presence in the unmade series makes sense of the emphasis put on him in *Queer as Folk 2*. Although there had been indications of the poor relationship between Alexander and his parents in the original run, the sequel had made this into a prominent storyline of its own. While it would have worked well in a longer series, it sat oddly amid the ongoing drama of Vince and Stuart. Retrospectively this seems to have been an attempt to beef up the initially rather two-dimensional character so that he could play a more prominent and nuanced role in the spin-off.

The first episode, written by Davies, opens with Des wrestling with a criminal, only to be distracted by Hazel tracking him down to confirm details of their plans for the evening. She finds him courtesy of Bernard's scanning of the radio waves ('Well, I'd dial 999, but you told me off last time,' she points out), and it's instantly clear that *Queer as Folk* 's blend of drama and comedy was to have been present and correct in its spin-off.

Most of the drama comes courtesy of the return of Vince and the introduction of Des' son Mickey. The Vince of *Misfits* is a very different person from the one who left with Stuart at the end of *Queer as Folk*. When Hazel tells a neighbour that he is staying for just a week ('all he could spare us'), the script describes her as 'smiling, but *too* bright, clipped, a lot going unsaid.' Evidently a lot has gone unsaid between Hazel and her son, with Vince finding himself lightly questioned by Des about the frequency of his communication with his mother. 'Come on though, couple of e-mails a month, is that enough? Every morning she checks the inbox,' he tells Vince. Vince insists that he and Stuart just don't stop long enough in one place to make communication that easy. 'I've got my laptop, I make a bit of money designing websites. You can do it on the move,' he points out.

But there's clearly more to his new life than he is letting on. Vince has a lot of money and is coy about exactly how a job designing websites would provide for him so well. In a bar later that evening the changes in Vince are made more explicit. Alexander gets sworn at by a man who barges past, which he takes in his stride, but Vince has a rather different perspective. There is 'a glint in Vince's eye, a coldness. Danger notching up with every line.' A brief argument ensues between Vince and the man, who claims that Alexander acts too much like a 'fucking poof'. 'So my friend's the wrong sort of gay, is that it?' says Vince, only for the man to call Alexander a 'freak'. The script specifies: 'Trigger word. For all the danger, it's a complete surprise as Vince swings a sudden expert punch, hits the bloke right in the face.' This is a new Vince; something has clearly changed, with this obviously not being a one-off occurrence for him. 'Vince just stands his ground, utterly unscared,' the script continues. Hazel is scared, 'like she doesn't know him at all.'

The burning question, of course, is what happened between Vince and Stuart after the events of *Queer as Folk 2*. Their relationship status is even unclear to Hazel but, true to form, Alexander has no qualms about being direct in his questioning. 'Look, I'm the only one who's gonna ask,' he says. 'What's going on with you and Stuart Jones?' Vince is evasive, so Alexander clarifies: 'Are you shagging?' Vince simply replies that 'We're together', saying that 'You've just got to be there.' Hazel, having had a drink, manages to be more direct than she had been earlier. ''Cept we're not, are we? So we're never going to know. End of story.' She is described as being 'like a time bomb', and explodes shortly after. 'You fuck off, you up sticks and fuck off and I don't know a thing, it's all gone and you don't give a *toss*,' Hazel shouts at Vince.

Unlike the Vince of old, who grumpily received insults from all and sundry, he retaliates when she complains that he hadn't just left for London, as was Stuart's initial plan, but left her outright. 'I'd get people laughing at me, d'you know that?' he says. 'Cos every night I'd go out and there was my mother, I'd get shags laughing in my face, you're the bloke with the mother, how embarrassing was that – ?' There is no apology, but they make up with each other later.

No further clarification of his relationship with Stuart or his changed character is forthcoming, which is perhaps fortunate for those who enjoyed pondering on the nature of the love between Vince and Stuart as finally manifested at the end of *Queer as Folk 2*. At one point Vince reads through the emails he has sent his mother. 'From: Stuart&Vince, the two names in a column, repeated over and over. On every subject line, a different city: Chicago, Boston, Los Angeles, Las Vegas, etc. [Close up on] Vince. Haunted by his other life.' Precisely what he was being haunted by is unclear, and the two finished scripts are tantalising in this regard. But even had a full series been completed it seems likely that there would have been no further clarification. Whether it was a sexual love, or a more complex form of deep friendship, is still open to debate. Indeed, the question is complicated even more by the appearance of new character Mickey.

Mickey Stroud is a 23-year-old junior doctor, 'full of energy, sexy in an untidy sort of way.' When we first meet him he is treating an eight-year-old girl, but he is more interested in her father, a 'sexy fucker'. He insists on checking out the father's groin strain, although not out of any concern for his wellbeing. Afterwards he says to the nurse, 'Just you wait, he'll go home, think about me, have a wank, then punch the wife. Guaranteed!' Highly sexed, Mickey lives with his boyfriend Steve, '29, tall, smart. Very handsome, but that's all.' But their relationship is an open one, on Mickey's side at least. When he meets Vince there is an attraction. Shortly after they are properly introduced, they go out onto Canal Street away from the others. 'Then with absolute confidence – the opposite of his old self – Vince reaches out, takes hold of Mickey's arm, pulls him in. Kisses him. Deep, strong, snog. Not just grappling for sex, a powerful connection.'

The two have sex, but it's always clear that there is no particular emotional attachment on either side. There is an implication that Hazel has manipulated the pairing in the hope that it will keep Vince in Manchester. But the man that Vince now is does not have any interest in standing still or settling down. Of course, the ease with which Vince sleeps with another man adds yet another complication to the question of exactly what the relationship between him and Stuart is. Vince finds the idea that there is a future between him and Mickey preposterous. 'Sod Stuart Jones, not him. I'm in love with Mickey Stroud. Thought you all knew that,' he jokes. 'You can forget America, I'm gonna stay and move in with him and live happily ever after. We could live down the road, pop in every day.' Then he makes his point more bluntly. 'I *mean*. He's a kid, he's nice enough but he's a kid. I've shagged him a few times, can I stop now?'

It's impossible to second-guess the likely reaction to *Misfits* had it been made, but certainly Davies' scripts are strong. Although very firmly placed within the *Queer as Folk* universe, there is enough of a shift of emphasis to mark it out as a separate entity to its forebear. Much of its black humour remains intact. (When Des speaks of his late wife, he tells the story of her death, when an elephant attacked her minibus during a visit to Kenya. 'Stamped on,' he tells Hazel's household. 'That's awful, that's completely awful,' Vince empathises. A beat, then he asks 'What happened to the elephant?') Its ability to mix bold and outrageous stories with potent character moments also seems to be in place, with Mickey being at least as sexually confrontational as Stuart. Despite this, it is also worth considering whether the shift of emphasis away from an almost exclusively gay cast of characters to more general 'misfits' would have allowed the series to cross over into the mainstream.

But perhaps the most problematic element of the programme would have been the initial emphasis on Vince. After such a deliberately enigmatic finale to *Queer as Folk 2*, it is difficult to accept the 'official' line on what sort of person Vince became. Although it is deliberately left vague, and there is no indication that there will be further clarification in later episodes, Vince is the character it was easiest to form an emotional attachment to. By developing the character, and stripping away so much of what made him 'Vince' in the first place, there is a chance that sections of the audience would have been disappointed.

By and large, though, the scripts strongly indicate that the show would have been very successful. The opening episode establishes the plot well. The story and characters are so clearly defined that there would have been no problem for new viewers, while the emphasis on Hazel opens up a myriad possibilities. Necessarily a supporting character in *Queer as Folk*, an exceptional performance from Denise Black hinted at depths to the character which went unexplored. As the central focus of a new series it would have been interesting to see how sympathetic the character remained. Thanks in large part to Black's performance, Hazel, despite several character flaws, is near impossible to dislike in the parent series. In *Misfits*, however, there's a strong implication that she's marrying Des for his money, and the security that it will bring her. When Vince offers her £8000 not to get married again, Hazel doesn't dismiss the idea. Clearly there would have been some interesting developments in her character had the series been made.

But, despite their initial enthusiasm for a sequel to *Queer as Folk* in any form, Channel Four suddenly seemed to lose interest in the idea. Work on the series was at an advanced stage, with the opening of a production office imminent, when the channel suddenly decided they no longer wished to make it. 'I don't know why that was,' says Paul Cornell. 'There was a brief period of time when Channel Four were looking for a laddish audience, and maybe they thought that *Queer as Folk* wasn't very laddish, I don't know. But I'm still very proud of the scripts I wrote for *Misfits*. It's a pity we're never going to see those in any shape or form.' Nicola Shindler broadly concurs with this assessment, finding the channel's attitude equally baffling. 'They weren't very appreciative, yet they still quote *Queer as Folk* as their best ever drama. They haven't ever done anything with Russell again, though.'

Davies himself was less concerned about the capsizing of *Misfits*.

'I'm always happy to move on,' he insists. 'I genuinely think nothing has a God-given right to get made. You should *never* try and make something for someone who doesn't want to make it. It was, like, move on. It was terrible personally, for people. Everyone was all right in the end, but a friend of mine had been brought on board as producer, and had given up her job on Sky and moved back to Manchester. That's how much they'd promised it to us. She didn't do that lightly.'

The news that Channel Four had pulled the plug on *Misfits* came through to the Red offices mere days before Christmas 2000. 'Murray Gold [composer] had come up,' Davies remembers. 'He was in the office to talk about something else, but also *Misfits*. We all went to Bar 38 just up from Granada. And just sat there! At Christmas! Like orphans!' He laughs. 'Unemployed! My producer friend *literally* unemployed, like, "How am I gonna pay for my house?" It was terrible in that sense. I felt like I should have been sadder! But I left and thought, "Oh well, I'll go and write something else." That's my job. Very strange.'

Davies was never told why, after five months' hard work, *Misfits* was rejected by Channel Four. He was free to offer the project to other channels after two years had passed, but in the event he demurred. By then too much time had passed since the end of *Queer as Folk,* and there were also potential legal difficulties in using characters that Channel Four could claim to co-own. And, soon after the cancellation of *Misfits*, plans for a *Queer as Folk* website, for which Davies had been preparing short stories, were quietly ditched by Channel Four without his knowledge or consultation. Not surprisingly, Davies' regard for the company hit an all-time low, and the relationship between the two parties became fractious.

Although the broadcast of *Queer as Folk* in North America initially attracted little attention, news of it spread through the continent's gay communities, and via bootleg tapes and, eventually, an official if overpriced limited VHS release it picked up a small but vocal following. Hollywood producers started to take an interest in the series, and it was soon announced that renowned director Joel Schumacher was to bring the series to North American television on the Showtime cable channel in the US and Showcase in

Canada. In some respects the show was a natural candidate for a US remake, given that for a British television production the series approximates the look of an American show, being shot on film and including bright colours and long lenses.

Proposed US remakes of British television shows are ten-a-penny, but most fail even to reach the pilot stage. At first, then, it may seem unlikely that one of the most popular North American remakes of a British production in recent years should be of a challenging and extreme show like *Queer as Folk*. It's important, though, that the UK original wasn't shown on one of the major networks. It ran for five successful seasons on a cable channel that, like HBO, was free of the restrictions imposed on the main networks in relation to language and sex. This meant that it was not a mainstream commodity but was nevertheless extremely successful. It's unclear for how long Joel Schumacher was involved, but by the time of the first episode's broadcast in late 2000 he was no longer linked with the production.

Perhaps the most surprising aspect of the US version is how close it is to the UK series, in its initial stages at least. Very often remakes keep the basic concept but are 'remakes' in name only, perhaps keeping only some key characters or plot points. However, the early episodes of the US *Queer as Folk* are nearly identical to the original in many respects. While Stuart may be called Brian, 15-year-old Nathan is now 17-year-old Justin and Vince has been renamed Michael, they are effectively the same characters. The opening episode's plot is identical too, with most of the series' plot lines appearing at some point, mainly early in the run. But not only the main characters recur; the series has its own versions of Hazel, Donna, Phil, Bernard, Alexander and Cameron. When Ted is taken home by a crystal meth user and encouraged to join in, it's a case of so far, so Phil. But although he falls into a coma, Ted does live through the experience and survives relatively intact. After this event, covered in the third and fourth episodes, the series starts to diverge from the original more and more. However, none of these fresh plots would have felt out of place in the UK version. It simply feels like a different telling of the same basic story.

Far from taking issue with what could be seen as a distortion of his 'vision', Davies enjoys the US *Queer as Folk* on its own merits. 'I just love the fact that it exists,' he says. 'I absolutely love it. No matter how much people say, "Gay characters are much more represented than they ever were," we're still massively under-represented. And I've been in America, in a hotel room, flicking through the channels. And suddenly you'll find the Showtime channel on which men are snogging. The fact that farmers in Iowa are watching that is a fantastic thing!

'The funny thing is,' he adds, 'the remake very much became a soap opera. It was funny reading quotes from the production team and they were saying, "Oh, we've moved on from the British original now." And what I love is the fact that it was *exactly* the same! It hadn't changed *at all*. It was the same characters acting in the same way in the same setting. They got up to episode 57, or whatever, and it was exactly the same. Stuart was sleeping with lots of men, there was a love story, Vince had got a boyfriend, his mother was outrageous, stuff like that. They kept saying how much it had moved on, but I love the fact that, like a good soap, it kept on regenerating itself but actually stayed the same.'

In all, Showtime's *Queer as Folk* ran for five seasons. 'What a compliment is that?' Davies says. 'You write a script and most of them just vanish into the ether. And you get lucky if you ever get to talk to anyone about it or anything. It's fantastic.'

Davies didn't push for a role as consultant, or decide to be at all hands-on in the process. He received a credit for the original idea and visited the set in Vancouver, but did not have any other involvement aside from some courtesy emails and viewings of early scripts. 'There might be things in it that I wouldn't do, or would,' he says. 'But actually sometimes there were things I wish I'd done. There's one episode set entirely in a nightclub. It's brilliant. I wish I'd done that!'

Although *Misfits* had failed to be reach the final stage of the commissioning process, Davies was hardly at a loss for something to do. He had been working with the channel on another major project, one that had been at the back of his mind for several years. A bold statement piece, it got the official green light from the channel. Legally it was guaranteed; Davies' next project was all set to bring him back to Channel Four.

Or so it seemed.

EIGHT:
I'M GAY NOW. I'LL DIE GAY.
I'LL HAVE A GAY GRAVESTONE.

With the breakthrough success of *Queer as Folk* under his belt, Davies had established himself as a TV writer to watch. This juncture of his career, then, can be summed up in just two words: 'Follow that!'

Certain factors relating to his next project fell into place of their own accord. His new working relationship with the Red Productions team had been immensely fruitful, and all concerned wanted it to continue. It also followed quite naturally that Davies would write more work set in his adopted hometown of Manchester. Indeed, he already had an idea in mind, ready to embark upon.

Many years previously, he'd taken a car journey to Liverpool with his Granada colleague Tony Wood, and found himself musing on the idea of Jesus returning to Earth – specifically, present-day Manchester. The Second Coming, done properly. How would people respond to his return? What would he do? What would become of him? That, Davies reasoned, was a great idea, loaded with dramatic potential. Years later, in the immediate aftermath of *Queer as Folk,* Davies discussed the notion with Nicola Shindler and, once she'd given her approval, he set about working on it in earnest.

So it was that Red proposed a four-hour drama serial, going by the name of *The Second Coming*, to Channel Four, who promptly commissioned it. (Neatly enough, the title had its own particular connection to the Manchester of recent times. The local indie band The Stone Roses, who'd been in receipt of a volley of frenzied critical acclaim, had used it with tongues firmly in cheek for their much-delayed second album, finally released in 1994.) Davies agreed to defer working on any other projects in order to set about writing it, and it became public knowledge that it would be his next major work.
For ten months, he poured his energies into developing the project.
Then, in October 2000, disaster struck.

With two hours' worth of script already written, there was a change in drama executive personnel at Channel Four. On these occasions, it's not unusual for the new broom to make his or her mark by sweeping their predecessor's projects away. After all, if they fail, who gets the blame? But, if they succeed, who gets credit for backing the idea in the first place? Sure enough, during a crucial meeting with Channel Four, a newly installed executive allegedly dismissed the part-written *Second Coming* script as 'a bit science-fiction'.

It's a curious criticism to have made. By the same yardstick, the bible could be considered a blockbusting space opera. But it should be remembered that, at that point in British broadcasting history, anything that smacked of fantasy, or indeed imagination of any kind, was a distinct no-no. Gritty realism was the order of the day. 'You're going to look stupid,' one senior Channel Four figure warned Davies. Suddenly, *The Second Coming* was off.

'It was supposed to be four hours long,' Davies recalls. 'I wrote the first two hours, and then, to be honest, they sort of laughed it out of the building! They didn't believe a word of it! I mean, it's a funny thing. It's so high concept. Either you get it or you don't. They just didn't believe he was the Son of God. And there's nothing more you could have done with that script to convince people that he was the Son of God. It's a choice you have. Everyone makes a choice when they watch a film to think, "Do I want to believe this?" My grandmother used to switch off Star Trek saying it was too far-fetched...'

In practice, though, this wasn't a clear-cut case of the plug being pulled. 'We were in a very interesting position when Channel Four turned that down, because they had actually commissioned it,' Davies points out. 'We could, technically, have insisted and said, "This has been green-lit." But that's where Nicola Shindler's very brilliant at saying, "You are *not* going to make it for someone who doesn't want it. It'll be a nightmare from beginning to end. Every day's rushes, every edit, every note will be terrible, and you'll just *fight* the entire time." If someone doesn't get something, fundamentally, give up and walk away. And take your script with you. But there's no point in bashing your head against the wall till you're bleeding.' Charitably, but perhaps surprisingly, Davies has since described this parting of the ways as 'amicable.'

Nicola Shindler suggests that 'Channel Four knocked it back for snobby writing reasons. They felt that if you're going to do something like that, it has to be more intellectual, a big *debate*: things that Russell doesn't write and I didn't want to make.' Coupled with the capsizing of the *Misfits* project mere months later, it's hardly surprising that Davies gave up on Channel Four entirely, and instead sought out opportunities in British broadcasting's mainstream.

In the immediate aftermath, as 2001 dawned, Red Productions set about approaching other broadcasters with *The Second Coming*. Meanwhile, Davies considered his next move. Ideas for a fresh script had already been bubbling away. The initial inspiration was a scandal which had occurred within his own social circle a couple of years earlier. His friend Thomas was, Davies says, 'the gayest man you'll ever meet in the world.' Entirely out of the blue, Thomas met, and fell deeply in love with, a woman, Rhian. The writer – whose own intimate experiences with women, as he admits, go no further than 'snogging one when I was 14' – was staggered by the sheer volume of sneering contempt and prejudice this caused amongst Thomas' (predominantly gay) friends. Indeed, he was guilty of it himself.

One night, Davies was invited to dinner with the couple. All present got wildly drunk and the writer took the opportunity to quiz Thomas until the wee small hours about the details of his unexpected relationship. Thomas insisted that he remained entirely, 100 per cent gay. It just so happened that he loved a woman. He had no great explanation for it, other than that it had happened, he hadn't lost his mind, and in fact he was very happy.

In the intervening period, Thomas and Rhian had married and even become parents. Here, Davies decided, was the 'couldn't-make-it-up' raw material for a great, unconventional love story. This dose of inspiration arrived at just the right time. In 1997, Davies' old friend Paul Abbott had written an off-beat love story of his own, the ITV drama *Reckless*. It told of a surgeon, Owen Springer (Robson Green), meeting a woman, Anna Fairley (Francesca Annis), quite by accident on a train journey to Manchester, where he's to take up a new job. There's clearly a powerful attraction between the two, which only grows deeper and more complicated when it transpires that

Fairley is married to Springer's new boss.

Davies and Shindler were avowed fans of *Reckless*, and keen to make something in a similar vein. This, then, was their chance to do so. Like *Queer as Folk* before it, the setting would be contemporary Manchester. Just possibly the romantic tone was informed by events in Davies' life, too. Since 1999, he'd been in a relationship with Andrew Smith, a customs officer from Hull.

Obviously, in becoming fiction, the true tale, and characters, of Thomas and Rhian would change. 'I came up with the names Bob and Rose,' Davies said. 'Simple, old-fashioned and right, just what you need for a love story.' Not surprisingly, given the bad blood over *The Second Coming*, the new project wasn't offered to Channel Four. Instead, rather more surprisingly, it was pitched to ITV. The network had already approached Davies about working with him, and in the wake of *Queer as Folk*, ITV Drama Controller Nick Elliott had taken the writer out to lunch to discuss the possibility.

Colleagues who worked in the industry expressed doubts about this new development. Surely the big commercial channel would never commission something with such a complex, possibly even controversial, approach to sexuality? In the event, though, ITV expressed no such concerns. 'I didn't change the content for them,' Davies insisted. 'It's just not about sex. It's about love, so the content reflects that.' It may have helped that ITV had received encouraging notices for a one-off drama, *Forgive and Forget*, that covered some of the same territory. First shown on 3 January 2000, the piece starred John Simm as Theo, a working class man secretly in love with his best friend David, played by Steven John Shepherd. In coming out to his friends and family, Theo faces the wrath of those around him, but ultimately feels he made the right decision. Davies' project was even less conventional, but having a successful precedent in ITV's recent schedules probably didn't hurt.

In making a judgment about *Bob & Rose*, the network did request a synopsis of the later episodes, but Davies, who preferred to allow the story to take its own course as he wrote it, refused to comply. Nevertheless, after only two days' consideration, *Bob & Rose* was commissioned by ITV. As Nicola Shindler explains, 'It's a romantic comedy, basically. Love stories have always been big. And ITV weren't scared of having a gay character at all – so long as there wasn't anything 'too gay,', which is fair enough. It was quite an easy sell in the end.'

Almost immediately, as though ready-formed, Davies found the key elements of the first episode falling into place. The couple would meet by accident late at night, he decided, in an incident featuring a taxi. In his mind, a key visual moment – of two taxis sailing off into the night in different directions – was in place before a word of the script was written. A first draft of the episode came together very quickly, with five further instalments planned. In the process of writing the first episode, though, Davies decided to abandon his initial plans for the series and change the whole emphasis of the story. 'I had intended to write six hours attacking prejudice, in all its shapes and forms,' he later wrote. 'I lined up cardboard characters in the script, all ready to attack the central couple. But typing away, I came to realise that prejudice is, of course, stupid.'

So, after writing around 20 minutes of the first draft of the opening episode, Davies scrapped it and began again. Six hours of drama that centred on prejudice, prejudice that he decided didn't even deserve airtime, would have made for a one-dimensional drama. The issues involved, he felt, were less vital than the characters themselves. They should form the core of the piece, and the issues involved should flow from them without being preachy or one-dimensional. The result was a light, character-driven piece buoyed with charm and humour.

The main substance of the plot evolved as Davies wrote it, too. He'd planned to give Bob a best friend, Louise, intended as an inoffensive work colleague – in other words, an almost functional foil. In the process of writing the first episode, Louise, now renamed Holly, changed radically. As Davies remembers, 'She was like, "Oh Bob, I hope you find someone nice to settle down with." She just fed lines to him. And then suddenly I came to this one scene where she just started lying. I was bored with her. Actually, on a completely practical level, I was sitting there thinking, "How the hell can I tell that love story for six hours?" You've got to generate plot. You've got to be a whore, and just give yourself story after story after story. Any love story needs an enemy, so you think, "Oh! Hello – enemy. Good. Right, that's something." Especially with *Bob & Rose*, where I couldn't let the sexuality be the enemy. It always sounds pretentious when writers say this, but she started to happen on the page. Literally, she started her life in this scene, and suddenly I could see six episodes ahead of me. I thought, "That's it. This is about Bob and Rose and Holly." But she wasn't invented like that.'

The scripts Davies came up with were replete with the themes and preoccupations that had been developing throughout his work. Rose's Mum has a boyfriend, Trevor, who's revealed to be an obsessive James Bond fan – just as Queer as Folk's Vince holds his Doctor Who video collection dear to his heart. Of course, Davies himself knows a thing or two about the world of cult fandom: we're talking about a man who installed a life-sized replica Dalek in his front hall. There's an ongoing fascination with television in Bob & Rose, too. Characters watch television avidly, and a key plot development, when Rose's family discover that Bob is gay, comes about when they see a TV news report. Like Queer as Folk, this serial revolves around Manchester's gay community.

The main character, Bob Gossage, is part of an extended 'family of friends', as well as his more fractured blood family. In particular, his relationship with his father is distant and uncomfortable, whereas his 'surrogate family' is, at least initially, more secure. Gay lifestyles are depicted, and sexuality handled, in a purely non-judgmental fashion. The message of Bob & Rose isn't, clearly, that all gay men can turn straight at the drop of the hat. Rather, it's about one gay man who just happens to fall in love with a heterosexual woman. It's just his life, and his feelings, and the piece isn't meant to speak for the experiences of all gay men in one fell swoop.

Nevertheless, some sections of the gay community responded with vitriol to Davies' latest project, interpreting it as an unwelcome blurring of gay identity. Davies has spoken of receiving highly critical letters and texts, suggesting that he deserved a fate along the lines of being 'burnt at the stake on Canal Street.' The writer himself did admit to some discomfort about the fact that one of the chief antagonists of the piece was Bob's ex-boyfriend Carl. A dour gay 'villain' might, he felt, be interpreted as sending out an unfortunate signal.

While filming on location at Canal Street's Hollywood Showbar, Davies had been harangued by a disgruntled customer taking issue with the safe community space of the Gay Village being invaded and turned into public property. It's an argument that's easy to sympathise with. In the wake of the area's appearance in *Queer as Folk* as a romantic, almost magical place, Canal Street had turned into a favourite drinking destination for Mancunians in general. Hen parties made a bee-line for it. The annual gay Mardi Gras became a weekend out for all the family. After *Bob & Rose*, there were even whispers that local single women were heading for the Gay Village in hope of bagging a gentle, well-dressed Bob of their own.

But right at the heart of Davies' new serial was his often provocatively progressive approach to sexuality. The piece looks at what it means to be gay, and concludes that it's not actually about who you sleep with. A gay man can have sex with a woman out of choice, and remain gay. It's the choice that's the point.

To more traditional members of the gay community, who'd battled to have their identity recognised, legally permitted and even celebrated, Davies' hatred of labels may well have seemed aggravating. Theirs was a label they'd fought for. The resulting debate and friction was inevitable. But in his writing, Davies was focusing on the complex, contradictory human individual beneath the issues and the labels. Labels, he suggests, are restrictive, unsophisticated and unnecessary.

Within the serial Bob Gossage is seen confessing to his parents that he has a girlfriend, a marvellous inversion of the classic 'coming out' scenario. But Bob insists that he's no less gay, and rankles at the suggestion that he must now be bisexual. As he makes clear, 'I fancy men. And her.' 'Go on, then. Label that,' says Davies.

On the face of it, *Bob & Rose* might seem to represent a departure from the tapestry of *Queer as Folk*, which featured three lead characters, whereas the new piece, as the title suggests, has two. But, as Davies himself says, it's actually about Bob and Rose and Holly – and in that respect it mirrors *Queer as Folk* almost exactly. The earlier serial told the tale of two best friends, one of whom has a profound crush on the other, while the other gets involved in an often rocky new relationship with an 'outsider'. Essentially *Bob & Rose* is the same story, but with the main focus shifted from the friends, with the outsider on the fringes, to the new couple, with the besotted friend marginalised. Plus, the friend in question, Holly, decides to sabotage the relationship, which drives the narrative forward.

It's another instance of unrequited love – a perennial Davies motif – taking centre stage in one of his dramas. There's perhaps a nod to the writer's love life in the character of Rose's boyfriend Andy, who, sweetly, shares his name with Davies' own partner – though, rather less sweetly, he finds himself out of the picture within three episodes.

Casting the serial posed its own problems. The leads would be required to handle an unconventional romantic comedy with a very particular lightness of touch. Alan Davies, cast as Bob, wasn't gay but brought with him a charm and sensitivity that were ideal for the role. Plus, he was ideally suited to handle the lighter, comic material in the piece. On first arriving in Manchester, the actor had taken the trouble to go out on Canal Street every night, often in the company of director Joe Wright, delighting in the fact that they were regularly assumed to be a couple. He only drew the line at portraying Bob as a Manchester United fan. It had been Nicola Shindler's idea to drop this into the script – as a fervent supporter, she hadn't christened her production company Red for nothing – but all references to the team were skilfully excised by Davies.

'Fantastic actors will take a script to places you've never dreamt of,' Russell says. 'Like a good director makes something far better than you ever thought it was, a good actor will do *astonishing* things. All an actor's got to be is intelligent, really, and Alan Davies is the most intelligent actor I've ever worked with. There is a man who knows why every line, every word is there – probably because he writes himself, I think. But he knows the structure, why a scene is there, why all the scenes are around it and what order they come in, what the tempo of a scene is. He's a brilliantly talented actor in a way that he's never given much credit for. It's unfortunate he's not.'

Red found their Rose Cooper in actress Lesley Sharp, who had already appeared in such Red productions as Kay Mellor's *Playing the Field* and Paul Abbott's *Clocking Off*. Prior to *Bob & Rose*, Sharp had never taken a lead TV role. By her own admission, she'd never sought one, enjoying instead a range of character parts and ensemble work. And it's exactly this unassuming quality that makes Sharp's performance so strong. Her Rose is tough and funny, but entirely believable and human. Davies has revealed that the character of Rose was drawn not so much from her direct true-life counterpart Rhian, but rather from his old school-friend Tracy. Rose's fiercely independent personality, and even some of her speech patterns, could apparently all be traced back to Tracy. According to Davies, Lesley Sharp even bears a resemblance to her.

The third key role, namely the devious Holly, was taken by Jessica Stevenson, who was the only main character not to be cast by Red. Instead, Nick Elliott, the then Head of Drama at ITV, had been so impressed with her performance in Channel Four's *Spaced* that he suggested her for the part himself.

The director assigned to the all-important opening episodes was Julian Farino, whom Davies had known since they'd worked on the Granada children's show *Allsorts*, Farino's professional directing debut, back in 1992. 'Julian's a lovely director,' Davies says. 'That was one of the most perfect collaborations. We got together and had long chats. Tone is the thing. It's not how quickly a character gets to the room, it's not what colour should the wall be, it's not, are they drinking gin or are they drinking vodka. Tone is it. And it was luck partly, but we'd both got the same tone in mind. He used to say, it's like it's slightly suspended. Because it's a love story, it's as though they're two inches off the ground. The whole emotion is lifted. And that is exactly how I used to think of it, as something very delicate and very precious. It's a beautifully light piece of work. So we were very much in synch.'

The second half of *Bob & Rose* was directed by another future luminary in the form of Joe Wright. Clearly, then, there was talent to spare behind the scenes of the new serial. It was shot mostly in and around South Manchester suburbs including Chorlton, Didsbury, Victoria Park and Rusholme between March and June 2001. The key scenes from Episode One in which Bob first meets Rose were, in fact, filmed on the same road as Davies' home, at his suggestion. The resulting night-shoot saw Davies' house used as base camp, with actors taking breaks in his living room. Indeed, at one point, as the hours drew on, Alan Davies took it upon himself to switch off the writer's

TV set, which caused mock horror when its owner returned. 'I didn't even know it *had* an off button', the writer spluttered.

Other scenes, involving Bob's adventures in gay nightlife, saw Red returning to Canal Street in Manchester city centre – specifically, bars such as Spirit, Via Fossa and The Slug & Lettuce. Scenes at the flat belonging to Bob's devious ex-boyfriend Carl were filmed in the real-life city centre home of Anthony Wilson, the TV presenter and record label boss subsequently immortalised by Steve Coogan in the 2002 film *24 Hour Party People*. Manchester's Town Hall in Albert Square became the backdrop for the eventful PAH demonstration that closed Episode Four.

Curiously, the tale of *Bob & Rose* had a recent high-profile fictional precedent. Independent American film director Kevin Smith had made *Chasing Amy* in 1997, in which a comic book illustrator, Holden McNeil (Ben Affleck) sets out on a relationship with the staunchly lesbian Alyssa (Joey Lauren Adams). Clearly they're a good match, and what plays out is a mature, well-observed, unconventional romantic comedy. Eventually, their own past experience breaks the pair apart. Specifically, Alyssa is ostracised by her lesbian friends, and Holden is mocked by his possessive best friend Banky. It's surely no more than a coincidence, and proof that similar ideas tend to circulate at similar times. But it's made all the more striking when one considers that Kevin Smith's next film was 1999's *Dogma* – an atheist's take on the return of the Son of God to the present day. It was a pet project of Smith's that had been on the drawing board for some time and which eventually provoked considerable controversy on release.

Another recent Hollywood movie was a more direct influence on one particular aspect of *Bob & Rose*. 'At the edit we all got on a treat,' Davies says. 'You could feel it working. When it came to the music stage, we didn't have Murray Gold. He wasn't available for that, so we panicked – a bit more than we normally do, actually. We'd normally leave Murray to his own devices. But we were faced with a new musician – Martin Phipps, who was very good – but we were nervous and wanted more of a say. So we had this music session, which happens when you come into the edit to watch the finished episode. You go through all your CDs at home and you bring along stuff that you think would work, roughly. This was the bizarre thing. Me and

Julian [Farino] both walked in with the same CD, and the same track. It's a glockenspiel track from the soundtrack of *True Romance*. Weird!'

Phipps took these pointers on board, and the resulting score plainly uses the *True Romance* glockenspiel track as a jumping-off point. 'That poor musician, I felt sorry for him in a way, because he actually didn't have much freedom,' Davies says. 'He was a lovely man, and I think he probably would have done his own thing if he'd objected. I think he did understand what we meant. But if you listen to it, it's very similar to that track. There's only a certain amount of tunes you can play on a glockenspiel! You can't vary it very much.' Overall, music seems to have been crucial to establishing the tone of *Bob & Rose*. Davies has since confessed that the writing process for the series was fuelled by endless repeat plays of Moby's floatation-tank gospel album *Go*.

ITV were pleased with the way *Bob & Rose* had shaped up and, in a show of confidence, shifted it forward from the November broadcast slot for which it had originally been earmarked. But when first shown at 9.00 pm on Monday nights during September and October 2001, *Bob & Rose* had a decidedly mixed reception. Critics found it charming, intelligent and beautifully observed. ITV audiences weren't drawn to it in huge numbers, though. As is the way in commercial television, ITV responded quickly, shifting the final two episodes into a later, less prestigious time-slot of 10.20 pm. There was no second series – but then, none had ever been planned, as it was always conceived as a self-contained six-part serial. The team did float the possibility of a spin-off show starring Holly, to be entitled *Hello Holly*, seemingly just for their own amusement.

But it would be very wrong to view the serial as a failure. It remains a favourite of many career-long Davies watchers, and indeed, its creator still adores it.

'Of everything I've done, I think Episode One of that is the most perfect little one-off thing,' Davies suggests. 'There's almost nothing you'd change. Well, there's always something you'd change, but there's *almost* nothing in that. I think it's the one thing I've had transmitted in which not a word's changed from the first draft, because I knew *exactly* what it should be. I was so chuffed with that.' Of the series as a whole, he's suggested it was 'absolutely the best set of scripts I've ever written. To be honest, it's just about perfect, the way it was directed and cast.' Speaking to interviewer Phil George, Davies confessed that 'I actually think sometimes, in my quiet moments, it's possibly the best thing I've ever written.'

Nicola Shindler shares Russell's affection for the show. 'I *absolutely* loved it. And if you look at it, the ratings it was getting would be considered a success now. It's just that it was a different time, I guess. I was very proud of it.' Nor were its creators alone in the regard in which they held the serial. At the British Comedy Awards in December 2001, it won 'Best TV Comedy Drama' category, and Davies' contribution saw him awarded 'TV Writer of the Year'. For her performance as Rose, Lesley Sharp received Best Actress nominations from both BAFTA and the Royal Television Society, and Alan Davies won Best Actor at the Monte Carlo TV Festival for his contribution as Bob Gossage.

Why, then, was such a winning piece treated by ITV as a misfire? Perhaps it just didn't quite belong on the commercial network at that time. ITV were keen to revamp and improve their drama output, and possibly they wanted to capitalise on the success d'estime that *Queer as Folk* had enjoyed. *Bob & Rose* reached a far wider audience than *Queer as Folk* – an average of 6.6 million viewers, around double *Queer as Folk*'s combined figures – but not large enough to be considered a hit on ITV's usual scale, despite a steady increase in ratings over the run. Although *Bob & Rose* saw Davies writing in a variation of the *Queer as Folk* mode, mainstream ITV viewers might not have been ready for a series along those lines, even if it was lighter and more accessible.

Davies himself has since identified one of the serial's failings. Light romantic comedies inevitably hinge on a question of 'Will they? Won't they?' – the standard answer being, 'After overcoming a host of almost insurmountable hurdles, yes they will.' In truth, *Bob & Rose* is no different, but stretching the quandary out over six weekly hour-long episodes might have dissipated some vital momentum. In Davies' own estimation, 'No story is six hours long', and by the serial's mid point, the characters of Bob and Rose have already pledged themselves to one another. The question that then arises – 'What's at stake for them now?' – is something that Davies struggled to resolve during the writing process.

In retrospect, though, he has admitted that, given the chance, he'd rewrite the troublesome 'second act' of the tale from scratch, to make the plot clearer, more compelling and less low-key. Nevertheless, the sheer quality of his writing – the charm of the tone, the humour and the characters – makes *Bob & Rose* as a whole one of Davies' most loveable pieces of work.

Transmission of the serial coincided with a personal tragedy for Davies. Back in Swansea, his mother Barbara passed away. As a result Davies spent more time in his childhood home town than he had in recent years. In the face of sadness he took some solace from the fact that his mother had died not long after transmission of Episode Four, and the last she'd seen of her son's work was the climactic PAH demonstration, concerning the solidarity between a gay man and his mother.

What, then, did Thomas and Rhian, the real-life inspiration for *Bob & Rose*, make of it? According to Davies, they didn't see the show. Instead, they recorded it to watch with their children once they'd grown up, by way of explaining exactly what they'd gone through. That, surely, is the highest compliment anyone could have paid to it.

NINE:
*DO YOU THINK YOU'RE READY
FOR THAT MUCH POWER, YOU LOT?*

Just six weeks after *Bob & Rose* finished its run, Davies had more new work
on television – this time, for the BBC. It was his first involvement with
the corporation in eight years. His old cohort Paul Abbott had been forging
a trailblazing career in television, working on the landmark ITV drama
Cracker as both writer and producer before penning *Reckless* and, for Red
Productions, the hugely acclaimed *Clocking Off.* Abbott's latest project was
another collaboration with Red, a comedy drama for BBC1 called *Linda
Green*, starring Liza Tarbuck in the title role. Claire Rushbrook took the
part of Linda's best mate Michelle. An initial run of six episodes had been
planned and written by Abbott. The BBC, strongly approving of what they
saw, increased the length of show's run before broadcast began.

Nicola Shindler recalls, 'They really liked the first series, but they wanted
more of it, so we had to do them very quickly. Paul couldn't write all of
them, and Russell's friendly with Paul, and friendly with me. He loved
the idea, and he loved what he'd seen, so he said, "Yeah, I'll do one." For
someone like Russell, when he's got an idea in his head, a half-hour show
can take days to write. He didn't mind writing for somebody else's show at
all, because he had the time, basically, and he's not a snob.'

Davies' contribution to *Linda Green*, entitled 'Rest in Peace', aired as the
fifth episode of the first series. A self-contained piece, it involves Linda and
her friends discovering that Debbie Mott, an old schoolmate they scarcely
remember, has died at the age of 32. For a wheeze, they decide to attend her
funeral, lured by the prospect of a good buffet and a nosy look at her family
home. Debbie, it turns out, remained a solitary soul her whole life. In the
aftermath, Michelle finds herself haunted by Debbie's fate and befriends
the late woman's mother Yvonne, played by Anne Reid. For the most part,
Michelle feeds Yvonne lies about Debbie's supposed impact on her life,
but ultimately Yvonne sees through her.

It's a distinctive episode, blending a good deal of irreverence towards death and funerals with more thoughtful scenes about wasted, or supposedly wasted, lives. Curiously, in amongst Linda and co discussing ex-classmates, there's a mention of one Robert Coles – just as, back in *Dark Season*, Reet and Thomas tried to differentiate between their contemporaries 'Robert Coles with no chin or Robert Coles with nasty shoes.' There's also a female character, unique to Davies' episode, by the name of Lucy Cooper, presumably unrelated to Rose before her or Gwen to follow.

Linda Green went to a second series in 2002, but Davies didn't contribute to it. The producer for the second run was Phil Collinson, who had been, earlier in his career, the script editor of *Springhill* and nearly featured in a leading role in *Queer as Folk*. 'When I arrived on *Linda Green*, Russell was on the list of writers but he was bogged down writing other things and simply couldn't spare the time,' Collinson recalls. 'I was sad because we hadn't worked together since *Springhill* and I was looking forward to what he might do with his episode.' It wouldn't be too long, though, before Collinson and Davies would work together again.

At this time, Davies was being courted by the BBC. They'd regularly approach him with the notion of, say, a new adaptation of *A Tale of Two Cities*. This was a time when period costume drama – always a BBC mainstay – was enjoying a massive new surge in popularity. Davies, though, wasn't to be drawn into it. Whatever the BBC offered him, his response was always the same: he only wanted to bring back *Doctor Who*. And whenever friends and colleagues such as Nicola Shindler went to meetings with BBC executives, Davies asked them to reiterate the message.

Eventually, in early 2002, Davies had a meeting with the BBC to discuss this very prospect, but it never got off the ground. The rights to the show were a minefield, not least because a film option had been sold not long before. Plus, BBC Films were poised to make their own film should the rights be freed up. In the meantime, one non-*Who* project by Davies managed to sneak through the net and find its way to the BBC. They were approached by Red with a view to picking up the still-unmade *Second Coming* scripts. In the event the corporation demurred, but the project still wasn't finished yet. 'We took it to the BBC, and they said no, thank you,' Davies admits. 'We just thought it was dead then. And it was Nicola Shindler who said, "I'm gonna take it to ITV!" Everyone was going, "They'll *never* make something like that!"'

It certainly seemed a long shot – would the commercial network really take on such a potentially contentious work? But then, similar doubts had been expressed over the channel accepting *Bob & Rose*, and they'd still gone for it. 'They're brilliant people to work for at ITV,' Davies says. 'As commissioners they're honest, and brutal, and fast, and *genuinely* supportive of you, if it works. And they said yes!' Sure enough, Red Productions were commissioned to make *The Second Coming* for broadcast on ITV1.

The very essence of the story had been in place since Davies had first discussed it with Shindler several years previously. It's encapsulated in a scene he envisioned, and which ended up midway through Part Two of the final product, in which the main character is in bed with a woman, and the following exchange of dialogue takes place.

> JUDITH: Do you love me?
> STEPHEN: Yes.
> (pause)
> JUDITH: Are you the Son of God?
> STEPHEN: Yes.

This then would be an exploration of a situation in which a man in the here and now discovers he is genuinely divine, and the impact this has on those around him, in particular the woman he loves. (Rather arrestingly, in creating this character of a divine Everyman, Davies named him Stephen, his own first name.) It was this initial inspiration that Davies and Shindler held on to through the protracted tribulations involved in getting the programme onto the screen.

'It was just such a brilliant concept,' Shindler says. 'And it was great that Russell was never saying, "Is this person or isn't this person a God?" He said, at the very beginning, "You've got to say, he absolutely definitely *is* the Second Coming." Now, how would the world deal with it? In fact, there were issues that we never even got in it in the end that always fascinated me. It was just really compelling. Also, Russell's ideology that the root of all evil is religion and Gods, and that the world would be a better place without them – that was so brilliantly radical to be putting on ITV.'

Although the subjects of religion and belief fascinate Davies, it's purely from the viewpoint of an avowed atheist, as his own upbringing wasn't of a religious nature. 'I couldn't even tell you what my parents believe, to be honest,' he admits. 'They never talk about it, never. Well, there's a bit of lip service. I think they probably do believe. My sister's an RE teacher, and she does genuinely believe in Heaven and stuff like that. Which is nice: you sort of think, "Good for her." But there's nothing religious about me at all.' As a child, though, he attended Sunday school, albeit not for long. 'I decided to stop going at a very young age, and the woman from Sunday school turned up at our house! It was like an avenging angel telling my father off, in the doorway. I must have been very young – must have been about eight. It bored me stupid, though. Fucking hell. Sunday school! School, on a Sunday! Who wants that?'

Religious undertones can be found in many of Davies' dramas. This, after all, was a writer who had once created a soap about a clergyman's family and named it *Revelations. The Second Coming*, as you'd expect, foregrounds the issue. Previously, *Springhill* had been his most concerted tackling of religion, albeit often in a sensationalist fashion. In its own way, though, the earlier series, with its battle between the forces of good and evil, with religion caught in the centre, was sowing the seeds for what was to come.

Back in 1969, Dennis Potter wrote a piece entitled *Son of Man* which centred on the character of Jesus. On many levels *Son of Man* and *The Second Coming* are wildly different, with Potter's play being far more traditional in approach than Davies'. It depicts the historical figure of Jesus as an impassioned, often tormented individual, ensnared by the politics of his day. But the all-too-human Christ that Potter presents, as highlighted in the title of the play, is nevertheless akin to Davies' own Stephen Baxter. Both struggle to reconcile their human feelings and desires with the unfathomable, divine purpose that sits on their shoulders.

NINE: *DO YOU THINK YOU'RE READY FOR THAT MUCH POWER, YOU LOT?*

The parallels between Potter's *Son of God* and Davies' programme are intriguing. Potter, who once described his religious inclinations as 'Christian-tinged agnosticism', told the *Radio Times* of the day, 'I wanted to write a play about a man deluded with the thought that he might be Christ ... We think of Jesus as being meek, gentle and mild. We have forgotten what the *man* might have been like.' To Potter, the main character of his play was 'this brave, witty, sometimes oddly petulant man.' Even the press reaction to Potter's play, with headlines ranging from 'Storm Over TV Christ' and 'Tough Guy Christ Shocks Viewers' to 'This Gospel of Our Times', seems eerily prescient of the manner in which *The Second Coming* would be received.

It's unlikely, though not inconceivable, that Davies, at the age of six, saw Potter's *Son of Man* on its original transmission. But the play was repeated in July 1987, in the wake of the success of Potter's *The Singing Detective* (about which Davies once wrote, 'Am I allowed to say that I find [it] a bit boring?'). It's almost unthinkable that Davies, an avowed admirer of (much of) Potter's work and himself an aspiring scriptwriter, would have missed out on seeing it the second time around.

The ideas at the heart of *The Second Coming* had particular currency in the late 1990s. As we've seen, Kevin Smith's film *Dogma* was dealing with very similar material. Similarly, Mark Millar, now one of the most acclaimed writers in the comics field, launched his career through the independent publishers Trident with the title *Saviour*. It told the tale of Jesus being reincarnated in the present day as a down-at-heel wanderer, whereas Satan has taken the form of a media celebrity with more than a whiff of Jonathan Ross about him. Because the publishers ran into difficulties, *Saviour* was never completed, so, despite being a keen comics reader, Davies himself was unaware of it.

On the other hand, he was very much a fan of another comics series, *Miracleman*, which started life in 1954 as a near-identical rip-off of the American character Captain Marvel for British publishers Miller and Sons. His adventures were lively but undemanding superhero fare that entertained readers until the early 1960s. *Miracleman* was later revived by the distinguished comics writer Alan Moore for the early eighties publication

Warrior, and subsequently reprinted and completed for American publisher Eclipse. In essence, Moore takes the previously one-dimensional fantasy character and plunges him into the modern world, asking what would it really be like to discover you're a superhero? And how would the existence of a genuine superhero impact on the world?

Davies has admitted that, in some respects, his own love of *Miracleman* fed into the writing of *The Second Coming*. 'A lot of that was in my thinking with it,' he says, 'about what'd happen if the world *really* changed.' Nor is it hard to equate Stephen Baxter with lorry driver Mike Moran, the ordinary British citizen who has to come to terms with the fact that he's actually the super-powered *Miracleman*. Moran then watches his entire relationship with the world and everybody in it change irrevocably as he engages in an epic struggle with his malign opposite number, Johnny Bates. Notably, Moran's wife Liz is unable to relate to her now superhuman husband and finds herself left behind. Distant echoes of this might be detected in the story of Stephen Baxter – who even has his own nemesis by the name of Johnny.

Another possible influence, on the drama's title if nothing else, may date back to a conversation Davies had with Frank Cottrell Boyce during production of *Springhill*. 'I remember a heated conversation with Russell about W B Yeats' *Second Coming*,' Cottrell Boyce says. 'Next thing I knew it was all in this domestic drama – the rough beast, its hour come round at last, and so on. With Russell, it all went in there – gay life, *Juliet Bravo*, W B Yeats – he has no barriers.'

Getting the tone of the new piece right was a tricky prospect. That's quite aside from its journey from broadcaster to broadcaster, with the running time in flux. As such, the script was reworked almost endlessly. As Davies remembers it, '*The Second Coming* was rewritten, like, 57 times! And I watch it, and I could still rewrite it now. I'm still sitting there going, "Ah, should have done this, should have done that..." I mean, you could keep telling it and still keep making sense of it. I wish I could write other drafts of that now.'

It's no idle observation. As Davies admits, he genuinely carries on coming up with new and better approaches for scripts he's long since written. In this respect, *The Second Coming* niggles away at him still. 'Oh my God –

do you know what I never did?' he says. 'I thought of this a year too late. When Steve did that big speech in front of thousands of people, he should have made *everybody's* mobile phone ring. Imagine if everyone's phone rang in the *whole world,* and he got everyone to hold their phones up. How brilliant would that have been? You think of that *afterwards.* Damn! Isn't that a great idea? A bit like a Barry Manilow concert with everyone holding up their phones... but with those CGI crowds, that would have been the most sensational moment. It's like, you just keep on rewriting them. In my head there's a programme that's getting better!'

In its eventual form, *The Second Coming* consisted of two 90-minute instalments. This represented a much smaller tapestry than that originally envisaged for its abandoned six-hour Channel Four incarnation. According to Nicola Shindler, that initial version 'was longer, obviously, but probably not to its advantage. There was a whole episode, I think, about the television transmission. There was a mass of talking around that, but then in the finished version Baxter just did it outside and took over very quickly. It was a lot more direct and full of action. It became more of a thriller, basically.' For quite a time, even up to the point of the ITV version being readied for production, much of the latter part of the tale was to be played out in a plush city centre hotel – shades of *The Grand*, perhaps. Unwilling simply to arrest Baxter and his followers, the police were to have emptied the hotel and installed their guests, with Baxter himself in the penthouse suite. A phalanx of police officers would then have made the building secure. Davies was fond of the surreal feel that the deserted hotel setting, akin perhaps to *The Shining*, lent the material. Apparently, Channel Four disliked it for exactly the same reason.

In the event, the location was shifted to the police headquarters seen on screen, though this required losing substantial subplots. Several employees of the hotel would have been revealed as silver-eyed demons. Before Judgment Day dawns, the demons were to have tempted, seduced and generally weakened Baxter and his friends, in a lengthy sequence that Davies has since referred to as 'the *Night of the Demons.*' Elements of this remain in the end result, notably the purposeful unravelling of Frank Baxter, but over ten minutes of similar material had been rewritten for the new setting, shot, and then edited out of the final transmitted version. It was, Davies decided, slowing the momentum down at a point when viewers want to get to the climactic Judgement Day.

Plus, time was tight in this three-hour ITV version: accounting for advert breaks, there was less than two and a half hours in which to tell the entire tale. As such, any material that was judged to be less than absolutely necessary had to go. Davies himself had no objection to such cuts. Indeed, he's all for concision in storytelling, and much prefers a narrative to rattle along. 'There's no four-hour drama in the world that couldn't lose an hour,' he suggests.

Casting Stephen Baxter presented its own very particular problems. More than ever before in Davies' work, this was an undisputed lead character. Not only that, but one who had to switch from being an unassuming everyday shop assistant to being the Son of God, with the entire world hanging on his every pronouncement. For the piece to work, the actor in question would be required to convince viewers utterly in both modes. Christopher Eccleston was to prove an inspired choice for the role. Among his many credits was the epoch-making *Our Friends in the North*, a drama once described by Davies as 'possibly the best series ever made.' He was also a close associate of Red's Nicola Shindler, and had come close to starring as Stuart in *Queer as Folk*.

Eccleston's performance in the role is magnetic, not least in the scene of Baxter's powerful address to the world. Prior to shooting, the actor had requested a significant alteration to the speech in question, feeling that the empathetic human side of Baxter was getting lost amid his loftier pronouncements. Eccleston's incisive observation won the admiration of Davies, who duly added lines in which the character draws on his own very human experiences ('I'm like you – I've been you!'), lines which Davies later judged were the most affecting in the entire scene.

The part of Judith was a hugely demanding one too, required as she is allow the viewer a way in to the tale, to ground the Son of God and, in due course, to destroy him. Davies and Shindler had been so taken by Lesley Sharp's performance in *Bob & Rose* that she was a natural for the part. Mark

NINE: *DO YOU THINK YOU'RE READY FOR THAT MUCH POWER, YOU LOT?*

Benton was chosen to portray *The Second Coming*'s demonic Johnny Tyler. In retrospect, Benton's character was another facet of the drama that had Davies kicking himself. 'Again, it's like, how mad am I that Chris Eccleston never met Mark Benton? The hero and the villain never fucking *met*! Jesus Christ almighty! How thick is that?'

Eccleston and Benton would fail to meet all over again in the opening episode of Davies' *Doctor Who* in 2005, which featured Benton as Clive, a character who obsessively stalks the Doctor but shares precisely no scenes with him. It's striking too that Benton's *Second Coming* character is called Johnny Tyler; another batch of Tylers would feature strongly in *Doctor Who*. Die-hard Davies surname watchers might also take note of the fact that the couple who discover the bedraggled Baxter on the moors are the Saxons.

With Adrian Shergold directing, filming of *The Second Coming* saw Salford University's Adelphi Building standing in for the police building within which Baxter and his followers are contained. An area of waste-ground by the University building was used for the iconic scenes of Baxter addressing the world via the medium of television. Other locations across South Manchester were used during the shoot, including the districts of Whalley Range and Chorlton. Perhaps most iconic of all, permission was granted to film within Manchester City's ground at Maine Road for the pivotal scenes of Baxter's first 'daylight at night' miracle. Originally, it had been hoped to film at the grounds of rival team Manchester United, but the club's bosses decided not to allow it.

Right up to the wire, the piece was still being reworked. Davies reveals that, at the editing stage, a lot of lighter, humorous material was excised, so as to keep the tone clear and avoid dropping into parody. The result – drier, pacier – lent the programme the feel of a thriller. In the process whole characters were lost, too. At the shooting stage, Stephen Baxter had an estranged mother, given to wearing a sandwich board and indulging in public 'fire and brimstone' sermonising. Her confrontation with her son, and realisation of his true nature, made for fine drama, but was eventually judged as slowing down the momentum of the plot. Similarly, actress Jo Joyner was set to appear as a maid who seduces Peter and turns out to be a scheming demon. Davies, a great admirer of Joyner's work, was heartbroken about the decision, but felt that the subplot interrupted the story's flow. All of Joyner's scenes were shot and then removed, though they did appear as extras on the eventual DVD release.

Perhaps Davies' most impressive achievement in *The Second Coming* is in getting right under the skin of the subject – a subject in which he has no personal stake whatever. As a non-believer, he nonetheless writes from a perspective in which God is very definitely real, and his son incarnate walks among us. Of course, once the piece plays out, it becomes clear that Davies' message is that mankind doesn't need a God, and should, indeed, actively choose to do without one.

It's heady stuff, especially for a primetime slot on a mainstream channel. Hardly surprisingly, then, the piece stirred up some very extreme reactions. Soon after it was first announced as a Channel Four project, Davies told website *PlanetOut*, 'There's been a whole page about it and me in the *Sunday Express* already. It's not on until next autumn; we don't start filming until March. And people are making a fuss already. The producer had to go on BBC Radio to defend the fact that we're making it.' On its eventual transmission, some Christian callers even saw fit to ring through to the Granada switchboard with death threats. To Davies, this wasn't so much disturbing as baffling. As he said, 'How can you be a Christian if you're issuing a death threat? It's like, how lonely are those minds? And how angry?'

A less hot-headed criticism that's often been levelled at *The Second Coming* is that the second episode fails to deliver a satisfying resolution to the first. Part One has the element of surprise and features several gripping, spectacular set pieces: the miracle in the football stadium, Baxter's impassioned address to the world, and the climactic explosion in the pub. Plus, the quest to find the Third Testament is set in motion. In comparison, Part Two boasts fewer memorable high spots and, as Davies has admitted, the character of Baxter, having announced his presence to the world, becomes essentially passive, sitting in wait for the arrival of the mysterious Third Testament. When it does arrive, it's in the form of a highly charged discussion between Baxter and Judith. Make no mistake, in Davies' universe all matters of life and death can best be represented by a scene of two friends talking over a meal, but it could never be mistaken for a spectacular finale.

It's also rather a desolate conclusion. Judith and Johnny are redeemed and there's a sense of hope, but it's low key and wilfully anticlimactic. In that respect, its bleakness goes against the grain of most of Davies' work. But that all ties in with the writer's own particular world-view, which *The Second Coming* certainly reflects.

In execution *The Second Coming* represented a significant shift in Davies' writing. Previously, he'd dealt with groups of main characters, even if in small groupings – the *Queer as Folk* triumvirate, for instance. But *The Second Coming*, although it features a central group of its own, has a very definite main character, a title character even, in Stephen Baxter, the unwitting Son of God. Baxter's a fascinating figure. Davies himself must have been sufficiently fascinated to have harboured his story for so long, and persevered with the project against all odds. In fact, it's fair to say that something of Baxter got under the writer's skin, or else was there under his skin all the time. Baxter-style figures, lonely Gods walking among us, crop up in everything Davies has written since, as we'll see.

Another device used widely in *The Second Coming* anticipates his subsequent work. Events of world significance are communicated to characters in the drama, as indeed they often are in real life, via the medium of television. Major developments in Baxter's story are shown as news reports, whether or not characters are seen watching them. Society's reaction to these developments often takes the form of TV discussion shows, from the high-minded to, well, *Richard & Judy*. To increase the impact, swift montages combine all these to spell out the sheer scale of events – with foreign news footage making the point doubly clear. It's a neat technique that Davies would go on to use many times when establishing extraterrestrial threats in the world of *Doctor Who*.

We even see Judith investigating Johnny's sinister behaviour by rewatching his dating tape. Baxter, meanwhile, grasps the power of television with enthusiasm, talking direct to camera – 'Coming soon. Stay tuned!' – during his miracle at Maine Road, and broadcasting to the world when announcing the quest for the Third Testament.

For a time, industry rumour had it that *The Second Coming* would be broadcast at the most contentious time of year possible, over the Easter Weekend. In the event, it went out at 9.00 pm on ITV1 over two consecutive nights, namely Sunday 9 and Monday 10 February. The two instalments won ratings of, respectively, 6.3 and 5.4 million viewers. For such a provocative, even challenging piece, in a primetime slot on a mainstream channel, this was some achievement. Prestigious commentators voiced their approval, too. Prior to transmission, critic Mark Lawson previewed the piece for the *Guardian*, under the heading 'Russell T Davies proves himself to be a worthy heir to Dennis Potter'. And in a lecture delivered to the Royal Television Society in September 2005, Davies' old friend and colleague Paul Abbott singled the drama out for praise, calling it 'a television masterpiece'.

For his towering performance as Stephen Baxter, Eccleston was nominated for a Best Actor BAFTA, with the piece as a whole nominated for Best Drama Serial. In the event both lost out, and the pattern was repeated when it was nominated as Best Drama Serial at the Royal Television Awards. However, assorted less prestigious awards were forthcoming; for instance, the piece received the 2004 Broadcast Drama Award.

Not without irony, *The Second Coming* did have an afterlife of its own. The electronic dance outfit Orbital incorporated elements of Baxter's 'You lot' address to the world in a track of the same name on their 2004 *Blue Album*. Yet more significantly, the format of *The Second Coming* was sold to the American Showcase network. Showcase had of course adapted the earlier *Queer as Folk* as an ongoing drama which ran for five full series. Rather improbably, the initial plan was for *The Second Coming*'s second coming to go the same route, and it was developed as a long-running series, much to Davies' (admittedly grateful) bewilderment. 'How can you make that as a long-runner? How? Miracle of the Week!? I *dread* to think. Although, actually, it's not impossible.'

In considering this, Davies draws again on his admiration for *Miracleman*, in particular the final run of the comic. After Alan Moore left the title, having established *Miracleman* as saviour and ruler of the planet, writer Neil Gaiman came on board to continue the tale, examining the new world that the character has forged. 'Those later *Miracleman* collections I've got are brilliant,' Davies says. 'Miracleman comes along, and he *does* solve the world's problems, and it becomes a Utopia. And then the comic *keeps going*, showing you what it's like living in a Utopia. It's an extraordinary imagination. You could tell a version of *The Second Coming* that way. If you were really brave and you keep telling the story, what actually happens to the world?'

In the event, the American adaptation of the piece has yet to surface. It's known that the HBO network, presumably working in tandem with Showcase, got as far as developing a trial script for the opening episode, which went against many of the painstaking choices of Davies' version. The central divine revelation was held back until the first episode's climax, allowing for half an hour's worth of back-story and build-up. Davies has declared himself an admirer of the script, and expressed the opinion that this slow-burning approach might even have been superior to his own. The project appears to have stalled, but it all goes to show that, on some level at least, the process of creating *The Second Coming* isn't entirely finished business for Davies.

It was, however, to be a major turning point in his writing career. *Queer as Folk* had established him as a name to watch. *Bob & Rose* had seen him shift towards the mainstream, but to mixed responses. There's also the fact that *Bob & Rose*, based as it was around contemporary Manchester's gay scene, could have given weight to the argument that Davies was a one-trick pony. *The Second Coming* proved in no uncertain terms that he was capable of writing in a variety of styles and genres. It also won major industry awards to fully cement Davies' reputation. Still, it did use a Manchester setting, and it was probably time the writer tried broadening the scope of his work. The subject he turned to next was, in many ways, even closer to home.

T IS FOR TELEVISION

TEN:
SWANSEA IS MINE!
OR, COME DRINK MY MILK

Imagine discovering that your family owned the city you lived in. A historical document that states as much is officially verified. Your life is changed instantly and immeasurably. Suddenly you have enormous wealth and influence. How would you cope?

Davies had been toying with this idea for several years. It was originally inspired by a genuine situation. Since the early 1980s, the many descendants of eighteenth century Welsh-born pirate Robert Edwards have been fighting a prolonged legal battle to prove that they own whole swathes of eye-wateringly exorbitant land in New York's Lower Manhattan. In return for disrupting Spanish lanes, Edwards was gifted 77 acres of the area by Queen Anne. Prior to his death he granted a century-long lease on the land, on the strict understanding that it would revert to his heirs in due course. Over the course of centuries, as Manhattan became one of the most heavily built-up areas on the planet, the matter of ownership, unsurprisingly, grew knotty and blurred. Those making claim to Edwards' inheritance have been mired in legal hell ever since. When the heirs' association was taken to court for mismanaging funds in the mid-nineties, the saga received a wave of fresh publicity and was featured in the BBC documentary series *Good Fortune*. Whether here or elsewhere, Davies got wind of the intriguing tale.

The writer's own take on it crystallised in circumstances that were far from happy, however. Around the time of the death of his mother in autumn 2001, he'd been visiting Wales more than he had in many a year. It struck him that he'd never really used his spawning ground in his own writing. He'd become accustomed to writing about his adopted home of Manchester, and using the rhythms of Mancunian dialogue. Yet clearly there was plenty of mileage in a Welsh-set series, drawing on his own life-long love of the place. At a stroke, he was inspired to use variations on his own home ground, and his own family, for the idea he'd been harbouring. After briefly entertaining the title *The Vivaldi Inheritance*, he christened the new series *Mine All Mine*.

Even aside from its basis in a true story, *Mine All Mine* slots into a long
TV tradition of 'hitting the jackpot' tales. In 1977, writer Jack Rosenthal
adapted *Spend Spend Spend*, the autobiography of pools winner Viv
Nicholson, as a BBC *Play for Today*. In a similar vein, a 1983 Sunday
afternoon serial entitled *The Boy who Won the Pools* needs little explanation
– it did what it said on the tin, with humour and imagination. Most recent,
and perhaps most intriguing, of these forebears was ITV's *At Home with
the Braithwaites*. Starring one-time *Doctor Who* Peter Davison and Amanda
Holden, it ran for four series from 2000, in which the titular family struggled
to come to terms with £38 million crash-landing into their lives courtesy of
the National Lottery.

The conceit of an independent state within the UK owes a debt to the
classic 1949 Ealing comedy *Passport to Pimlico*, which concerns a corner of
London declaring its independence after the unearthing of an ancient piece
of legislation. Free of the restrictions of post-war rationing, the area becomes
a desirable idyll. Like *Mine All Mine* which followed, the film centres on
the suddenly fortunate characters in the community, and comes compete
with bags of idiosyncratic humour – plus, it was extrapolated from its own
obscure real-life occurrence, whereby a single room in Canada became the
property of the Netherlands.

As far as characterisation was concerned, an influence seems to have been
ITV's smash hit of the early 1990s, *The Darling Buds of May*. The series
was adapted from H E Bates' series of novels about the lively, quirky Larkin
family. Country bumpkin farmers living in Kent, the Larkins find themselves
invaded by a tax inspector – who promptly falls for comely Mariette Larkin
(Catherine Zeta Jones) and elects to stay. No fortunes are made, but what
follows is a warm evocation of family life in all its wonder and strangeness,
instigated by the arrival of a city boy outsider, and that's certainly a template
that *Mine All Mine* borrows from. At one stage, Catherine Zeta Jones, by
then Hollywood royalty, considered appearing in *Mine All Mine*, in a cameo
role as herself, to read the mayoral election results. The plan fell through,
but nevertheless our subject took to calling himself Russell Zeta Davies
throughout production.

By its very design, *Mine All Mine* was meant to be a big, brassy mainstream primetime ITV hit. In itself this was perhaps a surprising career move for Davies to make, given that the success of *The Second Coming* had won him plaudits and established him as a more obviously 'serious' writer.

For Davies himself, though, it was very much a conscious departure. While the series was in production, he said, with heavy sarcasm, 'People have been dying for a Welsh comedy drama, haven't they? Battering down the doors for it! Actually I thought I was in danger of writing myself into a sort of esoteric corner – if there is such a thing as an esoteric corner! But, you know, writing very issue-laden things – gayness, sexuality in *Bob & Rose*, religion in *Second Coming* and stuff like that. It's a long game, writing. I want to be writing in 20 years. And there was a danger I was becoming sort of issue-led – slightly prestigious, dare I say, in tabloid terms, in a nine o'clock, BBC2, Channel Four-ish sort of way. I thought, you head in that direction too soon and you'll get one commissioned every two or three years. And that's not good enough. You've got to prepare for a long game, and get out there and write something every year.

'So it's a very deliberate step to take. And I love it. It's nonsense. It's a romp. It's like an Ealing comedy set in Wales. There's a family and they all make a lot of noise and shout and they run around. There's not a serious issue anywhere in there. There is a gay son – and a lesbian in a wheelchair! – but actually they're very funny, very sweet characters. They're not making issues about wheelchairs or lesbians or gay teenagers or anything. They're part of the plot.'

It represented a gear change for Davies, and an opportunity to use different writing skills. 'Sometimes I sit there and think, "Actually, I can write funny dialogue." And this was a deliberate decision to do a six-parter that's very, very dialogue-led,' he said. 'There are some nice visuals in it, but that's mainly down to the director to be honest. It's a very, very dialogue-y script. It's a cheaper script as well, taking a step back to people talking in kitchens. There's a danger of thinking that the more visual and silent it is the better, and that dialogue is like the last recourse of the bad writer, sort of stuff. It's not true.'

Produced, naturally, by Red, but with additional funding supplied,

unusually, by BBC Worldwide, there were grand plans for *Mine All Mine*.
As Nicola Shindler says, 'When Russell and I talked about *Mine All Mine* at
first, we talked about doing five years of it. It was meant to be a long runner.'
Having created and launched it, Davies would have stepped back, allowing
other writers to contribute while guiding the overall shape of each series and
writing maybe half of the actual episodes.

Needless to say, selecting the individual members of the ensemble cast,
with 11 key characters in all, was an epic task. There was no shortage of
wonderful Welsh actors, but few that were big, established stars. This being
an ITV production, though, big stars were a requirement. Davies appreciates
the argument. 'I can't imagine launching a comedy with a cast of unknowns
on ITV at primetime,' he says. 'That's the game you're playing. Things are
star-driven. Who wants to watch a cast of Welsh unknowns? I'm sorry, the
star system works, it does. And why fight it? Especially at ITV where they're
there to sell stuff.'

Faced with casting a name for at least one of the two biggest roles – Max
Vivaldi or his duplicitous wife Val – Davies suggested comedy star Griff
Rhys Jones as Max. 'I mean, he's not Welsh. He's got a Welsh surname but
he's not remotely Welsh! But he turned out to be absolutely fantastic, and we
wouldn't have got it made without him.' On the other hand, actress Rhian
Morgan, appearing as Max's wife Val, was a far less familiar face. Speaking
at the time, Davies said, 'It's a stunning performance, one of the finest
performances in anything you'll ever see. Rhian gets a lot of work in Welsh
theatre and on Welsh telly. I haven't seen her on mainstream nationwide telly
ever. I've actually known her for 20 years.' Indeed, this is the same Rhian
Morgan who was formerly a member of West Glamorgan Youth Theatre, and
Davies' one-off girlfriend, during the late 1970s.

Similarly, Sharon Morgan, cast as Max's acquisitive sister Stella, would
have been unknown to many viewers but had already carved an admirable
career in Welsh television and theatre. Playing the Vivaldi siblings, Matthew
Barry (as Leo) and Siwan Morris (as Maria) were relative newcomers. In
more recent times, though, Morris has attracted much attention with her
appearances in E4's popular youth drama *Skins*. For a time she was even
romantically linked with another of Davies' regular actors, Christopher Eccleston.

The production team went to some lengths to secure the services of Ruth Madoc as Val's sister Myrtle Jones. Enshrined in the minds of a generation of viewers as Gladys Pugh in the nostalgic sitcom *Hi-De-Hi!*, Madoc was one of the most recognisable Welsh actresses to the public at large and, despite her busy schedule, the team accommodated her restricted availability. Jason Hughes, in the role of Maria's boyfriend Gethin, had made his name as Warren Jones in BBC2's *This Life*. Welsh actress Joanna Page was cast, too, her role as Candy Vivaldi in *Mine All Mine* being not so different from her part in BBC Three's hit comedy *Gavin & Stacey*.

In fact, there are certain striking parallels between *Gavin & Stacey* and Davies' series. Both concern a Southerner falling in love with the daughter of a Welsh family, with a fond emphasis on the eccentricities of family, friends and local community. Just coincidence, surely, but it's as though *Gavin & Stacey* succeeds by refining what *Mine All Mine* tried to achieve.

With the initial block of episodes directed by Sheree Folkson and Tim Whitby handling the remainder, the series was filmed on location during late 2003 in areas Davies knew very well, in and around the Swansea area. Later, as a thank you to the local community, a preview screening of the first episode was held at Swansea Town Hall.

One prospective director, Euros Lyn, had failed to secure a gig on the series, despite his range of television experience – and his being Welsh. The following year, though, Lyn was engaged as a director on Davies' revival of *Doctor Who*, and went on to become one of the mainstays of the show.

A key element can be detected in the genetic make-up of *Mine All Mine*. Davies has confessed that his boyfriend refers to the show as 'The Private Joke'. 'It's true,' Davies has said. 'If you met my family, this is like a documentary.' The shape of the Vivaldi family, a Swansea couple with two daughters and a (gay) son, mirrors Davies' own exactly. That's not to say that Davies himself was a millionaire entrepreneur while still at school, nor that the Davieses owned any major Welsh cites. Rather, the frantic, busy atmosphere of the Vivaldi family home seems to draw on personal childhood experience for Davies.

It's not just his immediate family that played a part in *Mine All Mine*. Once again, Davies cited his lifelong friend Tracy, formerly the model for

Rose Cooper, as a major influence here. The Vivaldis' home was modelled on Tracy's, and in production was very nearly used as a location. Due to practicalities a different house was chosen, just three doors down – but Tracy's home found a use as the production's green room. Again, it's not so much the fine details of Davies' friend's life that provided the inspiration: it's not known if she's ever had a relationship with an estate agent or auditioned for *Pop Idol*, for example. It's more that something of her spirit has infused the piece and its characters. How the Vivaldis and co express themselves, how they feel, and how they live their lives, stands as a fond tribute, then, to Davies' own family and friends.

On the subject of friends, consider also that Davies' mentor Paul Abbott launched one of his best-loved series, *Shameless*, in January 2004. Set on a Manchester housing estate and featuring a large dysfunctional family – or rather a family that functions well, but in a deeply unconventional fashion – *Shameless* is, as Abbott has freely admitted, drawn from memories of his own childhood and family. The series has since established itself as a staple of contemporary British television and, although Abbott guides its progress, he contributes only occasional scripts, allowing other writers to take the reins. In other words, it's become exactly the sort of show *Mine All Mine* was intended to be. It might be pushing the parallels to say that *Mine All Mine* is 'Russell T Davies' *Shameless*', but certainly both Davies and Abbott had reached a point in their careers when it felt natural to write from the heart about personal experience, family and childhood.

Scratch the surface and *Mine All Mine* appears to be covering familiar territory for Davies. Max Vivaldi, an unexceptional Everyman, learns that he's a figure of special importance, and the story concerns the impact of this discovery on him and his nearest and dearest. In this respect it's a very different spin on the same basic story as *The Second Coming*, in which ordinary Stephen Baxter finds out he's divine and unique. Both Baxter and Vivaldi struggle to come to terms with what's happened to them; meanwhile, members of their inner circle respond to the development in their own ways, whereupon conflict, and therefore drama, is generated. In classic Davies fashion, Max, like Baxter before him, seizes upon the power of television, and begins broadcasting to his people through his own home-made broadcasting outfit, Vivaldivision. Max, in fact, is another entry in Davies' gallery of Lonely Gods. Being elevated above the masses, granted almost unearthly power, he reacts in very human, fallible ways, and his new-found estrangement from his intimates just highlights how alone his lofty status makes him.

The parallels between *Mine All Mine* and his previous production don't surprise Davies greatly. 'You are always writing the same thing, I think,' he says. 'It's weird, isn't it? There was a very big scene in *Mine All Mine* about which [Red] said, "Take that out, that's too much like *The Second Coming*!" I should never have taken it out, actually. It was a very good scene. You're always telling the same stories, though. You might be serious in tone, or you might be funny in tone. I think all my characters talk the same and sound the same. I quite seriously think they all live in the same world!'

Ultimately, the plans for *Mine All Mine*'s extended life went awry. During production in late 2003, there was general dissatisfaction with the second block of episodes, directed by Tim Whitby. In particular, Episode Five was judged weak, dealing with several plot lines – Max's broadcasting obsession, Leo's first date, and the revelation that Candy's wheelchair-bound manager was in fact hopelessly infatuated with her – that came across as incidental and rambling. When offered a five-week broadcasting slot leading up to Christmas, on Thursdays at 9.00 pm, the production team agreed to edit the final two episodes into a 90-minute conclusion, losing a huge chuck of material from Episode Five and bringing the tale to a slightly hasty close.

In general, ratings had been disappointing, beginning at five and a half million at the start of the run and dropping down to the two million mark by the final episode. At the same time, several of Davies' writer friends, including Sally Wainwright and *Royle Family* creator Craig Cash, confessed to him that they fundamentally didn't get *Mine All Mine*.

The bare-bones storylining for a second series was already in place, but a return engagement wasn't commissioned. It's rather a sad fate for a show with so much to recommend it, and oodles of potential. As Davies himself has confessed, the tone may have been too overwhelmingly madcap for the viewing public. It's also perhaps too specific a premise to have stayed the distance. Nonetheless it would have been interesting to see where the story would have gone. It's known that, had a further series gone ahead, Davies planned to introduce a new main character: a Chinese brother for Max, with his own claim on the family riches. This proposed plot line would have resulted in Swansea being split down the middle, complete with a checkpoint for those wanting to cross the boundary. Instead, the final scene of the show as transmitted insinuates that the spurned Eggman has poisoned the whole Vivaldi clan. This mealtime poisoning is yet another echo of *The Second Coming*'s Stephen Baxter and his fate, as well as bearing a distinct whiff of Davies' beloved *I, Claudius*.

In truth, the transmission of *Mine All Mine* was overshadowed by the mere prospect of Davies' next project. At long last, the balloon had gone up: he had been signed up by the BBC to bring back *Doctor Who*. Suddenly matters such as the casting of a new Doctor and his companion were generating more column inches in the press than poor *Mine All Mine* could ever hope for. Besides, even if *Mine All Mine* had been recommissioned, it's unclear whether Davies could have found time enough to devote to it and do it justice, once the juggernaut that is *Doctor Who* was in progress.

Davies himself became critical of the show. Mere months after transmission, he told BBC Wales presenter Sian Williams, '*Mine All Mine* didn't particularly work. It was sadly neglected by the great unwashed! It didn't do very well at all... I think people considered it to be too far-fetched an idea.' His big regret, he confessed, was that the series' excellent cast wouldn't get the opportunity to carry on their stirling work together.

The show didn't go entirely without supporters, though. Davies' colleague Paul Cornell was very taken with it. 'I loved *Mine All Mine*!' Cornell says. 'I thought it was an attempt to make quite light comedy about real people, and seeing real people in a non-soap opera context in primetime is still a shock! We need something Ealing comedy-esque that does that, that does it with some values. By values I mean some wholemeal crunchiness, some art, rather than one of these Sunday night 'covered in honey' shows. I thought *Mine All Mine* just went down the middle of that brilliantly.'

In retrospect, Nicola Shindler holds *Mine All Mine* in high esteem, while admitting to its shortcomings. 'I think we made some big mistakes in that,' she suggests. 'What Russell's decided is the big mistake is that not everyone wants to own their own town. It has to be something very desirable to make it work. And I think, at times, we just got a bit silly. If the basic premise had been stronger then the silliness would have been okay, but I think people found it hard to stick with and believe, because the level of comedy was too high, and too extreme. But I absolutely love it still, and it makes me laugh. I love the way people speak in it, that's gorgeous, and I love that cast and the way it looks. I think the first half's directed brilliantly. I'm really proud of it, and I'm disappointed more people didn't watch it.'

It's been remarked that Davies represents a new generation of television writers – one that has grown up as TV viewers. This might seem obvious, but it's worth remembering that television as a medium only dates back to the 1930s, and didn't really get any momentum going until well after the Second World War. The pioneering British TV dramatists of the fifties and sixties – Francis Durbridge, Nigel Kneale, Dennis Potter, Alun Owen, Jack Rosenthal – had come to the medium from other fields, including radio, the theatre, novels, politics and copy-writing. Television was then relatively new and was only slowly developing its own identity. As late as the seventies and eighties, major writers such as Alan Bleasdale and Alan Plater were quite capable of recalling a childhood spent before the full-on coming of television.

On the other hand, Davies, who was born in 1963, has vivid memories of watching television constantly from his earliest days. As such he's part of a wave of writers who've spent their whole lives steeped in the medium. Just as, across the Atlantic, Quentin Tarantino's movies emerged from a lifetime spent endlessly watching films, Davies' take on television is built on long years of absorbing his chosen medium. Unlike his scriptwriting forebears, he had no prior form in another field, and nor has he shown much interest in acquiring any. His theatre work was all on a non-professional footing; his illustration work never amounted to very much. The only prose he's written has been directly related to television, and he's never shown any desire to write for radio, the once-traditional breeding ground for TV writers. He's a keen viewer of popular cinema – *Back to the Future* is one of his favourite films – but he's been resistant to the common wisdom that writers who achieve success in television should 'graduate' to cinema work.

'I don't think it's easy,' Davies suggests. 'I don't think just because you can write telly it means you can say, "Oh, I'll write a film now!" It's a different language. It's like saying, "I'm good at drawing so I'll go and do a sculpture." It's really, really profoundly different. I'm not particularly a film watcher, strangely. I've got Sky Plus. I've had it for years and I must have watched three movies, seriously. I'm just not that drawn to movies, and if I do go to the cinema I'll go and see a blockbuster. Well, actually I like going the cinema, because it's the cinema I quite like as opposed to the film. I'll go and see all the big films, but you wouldn't catch me going to a world cinema season at the local art-house place. It's not the sort of thing I get off on. My mind is very television-shaped, I think!'

Previously he'd discussed potential film ideas with Nicola Shindler at Red, but nothing had come of them. He now came very close to branching out into film, though unsurprisingly, the project had firm roots in TV.

As soon as it was launched in 1998, the quiz show *Who Wants to Be a Millionaire?* was an instant hit. Stretched across the schedules by ITV, the Celador-produced show transmitted a new edition each night for its first run, allowing it to gain plenty of momentum. Davies became an enthusiastic viewer, telling journalist Katherine Bell, 'I think that's one of the best programmes on planet Earth. Literally, it's one of the best dramas.'

For some time the show's titular jackpot went unclaimed, but in November 2000 well-heeled gardener Judith Keppel became the first to scoop the top prize. By September 2001, the show had created its third millionaire, one Major Charles Ingram, but his success was tainted by allegations of cheating. His wife, stationed in the studio audience, gave a distinct cough as presenter Chris Tarrant read the correct answer to the Major, and this system netted them a cool million pounds – at least for a short while. The case went to court in April 2003, with the result that Major Ingram was jailed for 18 months and fined £15,000. The Ingrams became much celebrated in the British media. ITV even screened a special documentary about the events. In the press, Celador announced a feature film based on the Ingram case, set to go into production in 2004. At that point, Davies' interest was well and truly piqued.

'It's one of the few jobs in my life that I've ever gone to them for,' Davies admits. 'They announced, "We're going to do a *Millionaire* film" – and they were lying! They didn't have any writers or anyone on board. So I phoned up, going, "If your writer falls through, I'd be interested." And they said, "Oh, we haven't got one – come and do it!"'

Davies found the Ingrams' tale, and the real-life couple themselves, irresistible. 'I love them. When you read the full transcript of the trial, they are *so* funny. I mean, it's not a heist movie. It's not like *Ocean's 11* set in London or something. I thought it could be a beautiful Ealing comedy about trying to steal a million quid with 17 cameras and 26 microphones on you – by coughing! What could be funnier? No one dies, it's completely harmless, and they didn't go to prison. I think the shape of their lives has been ruined, actually. It's their fault, they did bring it on themselves, but it's actually quite a sad story in a way. It's got everything. What more do you want from a film? Funny and sad!'

Davies enjoyed his fleeting involvement with Celador, but the deal ran aground. 'They were very nice people. I let them down quite badly, I have to say. They paid me and waited for me because I was finishing off other things. I hadn't even started it – and then *Doctor Who* came along. I'd been waiting all my life to do *Doctor Who*! I would love to have done that film but there just wasn't time. I can't bear having too much work. It does my head in.' The proposed film has never gone ahead, but Davies retains a fondness for the idea. 'It's still sitting there, no one else has picked it up, so… one day. Maybe it needs a bit of time to pass as well. They thought I was mad, actually, to do *Doctor Who*. How wrong!'

For the time being at least, the lure of the film world is something Davies is quite happy to resist. 'I've got work for the next few years all lined up and I'm very happy with it all,' he says. 'It's all television, television, television. But you never know. The right thing could come along, or probably the right person could come along who I want to work with. I have to say, I'm happy with what I'm doing, so I'm not rushing to change.' He pauses for thought. 'Then again, you should change. I also think that, because I don't know how to write films, that's what I *should* go and do, actually. Start from scratch, write a bad one and get better. Then I might write a good one, so in the long term it's probably a good thing to do.'

A somewhat older source than *Who Wants to Be a Millionaire?* provided the springboard for Davies' next outing as writer. Giacomo Girolamo Casanova de Seingalt was born in Venice in 1725 and his freewheeling sexual exploits became the stuff of legend. One day, well over 200 years later, Julie Gardner, an English graduate, was leafing through *The Oxford Companion to English Literature* when the name Casanova leapt out at her. That, she decided, would make a great TV series. At the time Gardner was working as a drama development producer for the independent franchise LWT. Gardner's recent TV adaptation of *Othello*, a bold modern take on the play starring Christopher Eccleston, had been a considerable success, and she was on the look out for new ventures.

Aware that a major feature film version of Casanova's life was being planned, she fought shy of the idea and pitched instead for a TV version of *Don Juan*. In discussion her superiors, Michele Buck and Damien Timmer, insisted that Casanova was a more appealing prospect. Buck duly approached Davies to provide the script, and he leapt at the idea. 'Best subject in the world,' he said, 'men and sex!' In the event, Davies could only count his blessings that no other leading TV writer – Andrew Davies, say, or Stephen Poliakoff – had yet told Casanova's remarkable story for 21st century viewers.

The very name Casanova has become a byword for an experienced and irresistible male lover, but the fine details of Casanova's life aren't familiar to many. 'The whole point of writing it is to humanise it,' Davies explained subsequently. 'If you're describing someone as a Casanova then you're not being nice about them. It's a sort of cheap sleazy insult.'

Davies accompanied Gardner on a location recce to Luxembourg, and both gamely read through a mountain of research. Having devoured the multi-volume translation of Casanova's memoirs, the writer was rather surprised to discover that, despite his reputation as a sexual libertine, Casanova had never once dabbled with men. 'Nothing! The bastard was completely straight,' Davies said. 'Nevertheless, it's fascinating stuff. He didn't just fuck a lot of women, old Casanova. He loved them as well.' On the subject of the *Memoires*, Davies also noted, 'The most amazing thing about him is that he is nothing special. What you realise is that it's a highly sexualised age, and that everyone was doing it. He was just the only man who wrote it down.'

Keen to subvert audience expectations, Davies envisioned a serial anchored in character, rather than a tidal wave of nudity. 'I can't bear all that Nell Gwyn nonsense,' he admitted at the time. 'There will be no tits whatsoever!' Also, since ITV drama chief Nick Elliott expressed a particular dislike of comically long Italian women's names, Davies' Casanova found himself in the company of the likes of Bellino and Henriette.

Davies delivered scripts for three hour-long episodes that he felt told the story well, only for ITV bosses to demur. Though happy with the result, they didn't feel audiences would invest in the story sufficiently to return to it over three instalments. Instead, they suggested reworking it as a single two-hour piece. Davies was placed in a quandary. 'It was the usual nightmare,' he said, while asserting, 'ITV are lovely. I won't knock them, they've been very good to me.' But he couldn't help but disagree with the network's verdict on *Casanova*.

At the same time, Julie Gardner left LWT to take up a new appointment as Head of Drama over at BBC Wales. In her job interview, Gardner proposed that the BBC take on *Casanova*, which she was loath to leave behind. Sure enough, they concurred, and the series found a new home at BBC Wales.

Hardly surprising, really: the BBC's drama output was heavily dominated by period literary adaptations at the time. Switching *Casanova* over to being a BBC production wasn't entirely straightforward, though. The LWT executives who'd first championed the idea were credited as executive producers on the end result, along with Davies and Julie Gardner. To complicate matters more, the required budget could only be made available if the serial was produced for the BBC by a regionally based independent company.

Luckily, Davies knew exactly who to ask. Enter the fifth executive producer: Nicola Shindler. 'I'd do anything for Russell!' Shindler admits. 'I'd climb over anything to work with him. It was very different from anything we'd ever done at Red, and I only did it because the script was so fantastic. It was just brilliant. I'd read it all the way along, because Russell had always given me copies. He knew that I absolutely loved it so it was a logical thing for me to do it. It was a real challenge in that financially we didn't have masses of money for it. But we had enough, and we were so determined that it had to represent a different spirit from most costume dramas.'

Shindler, Davies recalls, was out walking with her baby by a reservoir when he called her with the news. So it was that *Casanova* was set up as a Red Productions venture, to be premiered on digital channel BBC Three with a BBC1 repeat to follow.

Davies' adaptation hinges on the conceit of two actors playing the eponymous character: one in the more substantial role of the younger Casanova, and the other as the older Casanova, recounting his exploits to a woman called Edith. As the older character, Red managed to secure the services of the legendary Peter O'Toole. Who, though, could match an actor of O'Toole's magnitude in the role of young Casanova? The search went far and wide, and several star names were considered. After all, Casanova's magnetism and star quality were perhaps his key attributes.

David Tennant, at the age of 33, was a rising TV star with a solid theatre background, having played leads for the RSC and the National Theatre and been nominated for an Olivier Award for his role in *Lobby Hero* at the Donmar Warehouse. He auditioned for the role of Casanova, despite having convinced himself, by his own admission, that he 'wasn't good-looking enough.' Nevertheless, the impression he made was immediate. 'As soon as David came in, he won the part,' Davies said. 'He can do big scenes, and then the next second he can make you cry with the subtlest of looks. Above all, he's wonderful at comedy, and it's important that this man can make women laugh.'

Bearing in mind Casanova's special relationship with women, it's telling that a female director was assigned to the project. Sheree Folkson had made firm fans of Davies and Shindler when she directed the first block of *Mine All Mine* episodes the previous year. 'She's completely mad,' laughs Davies, 'and we love her.' As a result she was entrusted with the complex and demanding *Casanova* gig. 'We're having a Technicolor ball,' Folkson told *Radio Times* during the shoot. 'Russell's script is so brilliantly imaginative that it's given us artistic licence to push everything – costumes, lighting, art direction and make-up – to extremes.'

Sure enough, the vivid period setting allowed for *Casanova* to be realised as a visual feast. A whole host of sources were plundered for inspiration by the design team, from Baz Luhrmann's *Moulin Rouge!* and the fashion work of Vivienne Westwood to Sir John Tenniel's classic illustrations for *Alice in Wonderland*.

The cast, too, was a remarkable assemblage of talent. The key part of the older Casanova's confidante, Edith, was played by young Australian star Rose Byrne, while Shaun Parkes featured as the younger Casanova's faithful companion Rocco. Of the many women who figured in Casanova's life, three assumed special importance. Accordingly, three accomplished TV actors were cast: Dervla Kirwan as Casanova's wayward mother, Laura Fraser as his true love Henriette, and Nina Sosanya as his enigmatic consort Bellino. Fittingly, many of the smaller comic roles in *Casanova* were filled by names from the world of British comedy, including Matthew Holness, Simon Day and Mark Heap. Appearing as Villars, Matt Lucas was right in the midst of the runaway success of his BBC Three show *Little Britain*.

The *Casanova* shoot took place over 53 days, taking in a stately home in Dubrovnik and, closer to Red's home base, Burnley's Townley Hall, Cheshire's Tatton Park, and Hoghton Hall in Lancashire. Scenes set on the seafront at Dover were realised at Liverpool's docks, and a Manchester studio was designed as a ballroom space, redressed as required to double for Naples, Paris, London and Venice. Naturally, some location work was done in Venice itself, where the production unit found themselves sharing facilities with yet another version of *Casanova*, the aforementioned lavish Hollywood film directed by Lasse Hallström and starring Heath Ledger. In acknowledgment of their more modest budget, the Red team in Italy dubbed their own version 'Little Casanova'.

There had in fact been a previous BBC adaptation of Casanova's memoirs. Shown in late 1971 (when, again, costume drama was all the rage), it was the first full-length TV serial to be written by Dennis Potter. Davies, as we've seen, is a fan of Potter. Indeed, Davies might well have caught a re-edited version of Potter's *Casanova* six-part serial that was broadcast in 1974, by which point he was a keen and active viewer of TV drama. Potter had spent 13 months writing his scripts, and later, despite claims of 'historical accuracy' in the *Radio Times*, he insisted he'd made virtually no reference to the memoirs themselves but instead extrapolated from the basic dates and facts of Casanova's life. The result was an often impressionistic piece with a fair degree of naked flesh on show; true to form, TV campaigner Mary Whitehouse protested publicly against its 'lewdness'.

Like so much of Potter's work, his take on Casanova explored misogyny. Davies, by contrast, presented Casanova as a man who genuinely and unconditionally loves and understands the fairer sex. As David Tennant explained while promoting the show, 'Casanova doesn't get women because he's handsome. He gets them through force of personality, through enthusiasm and through actually taking an interest in what they say... He listened to them when nobody else did.'

Davies was consciously setting out to approach Casanova from a different perspective to Potter's version, which, he recalled, 'famously had a lot of nakedness and shagging in it. I was more interested in the man's life... Sex scenes tend to stop things on television. Your brain sort of goes whuhh! – *sex!* Any viewer does that, and it actually takes you out of the drama... There's more to say about the man, about his attitude towards life.'

The dramatisation of *Casanova*, as befits the man himself, is chock-full of style and panache. The first word spoken is a decidedly non-period 'Bollocks!' The rapid-fire opening sequence shows young Casanova crashing through a window, failing to mount a house, cursing, and being chased through the canal-sides of Venice by a pack of irate, cuckolded husbands. As Casanova escapes their clutches, he delivers a speech that's more manifesto than apology.

> CASANOVA: Gentlemen, I'm sure we can sort this out amicably. Look at it this way: if you could do what I could do, you'd do it too! But you can't. I can. And I have. And I'll do it again. So you should be happy for me, just a little tiny bit, don't you think?

When Casanova adopts the lifestyle of a nobleman, he's seen in an impressionistic sequence with suitable garments and accessories hurtling

172

towards him as he stands stock still – a direct crib from the title sequence of Channel Four's recent hit *Da Ali G Show*. Even the televised trailers for the show featured Jamie Reid-style punk graphics to the sound of Sid Vicious singing 'My Way'. All the signs are there that this isn't intended as a gritty evocation of Casanova's life in eighteenth century Europe. It's heightened and stylised, and told using language and devices that a contemporary audience will appreciate. It's entirely appropriate, of course, as we're meant to be seeing the story of Casanova's life as he himself tells it in retrospect, complete with embellishments, exaggerations and flourishes. The framing sequences featuring Peter O'Toole are, suitably, much more mired in the grit and grime of real life.

To what degree, then, can we distinguish *Casanova* as the work of the same writer behind *Queer as Folk*, *The Second Coming* and the rest? Much of what Davies has written about in the course of his career has been thoroughly contemporary: popular culture, lifestyles and technology. For sure, *Casanova*'s the first major piece Davies has written that doesn't feature a single television lurking anywhere in the background. In many other respects, though, his particular preoccupations are marbled right through it. For Davies, Casanova's life is populated by a shifting surrogate family of friends. His real family, though, is a source of disappointment and pain. His mother abandons him, and his son reflects his very worst excesses back at him. And though he loves all women, pretty much in person, the great love of his life, Henriette, always remains just out of reach. Like so many of Davies' main characters, Giacomo Casanova's great weakness is a deep yet unrequited love.

'It really is my life in some ways, I'll be absolutely honest, and I think everybody recognises it because everybody has been in that state,' Davies says. 'Even the happiest married couple in the world had someone once who got into their brain in that way, someone special. So I think it's rather a beautiful thing even though it's also a tragedy. I have literally written it a hundred thousand times. Even in *Casanova*, even the world's greatest lover, I sort of wrote him in a state of unrequited love with Henrietta, because I think that every variation on the story is just fascinating and rich and recognisable.' It's clearly a matter dear to Davies' own heart. Speaking to *Doctor Who Magazine*, he once revealed, 'I just love writing about it, cos

I spend my life in a state of unrequited love. It's a healthy state to be in, I think – bitter, but good.'

It's pretty much par for the course that the story of *Casanova* deals frankly with issues of sexuality, but the attitude taken is never judgmental, and it's never allowed to be explicit or exploitative either. In many ways, Davies' Casanova seems to be an outwardly ordinary man who discovers that he has an extraordinary gift, namely an almost superhuman charm and magnetism, particularly where women are concerned. He then traverses the globe, always in company but, nevertheless, always fundamentally alone. In moving through the world blessed with gifts that make him the envy of mere mortals, Giacomo Casanova is, like Stephen Baxter and Max Vivaldi before him, one of Davies' 'lonely gods'. He's set to spend his days coming to terms with his own specialness, which could be seen equally as either a blessing from the gods or a dreadful curse.

Thus far, *Casanova* remains Davies' sole venture into the world of literary adaptation, although many commentators have spotted elements of another form of high art in his writing, namely opera. He agrees that this 'big' operatic quality runs throughout his work, but insists that his own tastes don't run to opera itself.

'I can't bear it!' he admits. 'Isn't that interesting? I've only ever been to two operas in my life and left in the interval in both of them. Fucking *hated* it! One was in Sydney Opera House – *Così fan tutte* … what a load of tosh! And then I went to the Millennium Centre. My friend bought me a ticket for a Christmas present. She said, "You're going to love opera. *Rigoletto* – you'll like that because it's sad. It's full of tragedy." And I couldn't stand it! At the interval I said, "I'm just going!" Because it's so *slow*! I mean, if someone's sad, they walk on and they sing about being sad for 20 minutes! And you think, "You're sad, I've got it! What happens next?" I really, genuinely – not just making it up to do a comedy routine out of it – hate it, as a form. No, no,' he shudders. 'My operatics are much better!'

For Davies, the frantic production period in 2004 was spent travelling back and forth between Red in Manchester for *Casanova* and Cardiff, where the first new series of *Doctor Who* was being made thick and fast. Speaking to BBC Wales' Sian Williams, he said, 'At one point I did the Manchester to Cardiff journey five times in three days. And that was enough, thank you very much! I just got shuttled to and fro like a baby in a pram!'

During this period, Davies struck up an excellent working relationship with Julie Gardner. Both were avid viewers of American fantasy shows like *Buffy* and *Smallville*, and bemoaned the fact that they had no British equivalents. Inspired, Davies dreamt up *Excalibur*, a proposed UK-based fantasy show about a team investigating extraterrestrial activity in a contemporary city setting. In retrospect, Davies told *Deathray* magazine that he'd envisioned 'a psychic cops show ... very urban, like *Prime Suspect* but with psychic powers.' A two-page pitch document was written to flesh the concept out. It wasn't to happen, though – at least, not in that form, and not yet.

The writer also bonded with actor David Tennant, sharing as they did a great love of *Doctor Who*. On set, they traded *Who* in-jokes – that, for instance, if Tennant's Casanova were to touch O'Toole's, the time differential between the two would be shorted out with cataclysmic results. The scene in which Tennant's Casanova begs for his life before an audience of three doctors also caused the pair much amusement.

When first aired on BBC Three on 13 March 2005, *Casanova*'s first episode claimed 940,000 viewers, a record for first-run drama for the channel. When it was shown on BBC1, hopes for success were high but the ratings for the terrestrial channel were less impressive. Again, Davies' other major project, then screening on BBC1 on Saturday evenings, had rather overshadowed it – and, indeed, virtually every other British TV show of that year. It had been a long time coming but *Doctor Who* was back.

T IS FOR TELEVISION

ELEVEN:
LOTS OF PLANETS HAVE A NORTH...

It might be unlikely that, at this stage in proceedings, the reader will require a brief history of *Doctor Who*, but it's worth looking at developments in context.

In the first instance, the series ran on BBC1 from November 1963 to December 1989, a curious blend of fantasy, science fiction and, in its early days, historical adventure, incorporating humour, horror, thrills and occasionally even the downright surreal, fit for all ages. It was an almost unique example of a thoroughbred winner being designed by committee. The original impulse for the show came from incoming BBC drama chief Sydney Newman, who wanted to create a new ongoing adventure series for Saturday tea-times to replace the children's literary adaptations that then held the slot. BBC staff writers researched the appeal of contemporary science fiction prose and, as the matter was debated back and forth, a format began to emerge. This was then passed to a production team to develop, and the team engaged writers, actors and designers to bring it to life.

The format continued to evolve. The show's second story introduced its first alien adversaries, the Daleks, who weren't instantly to Newman's taste – but viewers were bowled over. Slowly but surely, *Doctor Who*'s historical tales were phased out. Other hands left their own impression on the series. A string of producers, directors, writers, actors, designers and script editors came and went over the years. By 1966, all the lead actors, including William Hartnell as the Doctor, had left and been replaced, but nevertheless the show carried on. By 1970 – as Patrick Troughton, the second incarnation of the Doctor, moved on – the impenetrable mystery around the main character had begun to dissolve, and the series transferred to production in full colour.

During the mid to late 1970s, *Doctor Who*, by now an established fixture in the BBC's Saturday evening schedule, was winning some of its largest audience figures ever. By the mid 1980s, though, the series, for all its charms, had begun to run out of steam. The Doctor's now convoluted back-story, and the show's gallery of old monsters, were drawn upon with increasing regularity, but fresh inspiration was less forthcoming. In fact, by 1989, with the Doctor now in his seventh incarnation (Sylvester McCoy),

Doctor Who was enjoying a creative renaissance, but it went unseen by the viewing public at large, who had pretty much deserted the show. The 26th season ended its run that year, after which the BBC became cagey and non-committal about *Doctor Who*'s future. It would return, the corporation insisted, when the time was right, and they were actively planning for this. But as years went by with no solid news, most observers concluded that *Doctor Who* had been given a quiet burial.

Several developments kept the flame alive. The film rights to the series had been sold to a British company called Daltenreys who made considerable and very public efforts to get such a project launched, but without eventual success. Virgin Books, who had been publishing a series of novelisations of televised *Doctor Who* adventures, were granted a licence to produce new and original novels that carried on where the BBC series had left off. This range of prose 'New Adventures' thus allowed the saga to continue, in prose form at least. Similarly, an independent company called Big Finish began making commercially available, and officially authorised, audio adventures. These full-cast dramas featured original TV Doctors and companions from the original series reprising their roles.

Meanwhile, at the hub of this scene sat the monthly *Doctor Who Magazine* – initially from the Marvel UK stable, later published by Panini. The magazine helped publicise the output of Virgin and Big Finish, as well as featuring its own original *Doctor Who* comic strip, and reported any potential new developments about *Doctor Who* on television.

Come 1996, there was indeed news worth reporting. The BBC, teamed with Fox and Universal in America, embarked on a proposed new version of *Doctor Who*, guided into existence by executive producer Philip Segal. A feature-length pilot for this co-production relaunch was shot in Vancouver, with British actor Paul McGann cast as the official Eighth Doctor. Accompanied by a rash of merchandising, the TV movie aired on BBC1 on 27 May 1996, that year's Easter Bank Holiday. Truth be told, it was something of a curate's egg, making some excellent decisions about how to re-energise the format but also some plain baffling ones.

Reaction in fan circles was mixed, although Davies himself enjoyed the production. Indeed, he cites the scene where one-off companion Grace

Holloway dashes to the main TARDIS console room while the Doctor is trapped, his life force draining away, as one of his favourite moments in the whole history of *Doctor Who*. The production garnered very healthy ratings of 9.08 million in the UK, but when shown on the American Fox Network, viewing figures only reached a relatively poor 5.5 million. And the US reaction was deemed to be the most crucial. The pilot was never followed up, and Universal's option to co-produce *Doctor Who* expired at the end of 1996. The show appeared to be in suspended animation again.

By this time, the New Adventures novels range had been wound up and replaced by a near-identical series from BBC Books, featuring Paul McGann's Eighth Doctor. Over at Big Finish, McGann reprised the role for a number of audio adventures. Another option on the *Doctor Who* film rights was sold, this time to action film director Paul S Anderson. Again, it failed to come to fruition before the option expired.

Meanwhile, hopes were raised by an all-new animated *Doctor Who* adventure. Scripted by Paul Cornell, one of the most popular writers of original *Doctor Who* fiction, 'Scream of the Shalka' was first released as a webcast, with an additional, albeit limited, TV transmission for digital satellite viewers via the BBC's interactive service. Self-contained as a story, it was nevertheless designed to act as a springboard for more. In promotion materials it was announced that, in a completely official, BBC-approved capacity, Richard E Grant was the Ninth Doctor. Many observers, though, were left fundamentally unconvinced by the prospect of a web-based animation as a future for the brand.

Would anything concrete *ever* come of Doctor Who's future?

Enter Russell T Davies.

Davies had crossed paths with *Doctor Who* many times in the past. Let's not forget, the writer's earliest memory of watching television is very specifically of seeing *Doctor Who*. He insists that he can remember watching, at the grand age of three and a half, William Hartnell 'regenerate' into Patrick Troughton in October 1966. 'I was three, which is very young to be remembering stuff from,' Davies told a BBC Four documentary team in early 2005. 'It was terrifying, and my mother loved it.'

According to Christopher Eccleston, a young Davies even submitted an entry in a *Blue Peter* 'Design a *Doctor Who* Monster' competition. One such competition was held in late 1967, which would put Davies as less than five years old at the time. Given his youthful enthusiasm for drawing, it's far from impossible.

Davies has claimed on many occasions that, by the age of eight – so, by 1971 – he'd 'fallen in love' with the show. By that point, he was regularly writing up his verdict on individual *Doctor Who* episodes in his weekly school diary. He's since waxed lyrical about the mid-70s adventures starring Tom Baker's fourth Doctor, which would have accompanied his teenage years. Of the 1975 story *The Ark in Space*, Davies has said, 'Nothing creates terror and claustrophobia like the good old-fashioned walls of [a] BBC studio... I must have watched this a hundred times. It's not enough.' Similarly, he's suggested that episode one of *The Talons of Weng Chiang*, first shown in January 1977, boasts 'the best dialogue ever written. It's up there with Dennis Potter.'

In fact, both these stories were written by *Doctor Who*'s great perennial scriptwriter, Robert Holmes, during a time while he was acting as the show's script editor. In 1977, journalist Jean Rook interviewed Holmes for the *Daily Express*, then the Davies' family newspaper. 'I already knew that I disagreed with [the *Express*],' Davies has said. 'I loved the Jean Rook column though. The first woman in my world to stand up and criticise the Royal Family. Good for her.' In the course of the piece Rook sought to take Holmes to task for the supposedly terrifying direction in which he'd helped to guide the series. Holmes replied that he now considered the show to be 'geared to the intelligent 14-year old.' Davies, by then a declared *Doctor Who* fan and bright schoolboy, was himself just two months shy of his 14th birthday. He was, therefore, pretty much Holmes' perfect target viewer, never happier than when drawing *Doctor Who* comic strips for his own amusement.

Fast-forwarding to 1987, Davies was in the earliest stages of a career in television, with a developing interest in scriptwriting. On spec, he wrote and submitted a treatment for a four-part script to Andrew Cartmel, the incumbent *Doctor Who* script editor. Set on a space station housing an intergalactic news-gathering service, it followed the Doctor on a mission to unearth the sinister truth by befriending a journalist and venturing up to the restricted top levels of the station. Davies received a reply from the BBC Script Unit, suggesting he tried instead to write something more prosaic, about 'a man who is worried about his mortgage, his marriage, his dog.' Needless to say, no commission followed.

Clearly, Davies' early Children's BBC dramas *Dark Season* and *Century Falls*, the former in particular, betray his childhood love of *Doctor Who* and its ilk. In the early nineties, Davies suggested to his then boss, Granada's Head of Drama David Liddiment, that the company might consider reviving the show as an independent production for the BBC, but received very short shift. In due course, Liddiment told Davies he approved of the 1996 TV movie, but dismissed Paul McGann's Edwardian costume as 'fancy dress'. As Davies admits, he took this particular point to heart.

Some years later, while working as part of Granada's writing team, Davies was, as we've seen, commissioned to make his first professional contact with the world of *Doctor Who* as author of a novel in Virgin's New Adventures range, of which he was an admirer. The New Adventures range, which promised 'stories too broad and too deep for the small screen', aimed to be more sophisticated than the TV series that spawned it. Largely this was on the grounds that its readership had grown up with the show, and was eager for something more mature and substantial. In some hands, this approach freed the format from its shackles, but there was also a tendency, especially early in the run, for authors merely to bolt sex and swearing onto an otherwise standard *Doctor Who* adventure, to underwhelming effect.

Davies' *Damaged Goods*, published in October 1996, was certainly adult in tone, with its setting of a grimy Mancunian council estate populated by uncompromising drug dealers and closeted married men. The meat of the plot, which sees the Doctor tracking down a Class A drug across the galaxies, is miles away from Davies' later treatment of the *Doctor Who* format. Nevertheless, it's striking that the writer already chooses to set his alien clash in a contemporary housing estate, and centres it around a family who live there, specifically a mother and daughter named Tyler. The father of the family, notably, is absent. In this respect, at least, Davies was evidently thinking in a clearly defined direction already.

Lest we forget, *Queer as Folk*'s Vince is a rabid *Doctor Who* fan, given to mouthing lines of dialogue from the show along to his TV screen. From Stuart, he receives the remarkable birthday present of a full-size, remote control K9. In late 1998, while *Queer as Folk* sat awaiting transmission, Davies, with some engineering from his old Granada mentor Tony Wood, then a BBC drama producer, had a meeting about a potential full TV revival of *Doctor Who* with BBC drama executive Patrick Spence. The notion, unofficially dubbed *Doctor Who 2000*, never progressed beyond this initial meeting, and nothing of what was discussed ever made it onto paper. Davies, though, has since dismissed his approach at that point as 'unfocused and flimsy'.

In retrospect, however, it's easy to forge a link between what Davies was doing in *Damaged Goods* and what he ended up doing in 2005. By way of confirmation, consider that *Doctor Who Magazine* – which Davies had read and collected since it first launched and named without irony as 'my favourite magazine' – quoted the writer in a lengthy article in June 1999. The piece polled the opinions of several *Who* fans working in television as to the feasibility of the show actually making it back on air. Several of the figures quoted, including Steven Moffat, Paul Cornell, Mark Gatiss and Gareth Roberts, went on to work on the regenerated show itself.

In this forum, the most intriguing comments come from Davies. Quoted in the piece, he reasoned that an updated version of *Doctor Who* would have to be shot on film, rather than on videotape, and in 50-minute episodes, rather than 25-minute instalments as before. Mostly, his thinking was dictated by the norms of television production by 1999. 'I can't think of a filmed half-hour series,' he wrote. 'Is there one?' As regards the expense of sets – different for every story, each one centuries and/or galaxies apart – he mused, 'Maybe the solution is to go back to those [early 1970s] Pertwee years with the Doctor trapped on Earth. This is not my favourite formula, but it's more easily achieved using real locations.'

Stories with a recognisable contemporary setting would help engage an audience, too, he reckoned. 'If the moment the opening titles are over, you go into a Scene One that's set on a purple planet with three moons ... then the audience would switch off in their millions ... That's just an instinct, but I think you should set all that high-flown end-of-the-world stuff in a very real world of pubs and mortgages and people.' Warming to the theme, Davies argued for a more character-based version of the series than previously. 'It would have to be more personal, more emotional ... No more screaming girlies! ... An emotional content has got to be stronger, more interesting, more open, to grab a wider audience.'

Having asserted that the key ingredient in the show was 'death', Davies admitted, 'I'd chuck away half the background – the moment the Doctor started talking about Gallifrey and Time Lords, I'd just cut it. Excess baggage.' For good measure, he opined that Saturday tea-time would no longer be the natural home for such a show – 'that slot has been consigned to history now' – and summed up by saying, 'God help anyone in charge of bringing it back – what a responsibility!' It's safe to assume that these opinions weren't hugely dissimilar from those Davies expressed to the BBC at around the same time, especially in the light of what was to come.

In early 2002, Davies attended another meeting with the BBC, this time with executive producer Laura Mackie, discussing ideas for a potential revival of the show. At this point the notion was given serious, detailed consideration, but once again, it didn't immediately lead to anything. The film rights to the series had reverted to the BBC, and as their own BBC Films division was very much active, there was some internal politics regarding what form the series might return in. In addition, following the 1996 TV movie collaboration with Universal, the whole issue of rights was tangled indeed. But clearly a window of opportunity might open at any time, and Davies was only too happy to have his name in the mix. In retrospect, though, he's confessed that he never really believed any such revival would come to pass. As a *Doctor Who* fan, he felt duty-bound to lobby for its return. Privately, though, he felt sure the show was stone dead.

Around this time, there were actually said to be at least four separate proposals for a relaunch of *Doctor Who* circulating within the BBC. One came from Dan Freedman, an experienced radio producer who'd made *Death Comes to Time*, an ambitious new *Doctor Who* adventure – in audio only, with accompanying still images for webcasting – in 2001-2. Judging by the adventure, Freedman favoured a drastic reworking of the series format, developing the mythos of the Time Lords and telling an ongoing story on an intergalactic scale. It bore strong echoes of popular fantasy sagas including *Star Wars* and *Lord of the Rings*, but only scant resemblance to the *Doctor Who* of old. In publicising the venture, Freedman admitted to not being much of a fan of the original show, and favoured taking *Doctor Who* in a 'different direction'. He cited *Buffy the Vampire Slayer* as his ideal model for a new *Doctor Who*, and announced that as a consequence he was having discussions with the '*Buffy* people'.

Scriptwriter Matthew Graham – then an *EastEnders* alumnus, later to make his name as co-creator of *Life on Mars* and *Ashes to Ashes* – had also suggested reviving the Time Lord in discussion with BBC drama executive John Yorke. As he's since admitted, though, Graham would have felt obliged to retain key elements of the original run – multi-part stories with cliffhangers, and an older Doctor – but was tempted to suggest redesigning and updating icons such as the Daleks and the TARDIS, and in all favoured a dark, Gothic tone.

Similarly, Mark Gatiss, another outspoken fan of *Doctor Who*, pitched his own ideas for a *Doctor Who* revival to the BBC via Jon Plowman, then the corporation's Head of Comedy Entertainment. Gatiss had made his name as a writer-performer with the League of Gentlemen comedy troupe, who won the Perrier comedy award in 1997 before recording a series for BBC Radio 4 and then transferring across to BBC2. He'd also penned spin-off *Doctor Who* tales in the form of the Virgin New Adventures range and Big Finish's series of audio adventures. In writing a full *Doctor Who* pitch document, Gatiss brought in two other writers: Gareth Roberts, a fellow graduate of Big Finish and the New Adventures, and Clayton Hickman, then editor of *Doctor Who Magazine* and a sometime collaborator with Roberts.

The vision for the show that they devised contrasted somewhat with what was to come. 'It was broadly similar, but looking back it lacked the chutzpah of Russell's [2005] version,' Roberts admits. 'I guess back then it was inconceivable that the BBC would put serious money into it.' Some aspects of the team's proposal were highly refreshing, such as the conceit that the Doctor's memory had become extremely unreliable. New viewers would thus be on the same footing as the main character: should the Daleks arrive en masse come the first episode's cliffhanger, the Doctor would have no idea what they were.

Nevertheless, Roberts considers their approach too slavish to the original. 'I think we were far too wedded to some aspects of the original series – posh Doctor, 25-minute episodes, etc. I think we saw those things as untouchable, which we soon realised was nonsense as soon as the new show went out. Russell's version is so bold – ours was apologetic. *Who* fans – certainly back then – were sufferers of cultural cringe, kind of embarrassed by the wilder aspects of the series. I'd never have dared to write an episode as funny and strange as 'The End of the World', certainly not as episode two. That's a great thing with Russell – if you ever seem timid about a good idea he'll say "Why? Don't be a twit, if it's good, do it!"'

Come 2003, Lorraine Heggessey, the then-Controller of BBC1, was known to be a keen advocate of reviving *Doctor Who* as a Saturday evening show, even confessing her desire at the Edinburgh Festival. With the BBC taking such an active interest in bringing the series back it was now – pardon the pun – just a matter of time. It certainly didn't hurt that *The Second Coming* had been garlanded with critical acclaim, and as a result the BBC were as keen as ever to work with Davies. Behind the scenes, the knotty rights issues were resolved, and sure enough, in late August 2003, the writer finally got the call that he'd long been angling for.

Davies' agent Bethan Evans had been in attendance in her professional capacity at the press launch for the BBC's *Canterbury Tales*, a set of contemporary dramas modelled on Chaucer. At the event, in passing, Jane Tranter, the BBC's Controller of Drama Commissioning, told Evans, 'Russell. *Doctor Who*. We're doing it. Tell him.' The following day, Evans left a message to that effect on Davies' answerphone, but he took it to mean only that there was a new possibility of the show going into a long process of development. Consequently he didn't respond with any urgency, leaving it for over a week to follow it up with Evans. He then asked her to convey the message that he was definitely interested, but that currently he had a full workload.

In the meantime, Julie Gardner, with whom Davies had worked on

Casanova, took up her new appointment as Head of Drama at BBC Wales. At the start of September 2003, in her first meeting with new boss Jane Tranter, Gardner was told that she could instigate a proposed relaunch of *Doctor Who*, to be written, in theory, by Davies. Though BBC Wales had a rich tradition of TV drama production, their output was rarely broadcast nationally. The corporation was angling to build up its regional drama bases, with BBC Wales a leading light among them, and it was felt that anchoring a high-profile networked series like the new *Doctor Who* in Cardiff was an excellent example of doing so.

So it was that Gardner rang Davies direct to relay the offer from Heggessey and Tranter. Though delighted, he had his reservations, both in terms of his career and of the feasibility of actually bringing the show back. After three days' consideration, he decided to accept. Behind the scenes, Davies' deal to take on *Doctor Who* was interwoven with the simultaneous transferal of *Casanova* to the BBC.

Speaking some weeks after the announcement was made, Davies said, 'One of the reasons I chose to do *Doctor Who* is that – there are a lot of other things I could be doing – but it's *so* exciting, because it's like ratings *war*. It's going to be early on a Saturday night, at *Pop Idol* time. There is no greater white-hot nuclear fury in the ratings war than that slot. And to try and get a drama that works, it's like, we're going have to be so bold, and cheeky, and strong with it. No cod whimsy in some quarry, saying, 'Oh, isn't this nice, Doctor?' It's got to be *savagely* strong as a series – like no other drama.'

In some ways, of course, the project was a throwback for Davies. 'I've always worked in children's telly and it's a real chance to go back,' he said. 'Obviously I see a lot of adults watching that stuff for nostalgia, but I mean, I was eight years old and watching it – I was *four* years old and watching it – absolutely wide-eyed and entranced. I want to catch that audience again. There'll be a lot of adults watching, I think, who'll be appalled by some of the stuff we're going do because they'll find it silly or … or outrageous. And actually, you've got to get those kids watching. That's what it's there for. Otherwise we'd go out at six o'clock or eight o'clock on BBC2. It's *got* to get young people watching it. It's got to appeal to everyone.

'But, see, that's so frightening. Appeal to everyone: like, how do you do that? That's why it feels like going to war. And I'm not cynical about ratings wars and stuff like that. You do stand or fall by the ratings. If you get ten million, you've got something right. If you get four million, you've got something wrong, and you live or die by those rules. So, what a chance that's going to be. It's going to be brilliant.'

In the press, Davies exuded nothing but confidence and enthusiasm for the project but, after the event, he admitted, 'Even then, I wasn't sure it would work. I thought, if it died a death, that at least I'd get 13 episodes to hug in the old folks' home, under my rubber blanket.'

On reflection, Davies has said, 'I hate pitches. Always refuse to write them.' Instead, his preferred method was to outline an idea in person to commissioning executives and, if they were interested, to then write the script for the first episode of the piece in full. 'No synopsis, no outline. I feel like I'm killing the work, if I'm pinning it down well in advance.' Nevertheless, he recognised the necessity of such a document in this particular case. '*Doctor Who* was different. This was a gamble for the BBC. They'd commissioned it before a word was written.'

So it was that his first task on this new venture, while *Mine All Mine* was in production, was to write a 15-page pitch document, outlining his plans for a revived *Doctor Who*: the tone, the main characters, and idea sketches for stories. Within it, Davies posited a new Doctor, one who was 'your best friend. Someone you want to be with, all the time. He's wise and funny, fast and sarky, cheeky and brave. And considering he's an alien, he's more human than the best human you could imagine.' To accompany this Doctor, Davies created 18-year-old shop girl Rose Tyler, 'feisty and funny ... From the moment they meet, the Doctor and Rose are soulmates ... a perfect match.'

Davies' document went on to deal with the tricky issue of the *Doctor Who* universe's cluttered, convoluted history. 'The fiction of the Doctor has got 40 years of back-story,' he wrote. 'Which we'll ignore. Except for the good bits.' The police-box lookalike TARDIS was to be retained, as well as familiar elements such as the dreaded Daleks and the trusty Sonic Screwdriver. On the other hand, the Time Lords, the Doctor's people, were out, victims of an unseen Time War, at one stroke freeing the narrative from the shackles of continuity and providing a powerful new dramatic impetus. 'Last of the Time Lords' has a certain ring to it,' Davies wrote – and this would certainly prove true.

In another echo of the opinions he expressed to *Doctor Who Magazine* four years earlier, Davies argued that the series should centre on humans – if not the contemporary variety, then Earth colonists and descendants – whatever the setting might be. 'If the Zogs on planet Zog are having trouble with the Zog-monster… who gives a toss?' he wrote. 'But if a human colony on the planet Zog is in trouble, a last outpost of humanity fighting to survive … then I'm interested.'

This pitch document was submitted in time for the BBC's first major meeting for the return of *Doctor Who*, which took place on 8 December 2003. In attendance were Davies, Gardner, Tranter and Mal Young, who was at the time Controller of Continuing Drama Series for the BBC and a hands-on veteran of primetime shows including *EastEnders* and *Brookside*.

By that point, certain aspects of the project were already decided and others were still up for grabs. From the very start, the transmission slot, 7.00 pm on a Saturday night, and the format, of 45-minute episodes, were set in stone. Initially though, the BBC proposed a series of just six, or possibly eight, episodes, all to be written by Davies. It was also suggested that the episodes might break down into pairs, providing two-parters incorporating a cliffhanger, as per the original show. Davies argued against this on the grounds that self-contained 45-minute stories, with just occasional strategically placed two-parters throughout the run, might be more accessible to the casual viewer.

Similarly, he disagreed with initial suggestions that the Doctor's most familiar enemies, the Daleks, should return in the opening episode. Instead, he lobbied for their return to be held back until around the mid-point of the series, allowing for a flourish of new publicity once the initial rush of attention had died down, much in the manner of American television 'sweeps' weeks.

BBC Worldwide, the corporation's commercial division, was pushing for a longer series of 13 episodes, which lends itself nicely to foreign sales. (Thirteen weeks is exactly a quarter of a year, a neat television 'season'. In due course, four series of 13 episodes makes a total of 52, enticing foreign TV buyers with an episode a week for a full year.) Davies himself was enthusiastic about this prospect, and Julie Gardner duly calculated a workable budget for a longer run. Once this was approved, Davies was no longer responsible for penning every script for the show, although he was to provide a hefty eight of the 13 episodes.

For the balance, other writers that he suggested were brought in, namely Mark Gatiss, Robert Shearman, Paul Cornell and Steven Moffat. Each had experience in mainstream television drama, as well as a good working knowledge of *Doctor Who*. They'd all written for the franchise in different forms, from New Adventures novels and Big Finish audio dramas to online animations and, in Moffat's case, a beautifully judged *Doctor Who* spoof entitled 'Curse of the Fatal Death' for Comic Relief back in 1999.

Davies had also asked his friend Paul Abbott to script an episode. Initially Abbott agreed, supplying a storyline in which the Doctor's new companion Rose is revealed as having been created by the Doctor himself as an experimental 'perfect companion'. But within a matter of weeks Abbott, flushed with the success of *Shameless* and his political thriller *State of Play*, conceded that his schedule was simply too full and withdrew from the project. Similarly, Davies formally approached *Harry Potter* author J K Rowling, untested as a scriptwriter, with a view to her contributing an episode of *Doctor Who*, but she was swift to decline the offer due to existing commitments. (Davies subsequently confessed that he had no particular inclination to bring back scriptwriters from the show's original run – with one notable exception. Sadly his childhood hero Robert Holmes had died in May 1986. "If he'd been alive, my God, we'd have had him back straight away," Davies says ruefully.)

Much excitement was generated among his colleagues when Davies completed the full script for the first episode of the series, simply entitled 'Rose'. By necessity it was to be the template for all that would follow, not only as far as writers were concerned, but also BBC executives, design teams, and potential cast members – not to mention the budget. It was a mission statement of sorts, charged with rebooting the entire format, introducing the Ninth Doctor, Rose, her mother and boyfriend, and delivering an engaging adventure representative of what was to come – all this in the space of 45 minutes.

Subsequently, there were those who would complain that the plot of
the piece, about a foiled invasion of Earth by living plastic dummies, was
pretty slight. In truth, if ever a script had its work cut out for it, this was it,
and the fact that it achieves all its objectives, and in the process manages
to be fast, funny, thrilling and spectacular, was a remarkable testament to
Davies' writing skill. Recalling the initial buzz within the BBC when Davies
delivered it, Julie Gardner told *Doctor Who Magazine*, 'People were dropping
meetings just to get to that script! I could barely turn the pages fast enough.'
Meanwhile, Mal Young called it 'the most important script in my office.'

Gardner was to be credited as executive producer on the show, as was the
more experienced Young. After interviewing several candidates for the post
of the series' producer, they appointed Phil Collinson. Collinson had proved
his mettle on shows such as Red Productions' *Linda Green* and BBC1's
Born and Bred and *Sea of Souls*, aside from being an old colleague and
friend of Davies' from their days at Granada and a lifelong admirer of
Doctor Who. Collinson took up the post as the production office
started up in January 2004.

Officially speaking, Davies' own role on the new show became 'head
writer and executive producer'. In execution, though, he was working as
Doctor Who's 'show-runner', a term that's commonplace in American
television. Aside from writing his own episodes, Davies conceived the
overall shape of the series and assigned the bare-bones details for each
episode to the writers in question. Then he worked closely with the
writers in ensuring that their scripts proceeded as planned.

Ever convinced of the importance of getting the overall tone of a
production right – as he once asserted, 'tone is key' – Davies instigated
'tone meetings' for individual episodes of *Doctor Who*. Each production
department would be represented so that the required texture of each episode
would be set in stone at the earliest point, and even summed up in a single
word. (For Steven Moffat's 'The Empty Child', for instance, the chosen word
was 'romantic'.) Davies oversaw each stage of design, casting and scripting,
and during production, he received daily rushes of footage.

In short, where the return of *Doctor Who* was concerned, Davies was very
much the man in charge.

ELEVEN: *LOTS OF PLANETS HAVE A NORTH...*

Back in the 1970s and 80s, the British press traditionally had a field day each time it was announced that the hunt was on for a new Doctor Who. Encouragingly, this time-honoured ritual was revived along with the show. The fact that the names the tabloids were bandying about, including chef Ainsley Harriot and magician Paul Daniels, were so lightweight and unedifying was more dispiriting. 'That's how low it had sunk, and how cheap its reputation had become,' Davies told *Doctor Who Magazine*'s Ben Cook.

Speaking to the same publication four years earlier, the writer himself had suggested that ex-*EastEnders* star Michael French would have been a good choice. That was just idle conjecture, though. In late 2003, faced with actually selecting a new Doctor, Davies and the team, in conjunction with casting director Andy Pryor, brainstormed a vast list of possible actors, just by way of considering all options. 'There's a list of people at the moment,' Davies said at the time. 'Some of them are young. Some of them are old. There are all sorts of marvellous actors we could cast. We've got to be whores, actually, and really make it strong and sexy and powerful, to *get* people watching. We've got to *make* them watch. So, a lot of your normal drama considerations fly out the window with it. There are some great names on the list. But equally, there's some ... *cheeky* names.'

The process rolled on into 2004. Offers were made to some major names, among them British film star Hugh Grant. Rowan Atkinson, of *Mr Bean* fame, has since intimated that he was approached too. These, presumably, were among the 'cheeky' names Davies hinted at, but both declined.

More seriously, Mal Young had suggested offering the part to Christopher Eccleston. Davies, of course, admired Eccleston enormously, and had only recently worked with him on *The Second Coming*, but reckoned the actor wouldn't be interested in the series. Entirely independently, though, Eccleston e-mailed Davies asking to be kept in mind for the role, thus resolving the writer's reservations.

In early March 2004, the *Doctor Who* team met Eccleston at Manchester's Malmaison Hotel to discuss the role. The actor suggested filming a screen test to judge his suitability, which was staged at BBC Manchester ten days later. By this point, just two other candidates were in the running for the role. Although they've never been officially identified, press rumours suggest Bill

Nighy and Alan Davies were very strong contenders. In the event, though, it was Eccleston who was announced as the new, Ninth Doctor.

Strikingly, Eccleston later told several journalists that, in forging the character of the Ninth Doctor, with his overwhelming lust for life and unconditional intolerance of oppression, he drew from a real-life model: Russell T Davies himself. Speaking to the *Observer*'s Liz Hoggard, Eccleston said that the central message of *Doctor Who*, much like Davies' own world-view, was 'seize life, it's brief, enjoy it. The Doctor is always saying, "Isn't it fantastic?", which is one of Russell's favourite words. "Look at that blue alien, isn't it fantastic? Oh, it's trying to kill me. Never mind, let's solve it."'

Given its vast subsequent success, it seems hard to believe that the earliest days of making 21st century *Doctor Who* were dogged by problems. The first production block of Series One, which began in late July 2004, was assigned to director Keith Boak, who had directed some of Davies' earliest professional scripts back in the days of *Def II*. The block in question, though, seems to have been particularly hair-raising, as indicated by shooting over-running by a week – a huge and expensive problem for the producers. All concerned have since implied that, for all their careful planning, they were still knocked sideways by the scale and complexity of the shoot.

Location filming in Cardiff city centre drew hordes of onlookers, not least fans eager to report back to online forums, often with photographic evidence. The first night's filming, using Cardiff's Working Street for the Autons' shopping centre assault, required a great deal of stunt work and proved particularly problematic – yet was still covered by a live regional news report. Several scenes from this first block were deemed unsatisfactory and were subsequently reshot. Others, for which restaging would have been prohibitively expensive, had to be ditched. Rumours began to circulate of dissent and fraying tempers among the cast and crew.

Similarly troubled was the realisation of one of *Doctor Who*'s first new monsters, the Slitheen. Intended as a blend of CGI and prosthetic body suits, there were clear on-screen discrepancies between the two versions. All relevant parties were left dissatisfied by the end result. On reflection, Neill Gorton of prosthetics designers Millenium FX confessed to *Doctor Who Magazine*, 'When we started, I wish I'd turned around at a production meeting and said, "Look, I think I'm a bit insane trying to build these in the way we'd imagined, in this time frame. We're heading for disaster here."' Of this mixture of CGI and prosthetics, Davies has since acknowledged, 'We didn't get it right.'

Further headaches were in store, too. The Daleks, or more accurately a single Dalek, was now slated to return in the sixth episode, written by Robert Shearman, seeding a full-force Dalek fleet being revealed for the series climax. But ownership of the Daleks is a tangled matter. Though designed and realised by the BBC, the very concept of the Daleks was attributable to, and owned by, freelance writer Terry Nation, who first invented them for a *Doctor Who* story back in 1963. As such, the Daleks could only make *Doctor Who* appearances by agreement with the since-deceased Nation's estate. After Shearman spent four months writing successive drafts of his episode, the BBC's negotiations with the Nation estate broke down, and there was the serious possibility that the Daleks wouldn't figure in the new *Doctor Who* after all.

Under the direct aegis of Davies, Shearman reworked his script to feature an original race of monsters as an alternative. As a fall-back, Davies considered replacing the Daleks with the Cybermen, another classic *Doctor Who* foe, for the series' all-action climax. In the event, after almost a month, Julie Gardner managed to successfully renegotiate with the Nation estate and secure the full use of the Daleks as originally intended.

All the above came to pass within the first few weeks of production. In the face of this, and continued sneering from within the industry – even within the BBC itself – Davies and the team could have been forgiven for losing heart. As Phil Collinson has said, 'I did spend the whole pre-production period, and the whole first couple of months in the job, being absolutely, abjectly terrified.' At the time, Julie Gardner conceded, 'The first block was very fraught … There have been numerous tearing-your-hair-out moments.' Davies himself later admitted to *Doctor Who Magazine*, 'It was like hitting a brick wall … There were many moments when I thought, "We could just stop production and rewrite the scripts," but we didn't … No, we hit the wall and we kept going.'

Subsequent blocks of the production period brought their own difficulties, but none was as traumatic as the first. Lessons had been learnt on the job, and fast.

Nevertheless, there was still no guarantee of eventual success. *Doctor Who* combined two major elements – family drama and science fiction – which were poison in terms of British television at the time. Attempting to launch a big-budget entry in the field, in the dead centre of primetime, seemed like TV suicide. Since *Doctor Who* came off the air in 1989, examples of British telefantasy were exceedingly few and far between. None had really proved to be a success. Instead, the most recent trend in British television was reality TV, spearheaded by *Big Brother*, about as far from small-screen SF as it's possible to get. Davies confessed to *Doctor Who Magazine*, 'I was ready for a fall, absolutely … Seriously, I'm sitting there thinking, "What if only two million people watch?" Nicola Shindler … is one of the people I trust most in the industry, but she was the one saying to me, "It's niche, it's science fiction. It doesn't matter how hard you work, it's never going to be that big." I was really worried.'

All that worry, and the Herculean effort, paid off. 'Rose' was broadcast at 7.00 pm on Saturday 26 March, during 2005's Easter Weekend. Beyond even the most fervent hopes of all concerned, it won an audience of 10.8 million. It was a remarkable achievement. There remained some concern that audience figures might drop once casual viewers had satisfied their curiosity, but, in fact, though ratings fluctuated throughout the run, they were never less than extremely impressive, averaging out at eight million.

Critical response, too, was firmly favourable. The *Financial Times* declared the new *Doctor Who* to be 'fast, funny, scary and beautifully acted.' Charlie Brooker of the *Guardian Guide*, often a fierce and unforgiving critic of popular television, opined that the third episode 'The Unquiet Dead' 'may be the single best piece of family-orientated entertainment the BBC has broadcast in its entire history … TV really doesn't get better than this, ever.' According to the *Sun*, the series had made 'a triumphant return to telly', while *Heat* magazine dubbed it 'the most ingenious primetime drama in years.'

The immediate aftermath of the transmission of 'Rose' was almost bewilderingly eventful. As the saying goes, there was some good news and there was some bad news. After just four days, basking in the episode's hefty viewing figures, Jane Tranter announced a second series of *Doctor*

Who to air in 2006, to be proceeded by an extra-long Christmas special. The following day, the press covered the story – along with the leaked news that Christopher Eccleston wouldn't be returning for the second run. The BBC was forced to confirm this, but did so by issuing a statement without first consulting Eccleston, who took exception to the manner in which it explained his decision to leave.

The subject of the Ninth Doctor's departure has since remained a matter for conjecture. The BBC's official line is simply that Eccleston only ever intended to star in the role for one series, and that the climactic regeneration was always built into the plan. As such, the press were blamed for simply blowing the twist. This does beg the question, though, why a new Doctor was to be introduced ready for a second series when a second series had, at that point, yet to be commissioned.

Actor John Barrowman has made it clear that his Captain Jack character was at one time set to return for the proposed second series, but that the plan changed when Eccleston 'quit after only one season' – allowing a new Doctor to settle into an uncluttered TARDIS with just one companion. Lending further weight to the scenario, several writers who contributed to Series Two, Mark Gatiss and Tony Whithouse among them, have since stated that they began work on their episodes featuring Eccleston's Ninth Doctor, and only changed course in that respect once the news was announced.

One possibility, then, is that Eccleston only signed for one series, with the proviso that if further series were to go ahead, he'd consider them – and that, for whatever reason, he chose in the event to leave the role. That being the case, the fact that the shoot had been so gruelling, and not always smooth, may have played a part in this decision. Only the actor himself can say for sure, and, since leaving the show, he hasn't gone on record to give his reasons. Interviewed for a BBC Radio documentary *Project Who?* at a point between the series' shoot and its transmission, Eccleston bristled when asked if he would stay with the role of the Doctor for the long run, replying, 'I've *done* the long run!'

With *Doctor Who*'s immediate future secure, though, there was the question of who would play the next Doctor – the tenth, in fact. Though the search for each new Doctor has become a media event, in this case, it was almost a forgone conclusion. The earliest press reports of Eccleston's departure had suggested that David Tennant would take on the role, and a little over two weeks later this was formally verified by the BBC Press Office.

Like Eccleston before him, Tennant had worked with Davies before *Doctor Who*, starring in *Casanova*. At one point, he'd even been one of the names under consideration as the Ninth Doctor back in 2004, but it was judged that his name wasn't quite known enough at that point. Now, with *Blackpool* and *Casanova* under his belt, the timing was exactly right. There seems to have been not one ounce of doubt among all concerned at the BBC: Tennant was their first and only choice as Eccleston's successor.

Prior to *Casanova*'s transmission in March, the actor had been watching one of the finished episodes at Davies' home in Manchester when Julie Gardner whispered the magic words 'Doctor Who' in his ear. Later, once Gardner asked him outright and he realised the offer was serious – that, should *Doctor Who* be granted a second series, he was being asked to star in it – Tennant's initial reaction came in the form of gales of laughter. He went on to give the matter some days' serious thought before finally accepting.

Doctor Who had not merely staged a comeback. Now, it had a future.

TWELVE:
EVERYTHING CHANGES AND YOU'VE GOT TO BE READY

Even the staunchest optimist might have suggested that the extraordinary success of the 2005 series of *Doctor Who* wasn't a phenomenon that could be sustained and repeated. When Series Two went on the air in 2006, Davies himself expected a backlash and a downturn in ratings figures. It's testament to the sheer quality of what the BBC Wales team were producing that the backlash failed to kick in.

David Tennant was installed as a confident, vivid Tenth Doctor, and the nation's viewers took him to their hearts. The ratings also remained extremely strong, with in excess of eight million viewers for six of the 13 episodes. The 'Christmas Invasion' special, which aired at primetime on Christmas Day itself, introduced Tennant's Doctor to an audience not far short of ten million viewers. By the time 'The Runaway Bride' aired exactly a year later, *Doctor Who* Christmas specials were being talked of as a beloved British institution, when it was in fact only the second of its kind. Long-term, die-hard fans may still bear the woe of those lost, hopeless years, but to the average viewer it began to seem as though *Doctor Who* had never really been away.

Between the special and the second series, Davies wrote six of the sophomore *Doctor Who* episodes, on the face of it a lighter workload than the eight episodes he wrote for the first run. No one could reasonably accuse him of shirking, though. His involvement with the series as a whole – every script, and indeed every single aspect of production – made for a punishing schedule, particularly in light of the huge popularity that the revived *Doctor Who* had won.

As before, Davies sketched out the rough shape of each episode, its tone and the setting, before other writers began work. In the case of one episode, 'Tooth and Claw', one of these other writers – 'a great writer, in fact', Davies has since hinted – worked up a draft script that was quickly deemed unworkable. In the event, the writer pulled out and, at the eleventh hour, Davies himself penned a replacement script. It's since emerged that, of the

Series Two episodes credited to other writers, several were heavily reworked by Davies before shooting began. Indeed, those writers with relatively limited professional experience were contractually obliged to allow these rewrites.

Nor were these the only script worries facing Davies and the team. Celebrated performer and novelist Stephen Fry was signed up to pen an episode for *Doctor Who*'s 2006 run. The result, said to have centred on King Arthur, reached only an early draft stage when, for reasons of time, Fry was forced to withdraw. In its place, Davies brought forward 'Fear Her', a script by Matthew Graham initially pencilled in for the third series.

Speaking to *Newsround*'s Lizo Mzimba on the eve of Series Two's broadcast, Davies revealed that, perhaps surprisingly, his involvement with *Doctor Who* was not set down in any contract. In theory, he could have walked off the show, or the BBC could have dismissed him, at any time. Of course, given that the show had proved to be such a sizable hit, there was little chance that the corporation would dispense with the mastermind behind its revival. But by 2006, Davies, for his part, had a clear plan in mind for his future career, and for how long they would involve working on *Doctor Who*.

The overall quality of the second series was somewhat variable, but *Doctor Who* continued to thrive. By Series Three, it even survived the loss of one of its most iconic characters, Billie Piper's Rose Tyler. Initially, Davies considered installing a Victorian servant girl as the Doctor's new companion, but blanched when he realised this would mean all the series' ties to modern-day Britain would have to be severed. Instead, he devised Martha Jones, another, albeit slightly older, woman from contemporary London, adeptly realised on screen by Freema Agyeman.

Cannily, the impact of Rose was built into Martha's very character. The audience, like the Doctor himself, naturally mourns the loss of Rose, and keeps this new companion slightly at arm's length. Martha herself longs to be closer to the Doctor – as close, in fact, as Rose had been, if not closer. So it is that Martha's story is one of unrequited love, a Davies staple that can be traced back to *Queer as Folk*, *Bob & Rose* and *Casanova*.

Unrequited love isn't a state of affairs that can be sustained indefinitely, and sure enough Martha baled out of the TARDIS once she realised exactly where she stood, at the close of Series Three. For a time the replacement companion lined up for Series Four was known by the *Doctor Who* team as Penny, intended as an older, more self-assured woman who could stand her ground against the Doctor – with no obvious traces of love in the air. The sparkling screen chemistry between Spencer Tracy and Katherine Hepburn was the pattern from which the new Doctor/companion relationship might be fashioned.

Before long, Davies realised that Penny already existed. As a character, she was much in the same vein as Donna Noble, a one-off guest turn from BBC star Catherine Tate for the 2006 Christmas adventure 'The Runaway Bride'. At first, engaging an in-demand performer like Tate for a full series seemed unlikely, but when, in a wide-ranging meeting with Julie Gardner, the idea was put to her, Tate agreed enthusiastically. Thus was the embryonic Penny usurped by the returning Donna Noble as the full-time companion for *Doctor Who*'s Series Four in 2008.

The series in question proved to be another hit with viewers, and it seems likely that *Doctor Who*'s short-term – who knows, maybe even long-term – future on BBC1 is secure. With the demands of modern broadcasting, such things are never entirely certain, but Davies himself has asserted that *Doctor Who* could just conceivably run for another 20 years.

Davies has successfully revived many existing elements of the *Doctor Who* universe – the TARDIS, the sonic screwdriver, the Master, Davros, the Daleks, Cybermen, Autons, Sontarans, even Macra. But he's also added a handful of vivid new elements to the myth: the Time War, the Face of Boe, psychic paper, the Slitheen, Judoon and Ood.

As it stands, Davies' contribution to *Doctor Who* makes up a very considerable body of work. By Christmas 2009, he'll have written a grand total of 30 episodes of the show, eight of which are an hour in length, the remainder 45 minutes long. There are celebrated TV scriptwriters whose total career output can't equal this. For Davies, it's just one entry on his CV. However, no other show he's worked on can be compared to *Doctor Who* in terms of sheer numbers. Only *The Grand*, for which he worked on 18 episodes over two years, comes close. Even put together, *Queer as Folk*, *Bob & Rose* and *The Second Coming*, three of Davies' most celebrated pieces of work, run to less than 19 hours of screen time.

Not that these figures matter, of course. It's quality, not quantity, which really counts. Of Davies' *Doctor Who* scripts, the quality has varied quite a lot. Arguably, some of his episodes are rather makeweight and functional: for example, 'The Long Game', 'The Runaway Bride', and the series openers and finales might disappoint those expecting Davies at his very best. Others, however – such as 'Rose', 'The Christmas Invasion', 'Tooth and Claw', 'Utopia' and 'Voyage of the Damned' – rocket along with such wit and panache that only the stony-hearted could fail to enjoy them.

But some of Davies' very best writing for *Doctor Who* comes in the form of episodes that aren't so driven by high-octane comic-strip adventure. Rather, they take the series and its characters into stranger, more affecting territory. 'Boom Town' takes a returning villain, 'Margaret' the Slitheen, and shows her utterly defeated. Her beloved brothers are dead, and her deadly schemes for a new power plant are foiled without ado by the Doctor. Facing gruesome execution on her home world, Margaret spends an evening appealing to the Doctor for clemency in a Cardiff restaurant. Davies' working title for the episode was 'Dining with Monsters', and when Margaret attempts to fire a poison dart at her captor during the meal, the image – a poisoning over dinner – echoes both *Mine All Mine* and *The Second Coming*.

Series Two's 'Love & Monsters' divided viewers sharply by bending the format and indeed the tone of *Doctor Who* as never before. Certainly, it's an incisive depiction of how 'fan groups' work, but moreover it tackles human friendships in a manner that's otherwise unseen in the show. It's a demonstration of Davies playing to his true strengths. 'Gridlock' is much more imaginative and action-based, but by restricting most of the action to the tiny passenger communities within New Earth's fleet of trapped vehicles, and indeed the community formed between the vehicles, Davies is once again focusing on character, and notions of faith, with hugely satisfying results.

Prior to Series Four's blockbusting climax, Davies takes two episodes to examine the main characters in turn. 'Midnight', much like 'Gridlock' before it, is set on an immobile vehicle; in common with 'Love & Monsters', it's all about a mini-community. In the course of the piece, as the Doctor comes into conflict with the sourest edges of human nature, pure dialogue assumes new-found importance. Here, perhaps, are the fruits of those devised pieces

7/8/1993

Davies developed as a member of West Glamorgan Youth Theatre all those years ago. 'Turn Left' is much less enclosed, but in showing Donna in a more desperate, haunted light than *Doctor Who* usually can, the character, aided immeasurably by Catherine Tate's performance, engages the viewer in a way that the space opera trappings never do. In episodes such as these, Davies is writing at the peak of his powers, delivering remarkable material – powerful meditations on friendship, fate, faith and paranoia – for a mainstream family audience at Saturday tea-time.

On balance, Davies' particular take on *Doctor Who* – as he's said himself, he simply doesn't care about the Zog Monster on the Planet Zog – might be considered a double-edged sword. In writing powerful human, or at a push humanoid, drama, Davies' characters engage the *Doctor Who* audience on an emotional level that's rarely been attempted on screen before. On the other hand, there are times when, by its very nature, the series simply demands its Zog Monsters, and Davies appears less comfortable with such space opera trappings. Hence, perhaps, 'Love & Monsters' and 'Midnight' can seem infinitely more satisfying to the seasoned Davies fan than the likes of 'Last of the Time Lords' and 'Journey's End'.

It's entirely possibly that Davies' wide-ranging responsibilities on *Doctor Who* may at times have diverted him from the basic business of writing scripts. Moreover, his overarching perspective on the series seems on occasion to have reined him in as a writer. In the Series Two episode 'The Girl in the Fireplace', writer Steven Moffat created a scene in which the Doctor rode a horse through a huge mirror and crashes into a period ballroom, supposedly in Versailles. Realising this scene presented enormous problems to the production team. For a time, it was deemed impossible, and an alternative stunt was considered. In due course, though, a solution was found: the scene was shot as written. Reflecting on this, Davies acknowledged that, with his responsibilities as show-runner, he would simply have stopped short of writing such a demanding scene. The fact appeared to give him pause for thought.

There's a tight structure at work in each separate series of *Doctor Who*, as conceived by Davies. Each begins with an opening episode that emphasises the Doctor's character and his relationship with his companion – either introducing, or effectively reintroducing, the companion character. These opening episodes are light on plot and feature antagonists who are scheming and troublesome rather than utterly evil, and who are, eventually, quite easily despatched. The result's a breezy adventure full of spectacle that's intended to prove inviting to returning viewers. By way of reinforcing the show's format, the opening three episodes of each series alternate between a contemporary Earth setting, a futuristic setting, and a visit to Earth history, in some combination.

As the series goes on, a pair of two-part stories straddle the midway point, with darker, more involved stories held back until later in the run. Key elements including the return of the Daleks and the Cybermen are unveiled around the mid-series point, seeding their involvement in the finale. Other elements – the Satellite 5 station in Series One, or the species-altering chameleon arch in Series Three – make their first appearances around this juncture too. Running themes such as Bad Wolf, Torchwood, Mr Saxon and the phenomenon of missing planets begin to make their presence felt with more references as the series goes on, to come to fruition in the two-part series climax, most often set on contemporary Earth.

Davies has been very frank about the resistance he faced from fellow TV professionals when he took on *Doctor Who*. 'I had people in the industry looking at me in the eyes and saying, "What on Earth are you doing it for?" I had really big, important people saying, "Why? Why waste your time on that thing?"' On the same theme, in an introduction to the published Shooting Scripts of Series One, Davies wrote, 'There are some sniffy people in the TV industry who have asked, archly, why I'm now writing genre, instead of drama. Obviously they've never watched a single episode of *Doctor Who*. It's the best drama in the world.'

On the face of it, reviving an often-derided family SF show may have appeared an odd choice for the writer at that point in his career. But look a little deeper and it becomes clear that Davies' *Doctor Who* is very much of a piece with his previous work.

On an obvious level, a whole host of people he'd worked with before found themselves becoming part of *Doctor Who*. Christopher Eccleston and David Tennant, of course, had previous Davies form. But so too did numerous guest actors, including Penelope Wilton, Anne Reid, Daniel Ryan, Jo Joyner, Lesley Sharp, Jocelyn Stevenson, Jo Stone Fewings, Claire Rushbrook, Nina Sosanya, Dervla Kirwan and Debbie Chazen. In smaller roles, the cast list of virtually every episode of *Doctor Who* features performers who have appeared in earlier Davies ventures.

Davies had, of course, already worked with Julie Gardner on *Casanova*, and incoming producer Phil Collinson had been Granada's script editor back on *Springhill*. Composer Murray Gold had perhaps the richest pedigree of long-term Davies colleagues, having provided the music for all the writer's collaborations with Red Productions bar *Bob & Rose*.

There are tiny echoes of Davies' earlier work in his *Doctor Who* stories, too, from favourite recurring names – Tyler, Jones, Saxon, Harkness, even *Queer as Folk 2*'s Mickey Smith – to larger elements. The Editor of 'The Long Game', with his short blonde hair, dark clothes and sinister schemes, would appear to be a descendant of *Dark Season*'s Mr Eldritch. Both lurk in dark rooms peering at monitor screens with their minions. A device from *Springhill*, an attempted international exorcism in the form of mass emails all containing the phrase 'burn the witch', is mirrored by the worldwide chanting of the Doctor's name at the climax of 'Last of the Time Lords'. Even the acronym LINDA – the 'London Investigation 'n' Detective Agency', as seen in 'Love & Monsters' – was formerly the 'Liverpool Investigation 'n' Detective Agency' in an adventure for the *Why Don't You?* gang back at BBC Manchester.

But it goes even deeper. As we've seen, like any writer, Davies has favourite themes and preoccupations that crop up in everything he's written, and they're certainly present and correct in his version of *Doctor Who*. Television itself is used constantly. In the first episode, Rose Tyler follows developments around the fiery destruction of her workplace via the TV news, from the safety of her family sofa. 'Aliens of London' takes this further. When an alien spacecraft clips Big Ben and crash-lands in the Thames, the Doctor struggles to cross London to investigate, until Rose tells him, 'We could do what everyone else does. We could watch it on TV.' And that's exactly what they do. The Doctor quickly assimilates the importance of the medium: by the end of the episode, on arriving at Downing Street, he's waving for the cameras. By the time of Series Four's 'The Stolen Earth', Harriet Jones' broadcasts on the sub-wave network are actually of vital significance to the plot, allowing the Doctor and his associates to stay in contact.

An identical technique is used in several of Davies' *Doctor Who* episodes, including 'The Christmas Invasion', 'Army of Ghosts', 'Smith and Jones', 'The Sound of Drums' and 'The Stolen Earth': key plot elements are unveiled in the form of TV news footage that characters are watching. Montages of fake foreign news bulletins reinforce the idea that such events are of global significance. Also, these plot developments are echoed in other specially constructed TV 'excerpts': a recipe for a spaceship cake on *Blue Peter* or a scene of a ghost materialising in *EastEnders*.

In this respect, 'Aliens of London' begins to resemble a hall of mirrors. Having established that, even at the level of family entertainment, television draws on current events for inspiration, the plot builds up to a missile strike necessitated by the supposed discovery by 'our inspectors' of 'massive weapons of destruction, capable of being deployed within 45 seconds'. It's a blatant reference to the real-life reasons cited for launching the Iraq War in 2005: current events being echoed by family entertainment – which shows its own fictional current events echoed by televised family entertainment.

In the far future of 'The Long Game', the TARDIS lands on a news broadcasting space station. The setting is revisited in 'Bad Wolf', but by that time the station is making endless TV game shows. The episode 'Gridlock' even opens with a supposed news broadcast on New Earth in the far future. Admittedly, it's not unheard of for television to feature in *Doctor Who* episodes that Davies didn't write. But such instances are few and far between, whereas in a Russell T Davies story, there's usually something, be it a glimpse of *Trisha*, an election advert or a news bulletin, just around the corner.

Religion, another favourite Davies topic, crops up regularly both in episodes that he's written and those scripted by others which he has overseen. At the climax of Series One, the Doctor faces off against the Emperor Dalek, the self-styled 'God of all Daleks', intent on forging 'Heaven on Earth', to whom non-Daleks are 'heathens' capable of little more than 'blasphemy'. In Series Two's 'The Satan Pit', written by Matt Jones, the TARDIS crew encounter a vast demonic creature chained in the bowels of the planet:

it may be the source of every representation of the Devil, or it may
even be the Devil himself.

On a regular basis, even the Doctor is actually referred to as a deity.
According to Margaret the Slitheen, he 'might as well be God'; in the myths
surrounding The Face of Boe, the Doctor's identified as a 'lonely God'.
Often, the impact of his visits is comparable to that of a visitation from the
heavens. The final shot of Series Four's 'Fires of Pompeii' is of a shrine
depicting the Doctor, Donna and the TARDIS. At the conclusion of the
following episode, 'Planet of the Ood' by Keith Temple, the grateful Ood
tell the Doctor and Donna, 'Our children... and our children's children ...
The wind and the ice and the snow will sing your names forever.' In his own
words, spoken in the closing moments of 'The Satan Pit', the Doctor and his
companion are 'the stuff of legend'.

More general religious overtones are also rife in *Doctor Who*. In 'Last of
the Time Lords', the Doctor is only freed from the Master's tyranny when the
entire population of the Earth chants his name at exactly the same moment.
To all intents and purposes, as the Master himself points out, it's a 'prayer'
routed through the worldwide Archangel telecommunication network, which
transforms the Doctor into a spectral, floating being, charged with power.
Hot on its heels, in 'Voyage of the Damned' comes the image of the Doctor
ascending upwards borne by angels – actually the robot Hosts – to confront
his foe.

Clearly, Davies' *Doctor Who* isn't meant to come charged with pro-
religious ideology. The writer is an outspoken atheist. But he uses the ideas
and imagery of religion to explore how such ideas form, and just what it
would be like for such a being as the Doctor to exist. When questioned in
Doctor Who Magazine about his use of seemingly Christian imagery in the
show, Davies asserted, 'But that's mythological imagery ... that existed
way before Christianity – of the saviour, of the better being, of elevation.'
Nevertheless, the fact that his *Doctor Who* episodes use these ideas so freely
is extremely striking. That a primetime family TV show can, at least on
some level, explore what it means to be God-like, is greatly to be admired.
Just because Davies himself doesn't believe in it doesn't mean he can't
be fascinated by the implications of it. In 'Gridlock', when the trapped

inhabitants of New Earth are released from below ground, they are heard to sing the hymn 'Abide with Me', which Davies, intriguingly, considers to be 'one of the most beautiful songs ever written'.

But Davies' own world-view is present and correct in *Doctor Who* as well. In 2005's 'The End of the World', the Doctor shows Rose the sun-torched death of the Earth, before returning her, shell-shocked, to the safety of her own time and telling her, 'You think it's going to last forever, people and cars and concrete. But it won't. One day, it's gone. Even the sky.'

Of course, the Doctor is a prime example of Davies' use of 'lonely gods'. On the face of it, the Doctor looks human and behaves exactly like one. But he's special: centuries old, fiendishly clever, the last of an alien race able to change his physical appearance and cheat death – quite apart from his ability to travel through time and space. As Davies' Doctor says when we first meet him in the 2005 episode 'Rose', 'I can feel it. The turn of the Earth… That's who I am.' Being special elevates him above those around him, and being elevated makes him lonely. He craves companionship, but he can't easily connect with 'mere mortals'. His very 'specialness' is both a blessing and a curse. In this respect he's not so very different from *The Second Coming*'s Steven Baxter, or even *Mine All Mine*'s Max Vivaldi or Giacomo Casanova.

In the 2007 series of *Doctor Who*, the Doctor meets his match: a fellow Time Lord, thought extinct. The Time Lord in question, the Master, is, in his own way, just as much of a lonely god. In fact, at first he's an ordinary man, one Professor Yana. At the key moment, he realises his true identity in an extraordinary rush. It's a direct echo of Stephen Baxter's 'downloading' of his godly nature in the first moments of *The Second Coming*. Thereafter, the Master's tale concerns how he adapts to this revelation and how it impacts on those around him. In practice, the Master's a lonely god gone bad, who uses his gifts to lay waste to the Earth and subject its people to his tyranny. Similarly, Davros sets himself up as a lofty yet friendless creature, capable of acts of both breathtaking creation and literally limitless destruction.

The series acts as Davies' fanfare for the common man, in which the Doctor's greatest gift is his ability to bring out the best in the ordinary mortals around him – mortals who, on countless occasions, save his skin. As so often in Davies' work, *Doctor Who*'s main character attaches himself to a surrogate family of friends. The Doctor's own experiences of family are only hinted at, but seem laden with sadness. His family – his entire people – were lost in the Time War. In Series Four, he's seen to acquire a 'daughter', Jenny, but he loses her before the episode's out. (Although Jenny survives, the Doctor's unaware of the fact.) The companions he surrounds himself with have awkward family lives of their own: Rose's father died when she was a baby, Martha's parents are separated and at loggerheads, Donna's wedding day went spectacularly wrong and she's moved back in with her mother.

By contrast the surrogate TARDIS family seems to be less dysfunctional, and certainly it's much more exciting. Initially the 'family' has additional floating members (Mickey, Adam and Jack) and, in due course, the Doctor's various associates bond with each other. Martha joins Jack for a while in *Torchwood* and then works side by side with Donna when battling the Sontarans. For the climax of Series Four, a whole variety of companions and friends, from Rose, Martha and Donna to Jack, Sarah Jane, Jackie and Mickey, provide the Doctor with a vital support network. The ties that bind them all are not blood ties, but they're shown to be so important that life on Earth literally depends on them. (A version of this plays out, in miniature, in 'Love & Monsters', where the members of LINDA nourish and support each other until death.) The fact that these episodes see faces familiar from *Torchwood* and *The Sarah Jane Adventures* crossing over into *Doctor Who* seems to bear out Davies' assertion that he seriously believes the characters from his oeuvre as a whole 'all live in the same world!'

Much has been made of Davies' handling of sexuality in *Doctor Who*. To some observers, having made his reputation with the likes of *Queer as Folk* and *Bob & Rose*, he could be identified as a 'gay writer'. It's about as lazy and reductive an assessment of his output as can be. When the series was first announced, the least imaginative British tabloids even speculated that, under Davies' aegis, the new Ninth Doctor would surely be gay, which neatly sums up the small-mindedness at work. In practice, Davies' deployment of homosexual characters in *Doctor Who* is delicately judged. Simply by showing the occasional character to be gay, in a dialogue aside or a signal, Davies is endeavouring to 'normalise' it. So, in 'Midnight', Sky Silvestre says of her ex-partner, 'She needed space'; in 'The Stolen Earth', when facing death, Captain Jack holds and kisses his lover, Ianto Jones.

Captain Jack might be *Doctor Who*'s most utterly liberated character where sex is concerned, but in writing Jack's debut story, 'The Empty Child', it was Steven Moffat, rather than Davies, who fleshed Jack out in quite such open-minded form. In the same story, Moffat implies that married man Mr Lloyd is 'messing about with Mr Haverstock the butcher' – strong stuff for 1941.

In practice, Davies is highly conscious about how pervasive representations of homosexuality on television can be. Back before his ascension to *Doctor Who*, in early 2003, he'd lodged a formal complaint with the BBC about, of all things, an episode of the revived children's show *Basil Brush*. In the episode in question, during a scene at their local café, Basil's human pal Mr Steve decides to make a move on a long-haired woman stood at the counter with her back to him, and duly goes in to kiss her. Except, on turning round, it transpires that the woman in question is actually a long-haired man – who promptly punches Steve for his pains.

The fact that the incident is structured as a gag infuriated Davies, who later wrote a full-page piece for the *Guardian* explaining his reaction. 'The punch is literally a punchline ... I ranted to myself and stomped around the kitchen, reduced to Disgusted of Tunbridge Wells, despairing at the state of television today'. The writer of the controversial likes of *Queer as Folk* taking the makers of *Basil Brush* to task might, on the face of it, seem unlikely. Even Davies admitted as much. 'For me to complain about anything feels rather like poacher-turned gamekeeper,' he wrote, 'and I don't suit tweed.'

But while acknowledging that 'it seems pitiful to analyse such a slight joke', Davies felt that, at its core, the show was making a gag out of a violent homophobic reaction. 'In the eyes of Long-Haired Man, Steve was gay, and – perhaps the worst crime in the world of Long-Haired Men – he assumed Long-Haired Man to be gay also.' Most distressing of all to Davies was the thought that this dubious message would be imprinted on young viewers by the very nature of children's scheduling, wherein shows are repeated almost endlessly. 'Repetition is at the core of this ... The younger the audience, the more impressionable. They're learning behaviour and they learn a lot from TV.'

TWELVE: *EVERYTHING CHANGES AND YOU'VE GOT TO BE READY*

The writer was moved to complain to the BBC upon noticing that the episode was already being repeated heavily. The BBC, he wrote, had 'promised to investigate, and might well decide I'm talking nonsense, though I look forward to arguing the point.' In the event, Davies' oblique solution was neat and proactive. By the end of 2003, he'd been installed at the BBC to make his own family-viewing show, wherein he pursued a more responsible agenda than the minds behind all-new *Basil Brush*.

At the other end of the scale, on the death of gay TV star John Inman, a piece in the *Guardian* criticised Inman's best-known role, *Are You Being Served*'s Mr Humphries, as a one-dimensional gay stereotype. Davies was quick to respond, and his letter was published by the *Guardian* days later. 'As a young gay viewer I loved the character,' he wrote, 'and even watching it now, it strikes me that in a sitcom full of failure and frustration – as the best British sitcoms are – Mr Humphries was the only one with an active, successful sex life.'

Davies has cited a whole range of influences on his revival of *Doctor Who*. Some, like *Smallville* and *Buffy the Vampire Slayer*, are self-evident. A great admirer of these US fantasy TV series, Davies drew on their breezy, postmodern tone in reconfiguring *Doctor Who*. In particular he aped the structure of *Buffy*, wherein each season builds towards a climactic showdown against a major threat, known as the 'big bad'. (Even the phrase 'Bad Wolf' carries echoes of this.) And if Davies saw the new Doctor's companion as being just as important as the Time Lord himself, it's telling that the companion herself, Rose Tyler, was, like Buffy before her, a young blonde woman with remarkable reserves of intelligence, wit and stamina.

Another key influence is provided by the family-friendly films of Disney and Pixar. Davies is outspoken in his admiration for the likes of *The Lion King*, *The Little Mermaid* and *Toy Story*. The way that these films impact on *Doctor Who* is oblique (though *The Lion King* has even been quoted on screen by the Doctor), but it's their approach, rather than their content, that can be detected. Disney/Pixar tell stories for all ages in a bright, fast, very visual fashion, in a tone that can veer from dry and comical to highly emotive but never becomes mawkish. The mere fact that families across the country were sitting down together to watch, and indeed endlessly rewatch, these films helped convince Davies that the fabled family audience, long thought lost in TV circles, existed still, and could be tapped into by a fresh take on *Doctor Who*.

Davies' lifelong love of comics has fed into *Doctor Who*, too. The wildly imaginative storytelling of Marvel Comics and *2000AD* has always appealed to the writer, and a comics feel – bold, fast and vivid – suits the series down to the ground. Sometimes, the influence is specific, such as the resemblance of The Judoon to *2000AD*'s Judge Dredd or the consciously Marvel-esque mad scientist of 'The Lazarus Experiment'. Certain elements of 'The Voyage of the Damned', not least guest character Astrid Peth, are particularly reminiscent of *2000AD*'s 'The Ballad of Halo Jones', as written by comics maestro Alan Moore.

More than anything, though, it is the comics' grounding in a highly visual brand of storytelling that can be discerned in *Doctor Who*, with its arresting vistas of spaceships crashing into Big Ben, Cybermen marching on the Taj Mahal, and stolen planets hanging in space. 'I am a very visual writer,' Davies suggests, 'and I think very often *Doctor Who* gives you the chance to do pictures like you'd never have the chance to do on any other piece of television.'

Under Davies, *Doctor Who* has a very particular ethos, which naturally enough is very much in line with the world-view of the head writer himself. Speaking to Phil George in 2006, Davies said, 'The only thing I've banned [in *Doctor Who*] is the use of the word 'evil' ... The Doctor has never turned round and described someone as evil, because I just won't allow it ... It's the only thing I just won't have him say at any point.' In fact, the word in question has been used, in the Series Two episode 'Fear Her', written by Matthew Graham, but by another character, and it's quickly dismissed. Faced with an unknown threat lurking in the vicinity, the elderly Maeve insists, 'It's evil!' – only for her neighbour to counter, 'I don't believe in evil.' A little earlier in Series Two, in the episode 'The Impossible Planet', the Doctor discusses the notion of the Devil with guest character Ida, who professes instead to believe in 'the things that men do.' 'Same thing in the end,' reckons the Doctor.

It's notable, too, that many of the foes Davies has launched at the Doctor have very specific motives. It's not possible in all cases: the likes of the Daleks, the Cybermen and the Master, returning baddies from the show's past, were already established as being driven by pure megalomania, or a desire to conquer, survive and propagate themselves. But of Davies' own creations, the Slitheen are a space-going family business, the Judoon are yomping mercenaries, and the Ood are a slave-race – that is, a commodity. The Adipose's nanny Miss Foster and the cat-nuns of New Earth are basically over-eager professionals, happy to deploy catastrophic methods in maximising their productivity. Elsewhere, in 'The End of the World' Cassandra is prepared to slaughter her contemporaries on Platform One in the name of financial gain. In 'Voyage of the Damned', Max Capricorn plans to wipe out a ship full of passengers, not to mention the population of South East England, simply to avoid bankruptcy.

In other words, commerce, pure greed for hard cash, is the force that spawns much of the death, destruction, suppression and wrong-doing at large in the *Doctor Who* universe, at least as Davies sees it. In a similar vein, Davies' villains often gravitate towards the powers of public office, Margaret the Slitheen as Mayor of Cardiff, and the Master as Prime Minister.

Davies' *Doctor Who* is in fact a show about death. From the very start, the Doctor seems haunted and grief-stricken, somewhere below the surface. According to Clive, the Doctor's obsessive 'stalker' in 'Rose', death is the Time Lord's 'one constant companion'. Even the Doctor himself asserts grimly, 'Everything has its time, and everything dies.' But it's also a fundamentally optimistic show, as befits Saturday tea-time viewing. That might seem to be a contradiction, but ultimately it's about optimism in the face of death: the importance of friendship, wonder and beauty in an often dangerous universe. In 2005's 'The Long Game', set in humanity's far future, the Doctor himself sums this up: 'You lot, you spend all your time thinking about dying. Like you're gonna get killed by eggs, or beef, or global warming, or asteroids. But you never take the time to imagine the impossible. That maybe you survive...'

Estimating Davies' importance to the success of *Doctor Who*, producer

Phil Collinson puts it at '100 per cent. *Doctor Who*'s rebirth is entirely down to Russell's vision. I mean, a lot of us have worked very hard. But without his plotting, his vision of the characters, his help finding the look and feel of the drama, the balance of the comedy, and mostly without his brilliantly razor-sharp scripts and ideas, the show wouldn't be half as robust as it is. It could have gone so wrong in less capable hands. With Russell it soars, because even aged six you know when something is good.'

Davies, in his capacity as *Doctor Who*'s executive producer, is, Collinson explains, 'intrinsically involved with the whole running of the show, choosing directors and Heads of Department with me, watching cuts, dubs and grades. That means that we have a uniquely close working relationship, I think. His scripts are incredible, too. He's just so, so hard working and so, so clever. Usually when you read a first draft, no matter how good the writer is, you look for ways to improve it or take it closer to what you see as your vision of the piece. With Russell you can't do that because it's just well authored and I often find myself with not a single note. I'll ask questions, seek clarification on things – Russell's plotting is so tight and his storytelling so imaginative though and no one knows his scripts better than him. I know too that he's a ruthless self editor – often the script that lands on my desk is a third or fourth draft for him and stuff he'll have discussed with me during his planning process will just not be in there.

'Whenever I've asked him, "What about that bit where the Zog-monster uses the Thingummy to do whatsit?" he'll explain why that bit, brilliant though it was, didn't work and why he came up with this other idea that is much better. As a producer that has one main effect on you – it makes you want to do justice to his work. He toils so hard that you think, "I should work that hard too – make this the best thing he's ever had produced."'

Paul Cornell believes that Davies has stamped his mark firmly on the show, and applauds his willingness to work in the mainstream. 'It's Russell's show,' Cornell nods. 'It's like Johnny Cash playing pop music. I think it's fantastic that a writer as good as Russell wants to make pop music, and some of it is the best pop you've ever heard. You can detect him on *Doctor Who* keeping the Saturday night mainstream audience in mind all of the time, and I've never heard him using that tone of voice before. Even on ITV primetime shows he's written, you can't feel any kind of concession. On *Doctor Who* – and this is absolutely the right thing to do, by the way – I think he's tremendously aware that it could fail; that they might hate it. And so there are always two or three fail-safes. There's something that will keep people watching at every moment. I think that nervous energy is what's made it such a big hit. It's the first aerodynamically tooled big hit which television has ever seen!'

So resounding was the success of *Doctor Who* that it made waves far beyond the show itself. Sales of the official *Doctor Who Magazine*, to which Davies contributed a regular monthly behind-the-scenes piece called 'Production Notes', went through the roof. When the BBC launched another magazine, *Doctor Who Adventures*, aimed at younger readers, it managed to build up an even bigger readership. A new set of BBC spin-off novels sold remarkably well. For Christmas 2005, sonic screwdrivers, *Doctor Who* action figures and radio-controlled Daleks were the must-have toys for British children.

The impact was swift. Clearly, the fabled family drama audience was alive and kicking, and could be capitalised on. ITV commissioned *Primeval*, a Saturday night adventure show about a team of time-travelling dinosaur hunters. The BBC launched a fresh primetime version of *Robin Hood* and began developing a new series centred on Arthurian magician Merlin. Both shows were accompanied by a barrage of merchandising.

Almost inevitably, *Doctor Who* spawned direct TV spin-offs, too. The first, *Torchwood*, began production in April 2006. It was intended as a more adult equivalent of the *Doctor Who* experience, to be broadcast in a post-watershed slot due to its liberal 'sex and violence' content. Devised by Davies, it was a case of killing two birds with one stone. It provided the Captain Jack character, and thereby actor John Barrowman, with his own vehicle, and it did so by revitalising the *Excalibur* series idea that Davies had cooked up with Julie Gardner in the years before *Doctor Who*. Alongside Jack was a shadowy team of operatives based in Cardiff, monitoring extraterrestrial activity with an often ruthless eye.

To launch proceedings, Davies penned the opening episode himself, under the title 'Everything Changes' (although, until very near to transmission, it was to be called 'Flotsam and Jetsam', in reference to the ragbag Torchwood team.) The opening sequence, in which Cardiff policewoman Gwen Cooper accidentally witnesses the team bringing a murder victim back to life, had been in place since the earliest existence of the *Excalibur* pitch. Fascinated, Gwen manages to track Captain Jack down to the Hub, the team's HQ, and becomes embroiled in the search for an alien glove that can resurrect the dead. In time Gwen finds herself being invited to join Torchwood.

Structurally it's very reminiscent of Davies' first *Doctor Who* script, where Rose Tyler goes to similar lengths to locate the mysterious Doctor who so piqued her interest when their paths happened to cross, and in tracking him down becomes part of his 'team'. At the episode's climax, team member Suzie is revealed as the perpetrator, and is duly shot by Jack. Killing off a character who seems, until that point, to be established as a regular is quite a shock tactic. A precedent for this had been set by both *Spooks* and *Buffy the Vampire Slayer*, with both series electing to kill off a seemingly established lead character in one of the very earliest episodes of the run. In *Torchwood*, as in *Spooks*, this technique helps to establish just how hazardous being involved in the team can be.

Davies' opening episode of *Torchwood* is fast, stylish and involving, setting up oodles of dramatic potential for what's to come. Transmitted from October 2006, the show was a creditable ratings hit. It was hoped, at one stage, that Davies might pen at least one additional episode of the run, but in the event it proved impossible. It's unfortunate as the rest of the first series of *Torchwood* was often flat and uninspired, taking the dark, moody elements of 'Everything Changes' as a template but overlooking its streak of wit and cheek. The second episode, 'Day One', involved the arrival of an alien shape-changer who fed on the sexual energy of orgasm. While Gwen and her team mate Owen Harper conduct a secret pressure-cooker affair, their dialogue is laden with baffling expletives. A later episode, 'Countrycide' [sic], was rooted in fairly graphic depictions of cannibalism.

All fair game for a post-watershed series, of course, but at times *Torchwood* came across like an adolescent child swearing to prove how grown-up it was, succeeding only in looking hopelessly immature. With *Doctor Who* established as breezy, colourful, optimistic and family-friendly, *Torchwood* appeared to be straining too hard to forge its own very different identity, often to the detriment of the end result.

Later episodes in the run achieved a better balance, but in all the public reception to the show was very mixed. In his *Guardian Guide* reviews, though, critic Charlie Brooker opined of *Torchwood*, 'It's not really clear who it's aimed at ... Thirteen year-olds should love it; anyone else is likely to be more than a little confused. Which isn't to say *Torchwood* is bad. Just bewildering. And very, very silly.' Come the end of 2006, Brooker went on to appoint *Torchwood* 'Year's Most Jarring Show', concluding that it 'managed to feel like both a multicoloured children's show and a heaving sex-and-gore bodice-ripper at the same time.' In the wake of reactions such as this, the *Torchwood* format was rethought somewhat. On one point, though, viewers were in absolute accord: the show made Cardiff look amazing.

Just as *Torchwood* was aimed at *Doctor Who*'s older audience, another show was devised by Davies to appeal to the series' younger viewers. In the first instance, he was approached by CBBC, the Corporation's digital channel for children's programming, with a view to discussing a potential spin-off – a nice piece of synchronicity, as it turned out. 'I fancied the challenge of writing something for children based on *Doctor Who* at the same time as CBBC were keen on something,' Davies later told *Radio Times*. Initially, CBBC bosses mooted something along the lines of *Young Doctor Who*. 'There was talk of the adventures of the young Doctor on Gallifrey,' Davies recalls, 'but I said absolutely not.'

Instead, he made a suggestion of his own. Sarah Jane Smith, played by Elisabeth Sladen, had been a hugely popular *Doctor Who* companion between 1973 and 1976, a period of the show particularly dear to Davies' heart. The reappearance of the character in the 2006 *Doctor Who* episode 'School Reunion' had made a considerable impact, and Davies had tentative plans to bring her back for the show's third series. Now, though, there was a perfect opportunity to provide Sarah with her own spin-off vehicle, duly christened *The Sarah Jane Adventures*.

This had, in fact, been tried before, in 'A Girl's Best Friend', a pilot for a projected series to be called *K9 and Company*. It was broadcast over the festive period in 1981 and, as the title suggests, it teamed Sarah with another well-loved *Doctor Who* companion, the robot dog K9, whose popularity among young viewers ensured that he received top billing. In the event, although the ratings were healthy, a change of executives at the BBC meant that the project was canned before a series was made. In the *Doctor Who* universe, though, the two characters, Sarah and K9, were now stuck with each other. They appeared together in *Doctor Who*'s anniversary bonanza 'The Five Doctors' in 1983, and remained as such in 'School Reunion'.

But the rights to the K9 character lay with scriptwriters Bob Baker and Dave Martin, who first created him for the *Doctor Who* story 'The Invisible Enemy' in 1977. Baker and Martin had long harboured hopes of launching K9 in his own (non-BBC) animated show, and so his involvement in Sarah's latest spin-off was restricted to little more than a cameo – quite possibly, considering the prop's famous unreliability, to the relief of the show's directors.

In the final analysis, one of the most striking facts about *K9 and Company* is that it was the only concerted attempt to create a *Doctor Who* spin-off show during the series' original run – and didn't succeed. The 21st century version was more successful. Broadcast in a children's slot on 1 Jan 2007, during the same seasonal period as 'A Girl's Best Friend' before it, the series' hour-long opener, 'Invasion of the Bane', was a considerable success. Strictly speaking, it wasn't a pilot episode, as that would imply it was testing the waters for a full follow-up series that was yet to given the green light. In fact, by the start of 2007, the first series of *The Sarah Jane Adventures* was already in production: 'Invasion of the Bane' was merely an extra-length seasonal special to launch the show.

The series was set around a school, with Sarah Jane investigating mysterious (ultimately, alien and hostile) goings-on and linking up with some local schoolchildren in the process. In this respect, it was 'School Reunion' that acted, unwittingly, as the series 'pilot'. Back down the chain of evolution, Davies' *Dark Season* – which itself informed elements of 'School Reunion' – might seem to be the original granddaddy of *The Sarah Jane Adventures*, in which bright, troubled Maria and her school pals use their wits to defeat extraterrestrial menaces week after week.

With his career having gone stratospheric, and his schedule insanely busy, it proved impossible for Davies to write 'Invasion of the Bane' single-handed. Liaising closely with Julie Gardner, who was to act as co-executive producer on the show, he devised the series' format, and the recurring characters, even providing a bare-bones outline of the story for the special. Gareth Roberts was brought in to turn Davies' ideas into a full script. 'That was always the plan,' Roberts explains. 'Essentially Russell and Julie gave me the characters and set-up and a very loose story idea, which then went through two or three drafts at my hand. Then Russell came in and buffed it up.'

Initially, there were plans for Davies to contribute a pair of episodes to the series that followed, but, in the face of his already gargantuan workload, this fell through. Comprising ten episodes, made up of five two-part stories, the series was broadcast between September and November 2007 across the digital CBBC channel and an afternoon children's slot on terrestrial BBC1. Despite his lack of direct script input, Davies remained very actively involved in his capacity of executive producer. Gareth Roberts went on to write four episodes of the first series, and reckons Davies' contribution to the show was considerable. 'He's always there at meetings, and gives tons of feedback and advice,' Roberts says. 'Whenever I work with Russell I have a massive surge up the learning curve. He's been around, you know! He's either made the mistake you're making or he's seen somebody else make it. Often he's conscious of things that would never even cross my mind. I'm the Spike to his Ted Bovis.'

Aside from its popularity with its young target audience, *The Sarah Jane Adventures* has won many admirers among older *Doctor Who* fans, who have often likened it to the 1970s glory days of their beloved show. 'You know, I think that's largely because of two things,' Roberts says. 'First, the budget means we have to use less CG so we concentrate more on prosthetics. Second, there isn't really any sexuality – CBBC shows are aimed squarely at 12 and under nowadays, after all. That's not to say we shy away from the reality of emotions and relationships, it's more that we tend to focus on the emotional stuff that children are interested in. Parenthood, growing up, friendships…'

Davies' hands-on involvement with *The Sarah Jane Adventures* might not be easy to detect, but evidently the same fount of ideas and enthusiasm that brought forth the revived *Doctor Who* has touched its junior spin-off. Spirited, inventive and funny, it won very healthy ratings for its slot and inspired its own rash of merchandising – toys, books and DVDs. Unsurprisingly, a second series was commissioned for late 2008, with Davies staying in place as executive producer – but, once again, not involved as a writer.

Nor, despite early high hopes, could he find time to write the opening episode for the second series of *Torchwood*, which aired in January 2008. As late as April 2007, Davies was set to script the episode in question, to have taken place in the eerie setting of an all-night supermarket, before his workload simply became overwhelming. In promoting the second run of the show, there was a palpable sense of mistakes having been learnt from. Speaking to *Deathray* magazine, Julie Gardner explained, 'We wanted to warm up the second series … We needed to inject a bit more fun, a bit more charm, a bit more humour … In doing that, the tone has become more cheeky.' 'That,' Davies told *Deathray*, 'was the one thing we got wrong last year, where things just skipped a groove.' Setting out its stall, the first episode of the new series opened with a pensioner nearly being flattened on a pedestrian crossing by a sports car driven by an alien resembling a blowfish. As the car speeds off, the old dear mutters, 'Bloody Torchwood!' This distinctive pre-credit sequence was actually Davies' own work, a fleeting hangover from his plans to write the whole episode, and it acts as a bold, cheeky statement of intent for all that comes after.

The series that followed rejigged the *Torchwood* formula extensively, and proved eventful for the main characters. Captain Jack gains a recurring nemesis, one Captain John, a fellow Time Agent, and a slow-burning story about Jack's lost brother, Gray, threads through the series. Martha Jones, late of *Doctor Who*, is seconded to the Torchwood team for three episodes. Gwen's boyfriend Rhys is made privy to the truth about the nature of her job, and even becomes a semi-detatched member of the team himself. Gwen's affair with Owen has evaporated, and in a development echoing Suzy's death in the very first episode, Owen is killed – but resurrected as a virtual zombie. He's killed off properly, along with Toshiko, at the series' climax. Perhaps more significantly in production terms, episodes were repeated on BBC2 in a re-edited form suitable for its pre-watershed slot. Now, young *Doctor Who* viewers could track the activities of Jack and Martha away from the glare of their parent show.

TWELVE: *EVERYTHING CHANGES AND YOU'VE GOT TO BE READY*

Ratings were very healthy, and a third series was commissioned to air in 2009. Though planned as a shorter run of just five episodes, forming one overarching tale entitled 'Children of Earth', the third run of *Torchwood* will graduate, in *Doctor Who*'s absence, to BBC1, and Davies is slated to write the opening episode. Indeed, even after leaving *Doctor Who* itself behind, the plan is for Davies to stay at the helm of the spin-offs he's created, assuming they remain in production. 'I will, if they continue,' he told Radio 5's Simon Mayo. 'I love those shows and I feel honour-bound to the casts, Liz Sladen in *The Sarah Jane Adventures* and John and Eve in *Torchwood*. When we created them I sort of said, "I'll be here for you". So unless they want rid of me – which is possible! – I'll probably stick with those.'

Yet a further *Doctor Who* spin-off was suggested to the BBC by Davies, in the wake of his writing Rose Tyler's dramatic exit for the end of Series Two. With Rose, in story terms, stuck on a parallel Earth, fending off alien threats as part of a mirror-image version of *Torchwood*, the character was left in a situation rife with story possibilities. *Rose Tyler: Earth Defence* was proposed as a feature-length special following Rose in her new capacity, for broadcast on the May Bank Holiday of 2007, with the possibility of further such specials to follow every year. Sure enough, Julie Gardner pitched the idea to Peter Fincham, then Controller of BBC1, who commissioned the project and assigned a budget to it. Only then did Davies balk at the idea, feeling that, on reflection, Rose should remain off screen after her separation from the Doctor. As swiftly as it had been dreamt up, the project was abandoned.

It's telling, though, that a *Doctor Who*-related idea that even its creator had doubts about could come within a hair's breadth of going into production. The phenomenal success story of the show knew no bounds. In 2007, between the show itself, *Torchwood* and *The Sarah Jane Adventures*, BBC Wales was making a total of 37 episodes for network broadcast, as well as behind-the-scenes documentaries such as *Doctor Who Confidential* and *Torchwood Declassified*. *Doctor Who* and its spin-offs would be on air almost all year round. If Julie Gardner's mission had been to infiltrate the national mainstream with Welsh-made TV drama, no one could fault her for succeeding.

T IS FOR TELEVISION

After two years of filming *Doctor Who* in a converted Newport warehouse known as Q2, BBC Wales built a dedicated new production facility, housing, among other things, standing sets such as the TARDIS interior and Torchwood's Hub. For Davies, this development was a matter of almost confrontational pride. In his April 2006 column for *Doctor Who Magazine*, he wrote, 'I still find plenty of moaners complaining that the much-longed-for BBC Wales Drama Department isn't what they wanted, simply because it's making huge primetime dramas with worldwide sales, instead of small intense shows called *I Was Born in Wales and I'm Cross*. Episode One: 'Daffodil'. Well, sod your small-nation thinking. Camelot is here; we built it while you were whingeing.' Camelot was briefly an in-house nickname for the new facility, which was ultimately christened Upper Boat.

In terms of scripts, Davies might not have contributed much to *Torchwood* and *The Sarah Jane Adventures*, but he devised both shows, wrote (or co-wrote) their crucial opening instalments, and guided their progress in his executive role. Look a little closer, though, and even the series' formats are very Russell T Davies. The Captain Jack of *Torchwood* isn't quite the cheeky, good-humoured Jack of *Doctor Who*. In *Torchwood*, Jack becomes distant, mysterious and authoritarian. This aspect of Jack makes him another in Davies' pantheon of 'lonely gods'. He's travelled the galaxies, journeyed through time and can't die. As such he lives life at one remove from those around him – that is, the Torchwood team. His gifts and his experiences mean he lives his life in a heightened fashion, though it isn't always a happy place for him to be. We learnt a little about the families of the lead characters, via Jack's childhood and Gwen's home life, but their actual families are often troubled and dysfunctional. Their surrogate family, the Torchwood team, is where they seem most at home.

It would be pushing the point to tag Sarah Jane as one of Davies' 'lonely gods', but in many ways that's how she operates. Certainly, she's lonely. Her experiences with the Doctor (and beyond) mean she sees life in a special way, but a way that leaves her isolated from those around her. Her salvation is the surrogate family she forms – literally, in the case of Luke, but also in taking local children Clyde and Maria under her wing. Maria, too, is seen to have a troubled family at home that she escapes by pitching in with Sarah and company.

Inevitably, the team that first brought *Doctor Who* back to TV screens
in 2005 began to fracture, as the individuals concerned moved on. Mal
Young, one of the show's instigating executive producers, never had the
heavy day-to-day involvement with the production that his cohorts did.
Young left the BBC, and consequently *Doctor Who*, in early 2005, before
the series even went on air, while Davies and Julie Gardner stayed on as
executive producers. During the making of Series Three, the workload of
producer Phil Collinson was shared with the experienced Susie Liggat, who
came in to oversee two episodes. Liggat went on to shoulder responsibility
for five episodes of Series Four and, when production ended, Collinson
moved on from the series to take up a new post as Head of Drama in his
native Manchester. Meanwhile, Gardner announced that she would give up
her responsibilities as *Doctor Who*'s executive producer as of 2009, once
production of that year's run of four special-length episodes was complete.

The sheer volume of acclaim showered upon Davies' *Doctor Who*
must have left him astonished, and hugely gratified. A volley of National
Television Awards, Hugo Awards, Royal Television Society awards and
BAFTAs, both Welsh and national, was received by the show. Davies'
personal contribution was recognised, too. At the 2006 Welsh BAFTAs, he
was given the Siân Phillips Award for Outstanding Contribution to Network
Television. The following month, at the National BAFTAs, he received the
Dennis Potter Award for 'outstanding writing for television'.
By the time the fourth series was being previewed to the press, Davies had
become weary of incessant questions about when exactly he'd leave the
show. Finally, in May 2008, it was officially announced that he would step
down as *Doctor Who*'s show-runner after four extra-length specials to be
shown during 2009. Davies is to write all four, though two will be co-written,
the first with Gareth Roberts and the other with Phil Ford. Davies' departure
will also coincide with that of David Tennant's Doctor. As had been widely
mooted, Steven Moffat was announced as taking on Russell's role for the
show's projected fifth series, now set to launch the new, eleventh Doctor.
Davies himself confessed that his own private plans to leave had been in
place since 2006.

So, is this really the end of Davies' involvement in the show? When asked, on the eve of the broadcast of Series Two, if he'd continue to write for the series once he stepped down as show-runner, Davies replied, 'No. Once I leave, I'll … hmmm. I don't know. Who knows? Um … It's *so* much work. I don't think I could dabble in it. It is mountains of work. *Mountains* of work. And also there are other things I want to write. I think when I do leave, it'll just be a clean break, and … wish them luck!'

On the other hand, speaking to Mark Lawson for a BBC Four interview prior to the announcement that he was leaving, Davies confessed that he had firm plans for 2009 but, as to whether *Doctor Who* was involved, he teased, 'It … might be! It's far more complicated than you think, actually. It will be in all sorts of shapes and forms...' And when Lawson followed up with a question about a possible film version of *Doctor Who*, Davies gave a politician's reply: 'That would be nice ... Do you think the world's ready for that?'

THIRTEEN:
MOVING ON

On 14 June 2008, less than three weeks after it was made public that he would be moving on from *Doctor Who*, it was announced that as part of the Queen's birthday honours list Russell T Davies was to be awarded an OBE for services to drama. It's not an honour that's commonly afforded to TV writers. 'I'm delighted to accept,' he said, 'and I hope it does the whole industry a bit of good, for the writing of television drama to be recognised.' He's confessed that his decision to accepted the honour was heavily influenced by the knowledge that it would make his father, now 83, very proud. There can now be little doubt that Davies is currently the most high-profile writer in British television. His name does not seem to be losing its lustre, with the *Independent on Sunday* downgrading him just one place in their 2008 list of influential gay figures – from first place to second. According to his 2007 *Media Guardian* ranking, he's currently the 15th most powerful figure working in the British media.

Few TV writers or executives have ever been as publicly visible as Davies. In promoting *Doctor Who*, he has been seen as a guest on everything from *This Morning* to *Blue Peter* and *BBC Breakfast*. Whenever he's recognised in the street, he assumes that it's because of his regular appearances on BBC Three's *Doctor Who Confidential*. When he writes exclusive pieces for *Radio Times*, his name makes the cover. Curiously, though, he's admittedly that he has never joined the British Writer's Guild union, on the grounds that he can't quite see his profession as a proper job. Instead, to him it's a calling and an obsession.

Where Davies' career is headed from this point is anyone's guess, but in theory at least, his options must be almost limitless. Perhaps the most significant point about his success with *Doctor Who* in career terms is not the scale of the audiences, or the merchandising, or even the critical acclaim. It's the fact that many important industry professionals doubted that it could succeed, and Davies proved them wrong. He has demonstrated an almost magic touch, and it's surely that quality that broadcasters will be clamouring hard to secure in years to come. According to his friend and colleague Frank

Cottrell Boyce, 'Russell's magic is that he has genuinely populist tastes – he loves a good Saturday night – but he also has the courage and ambition of an artist. It's a Damon Albarn, Stevie Wonder, Hergé-like quality.'

As to the question of what happens next, the immediate answer would appear to be a return to Davies' favourite themes and people. For the whole time that *Doctor Who* has been conquering the airwaves, Davies has been formulating plans for a new drama, thus far known only by the codename 'MGM' – that is, 'More Gay Men' – with Nicola Shindler at Red Productions. Initially, it was hoped to go into production during 2006. The whirlwind success of *Doctor Who* put paid to that. 'We've got an idea which is like a more mainstream and updated *Queer as Folk*,' reveals Shindler, 'about 40-year-olds rather that 30-year-olds, but not about the same characters.' The initial inspiration for the premise, as it stands, was a comment made to Davies by his friend Carl Austin, who was named Mr Gay UK in 2001. As Davies told the *Guardian*, 'He asked me, "Why are so many gay men glad when we split up?" That remark's stayed with me for six years.'

Although Davies has said that 'MGM' will concern contemporary middle-aged gay men, he's made it clear that in the writing it could change completely. Indeed, in retrospect he's admitted that some of his comments to the *Guardian* – 'It's going to be about 40-something gay men and how jealous they are of gay teenagers' – were merely 'ideas' that he was 'throwing out' to see how they sound. 'I read that back in the interview and thought, "Well, that's boring isn't it?",' he later told Mark Lawson. 'So I don't know. But something in that area. Something domestic.'

The biggest complication will be the extent to which his current workload is so different from the majority of his career. *Doctor Who* has been a phenomenal success, and has rightly been hailed as introducing material to a mainstream family audience that simply had no parallels at the time. But it is still a very populist property, so will he be able to move back to writing projects that interest him, rather than ones that may be perceived as popular, or even 'safe'? Shindler's use of the word 'mainstream' in relation to 'MGM' might give us some indication. On the other hand, it's known that in May 2007 Davies was approached by Lucasfilm to write for their forthcoming *Star Wars* television series, and demurred. Clearly, he's looking to take on very different challenges from hereon in.

One of the greatest surprises of the success of *Doctor Who* is that it was a hit at all, given its patchy heritage. While all involved were hoping for a hit, it was never taken for granted until the new series had been seen by viewers. Even when writing dramas for primetime viewing on a mainstream channel, such as *The Second Coming*, there tend to be ingredients in Davies' work that might alienate the audience at large. But then, has he ever really written for anyone other than the audience at large? He's expressed his joy that *Queer as Folk* reached beyond a gay viewership, and his time at Granada consisted of attempts to make shows that were both interesting and popular. It's more the case that Davies has endeavoured never to alienate part of the audience or make a non-mainstream programme. He loves popular television.

On the topic of *Pop Idol* and similar ITV ratings-grabbers, he declares himself to be a huge fan. 'I do genuinely love it,' he says. 'You get a writer like Tony Marchant, who I've met lots of times, and he sort of dies inside when he hears me go, "Ooh, isn't *Pop Idol* marvellous?" He's genuinely affronted by that sort of material, for very good reasons. I can't describe his reasons very well because I don't agree with them, but he would put me in my place for saying this. So everyone's different. That's just my take on it. They're there, on ITV, to sell advertising space, and no one's denying that. If you get ten million, you've got something right. If you get four million, you've got something wrong, and I think you live or die by those rules.'

Indeed, Davies is also a fan of reality television, and will gladly watch anything that piques his interest on TV, whatever others' preconceptions may be. 'The producers and editors on those shows are great dramatists. They're telling stories, and they're completely honest about that. They talk about them as stories. On *Big Brother* they say, "What story are we telling today?" And they shape a story with what they've got. And you've got to soak it up. It's such brilliant stuff. You mustn't sit there as a writer thinking, "Oh, I'll just watch *Daniel Deronda* and one *EastEnders* a month."'

But this is more than just an interest in watching television in itself; Davies actually feeds off all types of programming as inspiration for his drama. 'You hear things on reality television that you would never write in a million years,' he says. 'That very first *Wife Swap* couple, they were sitting in their little flat and everything and the husband says to the wife, "I thought we weren't having any more pets?" And she said, she honestly said, "That was before I learnt a rabbit can be trained to live indoors." You couldn't make that up in a million years. What a fantastic thing to say! And I'll use that one day!'

To a degree, Davies' ear for comical but naturalistic dialogue may well have its roots in the grande dame of the style, *Coronation Street*. There's also the question of Davies' own heritage. Much of his dialogue is rhythmically similar to his own frenetic Welsh speech pattern, though he dismisses the suggestion that his Welsh identity shapes his writing to any degree. 'Sarah Harding, who directed the second block of *Queer as Folk*, always says that I write very musical scripts. Very lyrical, very rhythmic. But I don't know. There's that old cliché about the Welsh and lyricism. And there is a certain amount of language to it, and rhythm, which is why I wanted to write *Mine All Mine*. I wanted to get that rhythm out, slightly. But not really, no.'

Nevertheless, there is a strongly Welsh element in much of his work on the various *Doctor Who*-related spin-offs. Of course the series is predominantly shot in Cardiff, but that doesn't necessarily mean that it must have a Welsh flavour. (Consider the North American *Queer as Folk*, which was shot in Canada but was firmly rooted in the US on screen.) But there is a reason for the occasional highlighting of Wales.

'I do, politically, have an attitude on that,' Davies says, 'which is that I think the Welsh aren't on screen enough. You do *Mine All Mine*, and that fails, and now we do *Torchwood*. Something I love about that is that if something fails, you should do it again! You don't lick your wounds and run away. After *Mine All Mine* I remember people going, "There'll never be another Welsh drama on telly for 20 years." And I was like, "No – I've got another one!" Never give up. Never listen to all those people saying, "Oh, it'll never work." I genuinely get fed up of seeing plenty of Scottish and Irish characters on television, and not the Welsh. I think what you have to do is normalise it. A lot of episodes of *Doctor Who* have a Welsh accent in them. I do that on purpose. I'll write a character called Professor Llewelyn – you've got to make him Welsh then!'

Television itself was obviously an important part of Davies' cultural heritage, and his passionate love of the medium remains fundamental to his work. This fact is no mere side-note to his career. His knowledge of and interest in the whole of television underpins everything he writes, and the time he's spent watching it has helped him develop his style. 'They always say to writers, "Keep your ears open on the bus, and when you listen to your family" and stuff like that,' he suggests. 'But also, listen to television as well. Discerningly: you've got to filter out the shit. When you hear bad dialogue – "I feel hurt, betrayed, alone" – you've got to realise that's rubbish, but also, listen for the good stuff.'

However, the most visible aspect of this love of the medium is in the referencing of television programmes, both popular and obscure, among the everyday preoccupations contained in many of his scripts. 'I very much like that [2006] White Paper when the Government said they should put entertainment in the mission statement for the BBC. Which was very unexpected. You expect a White Paper to be saying, "Oh, politics … news … weather." And stuff like that. And I think it's funny putting a dividing line between entertaining and informing. Good entertainment is far beyond that.'

Indeed, Davies sees television as more than just a technical method of transmitting dramatic material. He embraces the way that it influences those watching it, and makes a genuine, lasting impact on their lives. Not just in terms of political opinion or thought-provoking dramas, but in every strand of entertainment. 'Phil Collinson and I were talking about *Only Fools and Horses* and that moment when Del Boy falls through the bar. It's like, how many times have you seen that? And it's still funny, after all these years. That's not just entertainment. That becomes a little part of your head. It becomes part of the colour of the way you think about things. It's actually part of your life, not just entertainment. There's no such thing as a piece of television that just entertains.'

Television, to Davies' mind, does not need to be worthy to be worthwhile. Of the celebrated *Only Fools and Horses* bar scene, he reasons, 'It hasn't educated me. Well, I suppose I've learnt not to lean on bars without looking! But the brain is so much more complicated than that. I think we're just all bits and sums of a thousand million things. This is silly, but Vanessa Feltz used to have a column in the *Daily Express*. She once talked about how her grandmother used to wash up, and it was very hot water so your hands are scalding. And that's the way I like to wash up. So now, every time I wash up, I think of Vanessa Feltz's grandmother! How random is the world that your connections are so barmy?'

Davies' dramas can have the same effect. Certain young viewers of *Dark Season* have eyed wooden stages in school halls with suspicion ever since. But more than this, his adult dramas can have a lasting impact on the viewer even if they aren't seeking to make a statement.

Regarding television as a whole, Davies is upbeat about its current direction. He probably has a better notion of how drama has progressed throughout television's history than most of his contemporaries, but he shies away from criticising the most recent trends. Quite the opposite, in fact. 'To be honest I think the state of television is quite healthy, and I get sick of people saying it's a terrible age. I'm always getting asked to give a speech at the RTS, or a speech at this, or a speech at that. And I'm always turning them down, because I can't fucking stand it when people like Jimmy McGovern are saying, "All drama on ITV is crap." What a load of bollocks. I love him for being so opinionated, but actually *The Grand* is the sort of show he's talking about. And maybe it was bollocks at the time, but if it wasn't for that, I wouldn't be where I am now. What a stupid thing to pipe up and say, "All those dramas are rubbish." Like all those writers have failed him.

'I know, in many ways, I'm lucky,' Davies admits. 'But actually, like all lucky people, all I did was work hard. There are a lot of opportunities. When I was starting out writing, it was the nursery slopes, of your soaps and your one-hour dramas, and when I was young, it was *Coronation Street* or nothing! And now there are a million things! All those shows packed with all sorts of children's stuff, and BBC Three stuff. I'm sure it's still hard, very hard to get into it, but actually, frankly, not as hard as it was. And if you really have sent off ten dozen scripts and never got anywhere, then your scripts are no good. Because there are so many outlets now.'

Sometimes Davies seems almost perverse in his refusal to agree with widely accepted definitions of 'quality' television. Most significant in this regard is his championing of ITV, but this may also have its roots in his previous criticism of aspects of the BBC. It has been widely speculated that the corporation used *Doctor Who* as bait for Davies to work for them. Whether true or not, it's unlikely he would have approached them under different circumstances at that point in his career. As he points out, ITV had treated him very well, never requesting that he toned down any of his projects. All his major ITV projects have been assigned to desirable 9.00 pm slots, at least at first, indicating confidence in Davies from the outset.

Davies rails against preconceptions of what is 'good' television. 'You've just got to get rid of that stupid notion of it's all bad, or it's all good,' he says. 'It's just all changing all the time. And it's completely beyond anyone's control as to where it's changing, but the one certain fact is that you get old. You get old, and whatever is coming up behind you will make you look old, and will be told in forms that you could never understand. Like your mum and dad can't understand how to operate the video. I remember thinking, "I understand videos. I understand this. I'm never going to let technology leave me behind." And it *is* now starting to leave me behind. We've got an MP3 player, and I'm still not quite sure how it works. It's the shape of the world. Whatever shape drama's going to take in the future is beyond any amount of prediction. One person can tilt it, or maybe a huge movement can tilt it, but you cannot predict where it'll go. You shouldn't even waste time trying to.'

Davies himself is rarely driven by trends. His dramas are always sufficiently distinctive to have little kinship with other hit programmes of the time, and as such could have been commissioned and written at any point. The key is a strong central idea, and beyond that Davies works out the rest of the drama. There is no check-list of plot devices or requirements. 'You read those interviews with people who go, "I get up at six and I have some muesli and I listen to Radio Four and then I will do 2000 words before 10.30." And you think, "Oh, fuck off!" I tell you who I once read saying that in an interview: Maeve Binchy. Have you ever read a Maeve Binchy book? Terrible. Absolutely terrible! The only time I read a Maeve Binchy book, I was in hospital with appendicitis. It was so bad it was making me hurt! And she talks about discipline like that.'

Davies' approach is somewhat different. 'I'm terrible. I treat it like homework,' he admits. 'I leave it and leave it and leave it, and then panic. That's the reason why being a writer's the best job in the world, because actually, for me, it doesn't happen that much when you're typing. It's when you're walking around, pottering about in W H Smith in a little world of my own. I can actually think about scripts while watching telly. I'm doing it now while I'm sitting here talking! I'm thinking, "Ahhh, I'll shift that scene…" That's why it's a brilliant job. It goes on all the time. And that's why it's a bastard job at the same time, because you go on holiday and it's still ticking away in there. But that's no hardship, that's brilliant.

'A lot of writers forget that it's a job,' he suggests. 'They get hung up on the artistic side, and think they're entitled to get drunk and storm through doors and say, "I can't possibly cope with this. I'm being creative." It's like, "Tough shit. Get real. It's a job." You get paid well, and I think you have a responsibility for that money to sort of behave, and be professional.' Understandably Davies favours the hands-on approach for the writer during filming. 'Writers should absolutely be on set, and it's happening more and more. With Red Production Company, it's Nicola Shindler's policy to encourage writers to be on set, unless they look like being loose cannons.'

Davies seems to advocate this presence on the set because it enables the writer to be involved in the process of presenting the story on screen; he is less keen on mixing with actors socially. On the topic of his working relationship with actors, he recounts a tale from early in his career. 'I was working with this woman. A terrible actress, but nice, sweet woman. We were all out for a drink once and her husband took me to one side. He was sort of physically threatening towards me, because I didn't give her enough dialogue. He was drunk, saying stuff like, "My wife's the best actress in the whole show!" Looming over me, and I'm hard to loom over! "She's brilliant, and you've got these scripts completely wrong. She's never in it."

'And literally an evening of my life was lost with this man having a go at me, quite aggressively. Do you know what? I never wrote another word for her again on that show! She vanished. And no one ever asked me why, because they knew what I'd gone through. As a writer you have a lot of *power*, in the end, so don't get too close to them.'

By the same token, he is keen that those working in television should never be too detached from the real world. He has a particularly strong memory of an incident that fuelled his antipathy towards what he sees as the irrationally high kudos attached to working in television. 'When I was back on *Why Don't You?* at BBC Cardiff, I remember casting a boy from up in the valleys who became the *Why Don't You?* book reviewer. He was just a little Welsh kid, and the night before he was due to come into the studio and do his piece to camera, his father drove him down to BBC Wales. They parked up the car and they sat outside, and his father said, "That's where you're going to be tomorrow." Now, I despise that adoration. I remember him telling me that and me saying, "But it's us! It's me, with a cup of tea!" It's just a building full of people who work. We shouldn't be put on a pedestal, and I'm so glad all that's fallen away.'

With Davies now so well respected, though, he's most likely on a pedestal of his own in the industry. What, then, do his colleagues make of his career path and his likely future? 'I don't know that he's necessarily followed a plan,' says Phil Collinson. 'I think his scripts have always been incredibly inventive. He's always been interested in the out of the ordinary, the unexpected, and he's always tried to find different ways to tell stories about ordinary people who become or are in some way extraordinary. He has a huge loud lovely family himself – and a happy one – and that's always been a fascination in his work. He writes families well, and understands the relationships that bind them and push them apart. The most successful part of the new *Doctor Who* is how he gives Rose a grounding, a reality and a sense of 'now' that it's never had before. She's a real young woman who comes from an absolutely real 2005. That's what Russell's always done – keep it real. No matter what' happening, hether it be inheriting a town, coming out or discovering you are the Son Of God, he absolutely convinces you of the plausibility of it.'

Certainly we have seen how thematically of a piece so much of his work has been. As Collinson points out, the grounding in reality has been a crucial aspect of his work. But equally interesting is the diversity of the types of drama he's made, from the dark and foreboding to the light-hearted. When asked if she has a preference for the type of project she would like to tackle with Davies in the future, Shindler is happy simply to wait and see. 'I think Russell should write whatever he wants to write!' she says. 'That's the brilliant thing about him. He should go wherever the ideas send him. If he next has an idea that is a huge mainstream idea, he should do that. If he next has an idea that is a tiny dark obscure thing that he has a passion to write, then he should make that. With Russell it's all about his drive and his desire to do it, and that's all it needs. That's true of any writer. You shouldn't ever push them in a certain direction.'

Shindler highlights Davies' most recent work as perhaps his most influential. 'He's made a lot of good stuff. I think with *Doctor Who* especially, he's made it more possible for people to do mainstream drama that has quality to it, with ideas and humour in it. I think he's brought humour to a lot of dark subjects. If writers watch that carefully, they'll see that if you work really hard and make yourself a producer on something and stay at the centre of it, then you can really make a difference. But most writers are lazy, and they'll probably ignore that!'

Paul Cornell is intrigued about what Davies' next move will be in the wake of the vast acclaim and media attention afforded *Doctor Who*. 'It's going to be seductive, isn't it?' Cornell says. '*Doctor Who* is his only primetime hit. And it's an enormous hit, a broadcaster-changing hit. You wouldn't have got *Life on Mars* without it, or any of the other telefantasy shows that have come along since. But what he does next is going to be really interesting. He could go on and be Dennis Potter, or a Stephen Poliakoff, and get the best of both worlds. I'd like him to go and kick a few doors down again. *Queer as Folk* changed the world. Saved people's lives. I'd love to see him do something that would be shown at 4.00 am on Channel Four. Other than *Springhill*!'

However, Davies has now proved that he doesn't need an obscure place in the schedules on a non-mainstream channel to write an interesting and different, or even groundbreaking, drama. He simply does not accept the perceived restrictions of writing for 9.00 pm on ITV. And when he did, with *The Grand*, the results did not play to his usual strengths.

There's a (not always glorious) tradition of successful TV playwrights turning their hand to directing their work. Is Davies tempted to follow suit? Let's not forget, he trained, during his Children's BBC days, as a director, and went on to gain some hands-on experience. 'I was a full sort-of four-camera studio director, and I did some single camera directing as well,' he recalls. 'I loved it, and I'm sure I will direct one day. The collaboration between writer and director is marvellous, though, and although it can be painful sometimes, it can work when you actually get someone else's genius thrown into it.'

But Davies confesses to the first stirrings of a change of heart. Matt Greenhalgh, Nicola Shindler's husband, had worked as third assistant director on *Queer as Folk*, rising to first assistant director status on *Queer as Folk 2*. In the years since, Greenhalgh has gone on to make his name as a scriptwriter. He won much acclaim for his script for the big-screen Joy Division biopic *Control*, and once wrote a BBC Three drama, *Burn It*, for Red. Greenhalgh directed, as well as wrote, the final three episodes of the show, and Davies was mightily impressed. 'For a start he directed them brilliantly, but the most interesting thing was that there were things he had written that he wouldn't have written if he wasn't directing it. And that really opened my eyes. They were beautiful, beautiful scenes. Actually they were silent, completely visual scenes. I've always sort of gone, "Oh, I'll direct one day, but I'm not bothered with it really, let's trust the professionals." Watching those three episodes started to shift my head.'

Of course, at this stage there's no reason to assume that Davies' future career will stay entirely within the boundaries of broadcasting. 'I'd love to do a graphic novel,' he reveals. 'The world of graphic novels has changed so much now. Ten years ago I'd have said I didn't have the skill to draw it. Now, it's much more relaxed and there's all sorts of badly drawn things! There are more honest graphic novels now. You can have stuff published that might not be polished, but has got something to say. So, one day!'

He seems to have little interest in building on his youthful experience and writing for the theatre. 'I wouldn't even know how to get people on and off stage,' he claims. 'I'm so used to television script language now. I should have a look at that.' Instead, it's possible that Davies has a novel in him. His two books thus far, namely the *Dark Season* novelisation and the *Doctor Who* adventure *Damaged Goods*, may not have been of enormous literary significance, but they certainly proved fun to write.

'I loved doing those,' he admits. 'That was genuinely brilliant to do, to just sit there on your own … It's the most solipsistic form of work you can do. It's limitless, absolutely limitless. What I liked about that was you could have a character walk from his front door to his television. And in the space of him walking from his front door to his television in his head he could have been thinking about his childhood, what he was doing tomorrow, who he loves, who he doesn't … Extraordinary thing to write actually. Not that I'd mastered it at all, but that was fascinating to write. Probably the most tempting thing to look at, one day. But I have to say I'm happy with what I'm doing, so I'm not rushing to change.'

Davies' one-time CBBC mentor Ed Pugh reckons that his possibilities are almost limitless. 'I kind of imagine,' Pugh says, 'that he might go off and write a musical, or something like that. I think he'd write a bloody good one. He's still young. Frighteningly!'

It's fascinating to speculate on the course of Davies' future career. Can we expect *Bob & Rose: The Musical*, perhaps? Then again, his choice of projects has never been predictable. To move from an uninhibited late-night drama about gay men to a family drama about a man who travels the universe in a Police Box would be remarkable enough. But for the intervening years to encompass the bawdy adventures of Casanova, a family inheriting the whole of Swansea and the second coming of Jesus makes for a uniquely diverse portfolio

Nevertheless, the recurrent motifs and distinctive dialogue demonstrate that Davies has an identifiable voice that's present throughout his work. Whether a critical success or not, his projects almost always provoke strong reactions from the viewing audience. In many cases, those projects seen by the fewest viewers, like *Springhill* and his work for Children's BBC, are particularly important examples of Davies telling the stories that he wants to tell in the manner he wants to tell them. These more obscure works contributed to his development as a writer, but his more high-profile successes have helped to shape British TV drama as a whole.

Davies is the best-known 6'6", bespectacled, gay, colour-blind Welsh atheist in the business, and at this point television is his oyster. He's still struggling to give up smoking, and has the telly on all day long. 'Never has it off,' clarifies Collinson. 'Even when he's upstairs writing he still has the TV on downstairs. It's his hobby and his life. It should be, though. How can you be in the TV industry if you don't watch what's being made? What people are saying and doing.' Indeed.

The last word, however, should go to Frank Cottrell Boyce. Asked what Davies' greatest contribution to British television drama has been, he says simply, 'Saving it from extinction.'

APPENDIX

FILMOGRAPHY

As writer unless otherwise stated; original tx dates in brackets.

Why Don't You? (various roles including assistant floor manager,
   studio director, producer and writer, BBC 1, 1985 – 1990)
Play School (as presenter, BBC 1, 01.06.87)
On the Waterfront (sketch material, also script editor, BBC 1, two series, Apr 1988 – July 1989)
Def II (uncredited sketch material, dates unknown, BBC 2, c.1989)
Breakfast Serials (also producer, BBC 1, September – December 1990)
Children's Ward, aka *The Ward* (assorted episodes as script editor, producer and writer,
   ITV / Granada, 1991 – 1996)
Dark Season (BBC 1, six episodes, 14.11.91 – 19.12.91)
Families (as storyliner, ITV / Granada, c.1992 – 1993)
Chucklevision (BBC 1, episodes 'A Lazy Day', 24.10.92;
   'Rich For a Day', 28.11.92, 'Spooks and Gardens', 26.12.92)
Century Falls (BBC 1, six episodes, 17.02.93 – 24.03.93)
Cluedo (Series 4 opening episode 'Finders Keepers', ITV / Granada, 19.04.93)
Do the Right Thing (uncredited script material, exact dates unknown, BBC 1,
   two series, March 1994 – May 1995)
House of Windsor (various episodes, not all as credited, ITV / Granada, May – June 1994)
Revelations (co-creator and writer of several episodes, ITV / Granada, two series, 1994 – 1995)
Coronation Street (ITV / Granada, brief stint as storyliner, 1996;
   also writer of video-only special 'Viva Las Vegas', 1997)
Springhill (storyliner, also writer of five episodes in Series 1, two in Series 2,
   Sky / Granada, two series, 1996 – 1997)
The Grand (various episodes, not all as credited, ITV / Granada, two series, April 1997 – April 1998)
Touching Evil (writer of Series 1 episode 'What Amathus Wants: Part 1', ITV / Granada, 27.05.97)
Queer as Folk (also co-producer, Channel 4, eight episodes, 23.02.99 – 13.04.99)
Queer as Folk 2 (also co-producer, Channel 4, two episodes, 15.02.00 – 22.02.00)
Bob & Rose (also co-producer, ITV1, six episodes, 10.09.01 – 15.10.01)
Linda Green (fifth episode of Series 1, 'Rest in Peace', BBC One, 27.11.01)
The Second Coming (also executive producer, ITV1, two episodes, 09.02.03 – 10.02.03)
Mine All Mine (also executive producer, ITV1, five episodes, 25.11.04 – 23.12.04)
Casanova (also executive producer, BBC Three, three episodes, 13.03.05 – 27.03.05,
   with subsequent BBC One repeat)
Doctor Who (head writer and executive producer: BBC One, 2005-2009): As writer –
Series One: 'Rose' (26.03.05), 'The End of the World' (02.04.05), 'Aliens of London'
   (16.04.05), 'World War Three' (23.04.05), 'The Long Game' (07.05.05), 'Boom Town'
   (04.06.05), 'Bad Wolf' (11.06.05) and 'The Parting of the Ways' (18.06.05); also mini-
   episode for Children in Need night (18.11.05);
Series Two: 'The Christmas Invasion' (25.12.05), 'New Earth' (15.04.06),
   'Tooth and Claw' (22.04.06), 'Love & Monsters' (17.06.06), 'Army of Ghosts'
   (01.07.06) and 'Doomsday' (08.07.06);
Series Three: 'The Runaway Bride' (25.12.06), 'Smith and Jones' (31.03.07), 'Gridlock'
   (14.04.07), 'Utopia' (16.06.07), 'The Sound of Drums' (23.06.07) and 'Last of the
   Time Lords' (30.06.07);
Series Four: 'Voyage of the Damned' (25.12.07), 'Partners in Crime' (05.04.08),
   'Midnight' (14.06.08), 'Turn Left' (21.06.08), 'The Stolen Earth' (28.06.08) and
   'Journey's End' (05.07.08);
Forthcoming: Christmas 2008 special 'The Next Doctor'; Easter 2009 special
   (co-written with Gareth Roberts); a further three special-length episodes during 2009,

one to be co-written with Phil Ford.

Torchwood (creator and executive producer; also writer of Series 1 opening episode 'Everything Changes' (BBC Two, 22.10.06) and Series 3 opening episode, forthcoming in spring 2009).

The Sarah Jane Adventures (creator and executive producer; also co-writer, with Gareth Roberts, of special-length debut episode 'Invasion of the Bane', CBBC / BBC One, 01.01.07)

SOURCES
by or with Russell T Davies unless stated

BOOKS:

A Licence To Be Different: The Story of Channel 4, Maggie Brown (BFI Publishing, 2007)
Dennis Potter, Humphrey Carpenter (Faber & Faber, 1998)
Dennis Potter: A Life on Screen, John R Cook (Manchester University Press, 1995)
The Crystal Mouse, Babs H Deal (Doubleday, 1972)
Dark Season (BBC Books, 1991)
The New Doctor Who Adventures: Damaged Goods (Virgin Publishing, 1996)
Queer as Folk: The Scripts (Channel 4 Books, 1999)
Doctor Who: The Shooting Scripts, Russell T Davies et al (BBC Books, 2005)
Doctor Who: The Writer's Tale, Russell T Davies with Benjamin Cook (BBC Books, 2008)
BFI TV Classics: Queer as Folk, Glyn Davis (BFI Publishing, 2008)
The Hill and Beyond: Children's Television Drama – An Encyclopedia,
    Alistair D McGown & Mark J Docherty (BFI Publishing, 2003)
Doctor Who: The Inside Story, Gary Russell (BBC Books, 2006)
Potter on Potter, ed. Graham Fuller (Faber & Faber, 1993)

MAGAZINE AND NEWSPAPER ARTICLES:

'The Media: Can the Ambridge touch save the motel?',
    Crossroads article by Peter Fiddick (*The Guardian*, 12.01.87)
'Media File', follow-up *Crossroads* piece by Peter Fiddick (*The Guardian*, 06.07.87)
'Uphill Struggle', an article on *Springhill* by Paul Cornell (*Dreamwatch*, March 1997)
Doctor Who Magazine, assorted issues, notably 'We're gonna be bigger than Star Wars!',
    on the potential future of *Doctor Who*, by Gary Gillatt with contributions from
    Russell T Davies et al (June 1999); and Davies' monthly 'Production Notes'
    column (March 2004 to present).
Heat magazine, assorted issues
'A Rose by any other name', *Bob & Rose* preview piece (*The Guardian*, 02.09.01)
'Boom boom and bust' criticising *The Basil Brush Show* (*The Guardian*, 31.03.03)
'Have a Russell T Davies TV festival' (*The Guardian*, 01.01.05)
'The thrill of the chaise', David Tennant interview with Lesley White (*The Sunday Times*, 06.03.05)
Radio Times, assorted issues, notably 'Love machine', *Casanova* preview piece
    by Sarah Dempster (issue dated 12-18 March 2005)
'Doctor in the house', interview with Christopher Eccleston by Liz Hoggard
    (*The Observer*, 20.03.05)
'Screen Burn' TV reviews by Charlie Brooker (*The Guardian Guide*: *Doctor Who*,
    'The Unquiet Dead', 09.04.05; *Torchwood* Series One, 26.10.06 and 16.12.06)
Annual *Doctor Who Magazine* specials published as *The Doctor Who Companion Series
    One – Four* by Andrew Pixley (Panini Magazines, 2005 – 08)
Introduction to booklet within Complete *Doctor Who* Series One DVD box-set (2Entertain, 2005)
'Flood Barriers', commentary article by Clayton Hickman within *The Flood* graphic novel
    (Panini Books, 2007)
'Sexy Beasts', *Torchwood* Series Two preview, by Matt Bielby (*DeathRay*, February 2008)

INTERVIEWS AND DOCUMENTARIES:

Russell T Davies & Matt Jones webchat (www.channel4.com, 02.03.99)
Russell T Davies & Nicola Shindler webchat (www.channel4.com, 13.04.99)
'Audiences are smart', interview with Brent Ledger (*Xtra! Magazine*, 01.06.00)
Interview with Katherine Bell (*PlanetOut.com*, 2000, accessed 20.02.06)
Interview with Jane Marlow (*Scriptwriter* magazine, March 2002)
Interview with Alan McKee (*Continuum*, July 2002)
Scriptwriting masterclass as part of Exposures student film festival
    (Manchester Cornerhouse, 04.12.03)
'Gay life', interview with Wayne Clews (*The Guardian* 'My Manchester' supplement, 10.05.04)
'Sitting Pretty', interview with Nick Duerden (*The Observer*, 07.11.04)
'Gardner's World', Julie Gardner interview with Clayton Hickman
    (*Doctor Who Magazine*, March 2005)
'Doctoring the Tardis', interview with Gareth McLean (*The Guardian*, 07.03.05)
On Show, with Sian Williams (BBC Wales, tx.17.03.05)
Russell T Davies: Unscripted (BBC Four, tx.11.04.05)
Project: Who? (BBC Radio 2, two parts, tx.22.03.05 – 29.03.05)
Doctor Who Confidential (BBC Three, four series, 2005 – 2008)
Annual interviews with Benjamin Cook (*Doctor Who Magazine*, August – September 2005;
    September – October 2006; September 2007; October 2008).
Interview with Lizo Mzimba (*Newsround*, BBC One, 12.09.06)
'One of Britain's foremost television writers', interview with Cathy Prior
    (*The Independent*, 22.10.06)
Value Judgements, with Phil George – courtesy of Green Bay Media
    (BBC Radio Wales, tx.29.12.06)
'The Russell T Davies Effect', interview with Richard Johnson (*The Daily Telegraph*, 12.03.07)
Letter on the occasion of the death of John Inman (*The Guardian*, 12.03.07)
'Russell T Davies: My Life in Media' (*The Independent*, 26.03.07)
'I can be very bolshie', interview with Stuart Jeffries (*The Guardian*, 20.10.07)
Russell T Davies Talks to Mark Lawson (BBC Four, tx.16.01.08)
Russell T Davies, Phil Collinson & Julie Gardner interview by Benjamin Cook
    (*Doctor Who Magazine*, April 2008)
Scriptwriting masterclass conducted by BBC writersroom as part of Manchester Literature
    Festival (Manchester Cornerhouse, 20.10.08)
Russell T Davies & Benjamin Cook interview with Simon Mayo (BBC Radio 5, 22.10.08)

MISCELLANEOUS:

Author interviews with Phil Collinson, Paul Cornell, Frank Cottrell Boyce, Russell T Davies,
    Godfrey Evans, Ed Pugh, Gareth Roberts and Nicola Shindler, between 2006 and 2008
Misfits scripts, courtesy of Russell T Davies / Red Productions
Century Falls fansite (www.centuryfalls.co.uk)
West Glamorgan Youth Theatre website (www.wgytc.co.uk)
Swansea Rugby Club website (www.swansearfc.co.uk)
'Encyclopedia of Fantastic Film and Television' website (www.eofftv.com)
Unofficial Russell T Davies site (www.russelltdavies.com)
DVD audio commentaries for *The Complete Queer as Folk* (Channel 4 DVD), *Bob & Rose*
    (Carlton Visual Entertainment), *The Second Coming* (Carlton Visual Entertainment),
    Mine All Mine (2Entertain), *Doctor Who* Series One to Four (2Entertain)
Podcast commentaries for *Doctor Who* Series Two to Four
    (downloaded from www.bbc.co.uk/doctorwho)

INDEX